Advanced English Reading and Comprehension

Also by Diane Engelhardt

Practice Makes Perfect: Intermediate English Reading and Comprehension
Perfect Phrases for ESL: Conversation Skills

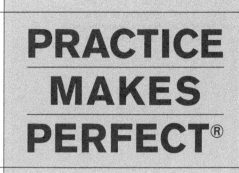

PRACTICE MAKES PERFECT®

Advanced English Reading and Comprehension

Diane Engelhardt

New York   Chicago   San Francisco   Athens   London   Madrid
Mexico City   Milan   New Delhi   Singapore   Sydney   Toronto

5 6 7 8 9 10   QVS/QVS   21 20 19 18 17

ISBN   978-0-07-179886-0
MHID   0-07-179886-2

e-ISBN   978-0-07-179887-7
e-MHID   0-07-179887-0

Library of Congress Control Number 2013930088

McGraw-Hill Education, the McGraw-Hill Education logo, Practice Makes Perfect, and related trade dress are trademarks or registered trademarks of McGraw-Hill Education and/or its affiliates in the United States and other countries and may not be used without written permission. All other trademarks are the property of their respective owners. McGraw-Hill Education is not associated with any product or vendor mentioned in this book.

Interior design by Village Bookworks, Inc.

McGraw-Hill Education products are available at special quantity discounts to use as premiums and sales promotions or for use in corporate training programs. To contact a representative, please visit the Contact Us pages at www.mhprofessional.com.

This book is printed on acid-free paper.

Contents

Contents

Preface

Practice Makes Perfect: Advanced English Reading and Comprehension contains 15 reading texts based on contemporary subjects. The book is designed to:

- Build academic and nonacademic vocabulary
- Develop reading comprehension skills at an advanced level
- Stimulate creative thought on the subject matter and the problems that each topic poses to human society

Each chapter is between 1,450 and 1,900 words long and contains the following sections:

1. **Pre-reading** As an introduction to the topic, you can use the questionnaire provided to interview classmates, colleagues, family, and friends. Column heads A, B, and C are provided for you to record the answers of each person you interview. In a brief exercise, you will predict the content of the reading text.
2. **Reading text** Following the theme of "think about it," the texts in this book cover a broad range of current topics having to do with technology and human interest. The reading text is followed by a short "After reading" exercise, in which you will confirm your predictions about the text.
3. **Vocabulary** Understanding and learning vocabulary can be a daunting task. In addition to its academic and nonacademic vocabulary, each reading text contains many other useful words and phrases that may be new to you. Because not every new word can be included in a vocabulary list or exercise, I encourage you to use an English language dictionary and to keep an independent vocabulary journal to record new words that are not included in the vocabulary exercises. The vocabulary exercises are broken down as follows:
   - **Thematic vocabulary** In this exercise, you will write down 10 words or phrases that relate to the subject matter of the reading text.
   - **Academic vocabulary** Each chapter focuses on 20 academic words (in **boldface** type) and 10 nonacademic words (in ***boldface italic*** type). The academic vocabulary comes from the Academic Word List (AWL) developed at Victoria University of Wellington, New Zealand. The AWL contains the 570 word families that students need to know how to use when studying at the university level. Here's an example:

     theory (n.), theoretical (adj.), theorize (v.): a set of ideas intended to explain something

In the academic word exercises, you will be required to write down the noun, verb, or adjective form of each word and its dictionary definition. In other exercises, you will write down the part of speech and a dictionary definition.

+ **Using vocabulary** You will complete each sentence of these exercises with the correct word, or form of the word, from the academic word list.
+ **Nonacademic vocabulary** You will identify each word's part of speech and match the word with its dictionary definition or with a synonym.

4. **Reading comprehension** This section tests your comprehension of the text under the following headings:
   + Reading for main ideas
   + Reading for details
   + Reading for interpretation and inference
5. **Reading strategies** In this section, you will practice various techniques that will help you process what you have read and enable you to take notes, paraphrase, organize information, and summarize a reading text.
6. **Critical thinking** It is important not only to understand what you read but also to engage in critical thinking, that is, to evaluate information in the reading text and relate it to other issues.

An answer key is provided at the end of the book. If specific answers cannot be provided for some exercises, suggested answers are given where possible.

◆ ◆ ◆

Reading is a great source of knowledge, but—more than providing facts, figures, and a wealth of information—reading can broaden our minds and make us reflect on issues that affect our lives and our future. The reading texts in this book were written not only for your skill development, but also for your pleasure. Read them and share your thoughts!

Acknowledgments

I thank my editor, Holly McGuire, for the opportunity to write this book, and my husband, Erich, for his considerable support.

Advanced English Reading and Comprehension

Ecotourism
Another way to see the world

Pre-reading

Using the following questionnaire, interview your classmates, colleagues, family, and friends.

Questionnaire	A	B	C

What kind of vacation do you prefer?
a. All-inclusive
b. A package deal that includes hotel and transportation
ⓒ Traveling on your own

How do you like to travel on vacation?
ⓐ By airplane
b. By car
c. By bus or train

Where do you go on vacation?
a. To a foreign country that is far away
ⓑ To a foreign country that is close
c. To a place in my own country

Where do you stay?
a. In an international chain hotel
b. In a small, locally owned hotel or inn
ⓒ In a hostel or bed-and-breakfast
d. Other (specify: _____)

What do you like to do on your vacation?
a. Relax and have a good time
ⓑ Visit famous buildings and historic sites
c. Travel and enjoy the scenery
d. Other (specify: _____)

When you travel to a foreign country,
    do you learn some of the language in advance?
        Ⓨes | No
    do you get information about the culture in advance?
        Yes | Ⓝo
    do you eat local food? Ⓨes | No
    do you buy local products? Ⓨes | No
    do you always clean up after yourself? Ⓨes | No

Predicting content

Considering the title of the chapter, predict the content of the reading text. Which of the following topics do you think will be included in the reading text?

- ☑ How tourism affects the environment
- ☑ How tourism began
- ☐ How you can travel cheaply
- ☐ Places you can visit on a vacation
- ☑ How tourism is changing

Reading text

1   The world has shrunk dramatically over the past 60 years, because people can travel farther, faster, and cheaper than ever before. Distant destinations that once took weeks to reach by ship are a few hours away by airplane. Exotic places that people used to only dream of or read about in books are as close as the nearest travel agency or online booking service. Luxurious locations on the Mediterranean are *affordable*. Exciting adventures in the Amazon Rainforest or in the Himalayas are possible. Cultural *immersion* experiences for sightseers and globetrotters are available, all because of one of the world's largest and fastest-growing industries: tourism.

The growth of tourism

Year	Number of tourists (millions)	Revenue generated, excluding airfare ($ billions)
1950	25	12.5
1980	277	200
1990	435	262
1996	592	423
2000	675	475
2005	797	679
2010	939	919
2020	1,560 (projected)	2,000

SOURCE World Tourism Organization.

2   Despite the dips and swings caused by political turmoil, economic downturns, and natural disasters, tourism's growth rate is not about to slow down. The number of tourists traveling every year has exploded from 25 million in 1950 to 939 million in 2010. For 2020, the World Tourism Organization estimates 1.56 billion international arrivals and an annual growth rate of 4 percent. Growth rates in increasingly popular developing countries are **projected** to *surpass* 6 percent a year through 2020. South Asia's annual growth rate has already reached 6.2 percent, and by 2020, Asia is expected to be second only to Europe as the most popular tourist destination.

3   Making up 11.4 percent of the world's gross domestic product (GDP) in 2005, tourism has become a major economic player for developed and developing nations alike. In France and the United States, international tourism's top two destinations, tourism accounts for 6 percent and 2.7 percent, respectively, of those countries' GDP. For countries such as Mexico, Malaysia, Thailand, Egypt, and Kenya, which depend heavily on tourism for employment and development opportunities, as well as for **revenue** and foreign investment, tourism can constitute 10 percent of GDP. For small Caribbean and Pacific islands, tourism can account for as much 40 percent of GDP.

Smaller and poorer countries depend on tourism as a major source of employment and as their only means of economic **diversification**.

4   The future of the fourth-largest global export activity (after fuels, chemicals, and automotive products) looks bright for travelers, airlines, commercial tour operators, hotel chains, hospitality businesses, and governments—but what about the future of coral reefs, sandy beaches, national parks, and the *pristine* natural treasures that attract experience-hungry tourists by the thousands? The red flags are already appearing: quaint fishing villages turned into sprawling tourist playgrounds, shorelines ribboned with high-rise hotels, agricultural fields plowed under and **converted** into golf courses, coastal waters polluted with sewage, beaches littered with garbage, and noisy streets plagued by traffic congestion. To make way for airports, roads, and tourist complexes, forests have been cleared, fragile ecosystems destroyed, wildlife dispersed or decimated, and indigenous peoples displaced and dispossessed.

5   If tourism's growth is unstoppable, can it continue on an upward path, or must it take a gentler, more **sustainable** course? Is there a different kind of tourism that lets everyone have their cake and eat it too?

The growth of ecotourism

6   An offshoot of the environmental movement of the 1970s, ecotourism has come into its own over the past two decades. Thanks to an increasing awareness of environmental issues such as climate change, combined with a high demand among European and North American travelers for unspoiled locations, authentic cultural experiences, and recreational challenges, ecotourism is growing at a rate of 20 percent annually, making it the fastest-growing sector in the tourist industry. The International Ecotourism Society defines *ecotourism* as "responsible travel to natural areas that *conserve* the **environment** and the welfare of local people." The International Union for Conservation of Nature characterizes ecotourism as economically sustainable, ecologically sensitive, and culturally acceptable. Closely related is the concept of sustainable tourism identified in *Our Common Future,* the Brundtland Commission's report to the 1987 World Commission on Environment and Development: development that "meets the needs of the present without **compromising** the ability of future generations to meet their own needs."

The principles and challenges of ecotourism

7   Ecotourism's principles clearly *distinguish* it from **conventional** mass tourism. Instead of classic tourist meccas, ecotourism seeks out remote locations with strict environmental protections and operates on a small scale. Tourists, businesses, and local residents are encouraged to **minimize** their **impact** on the environment by recycling materials, conserving energy and water, safely treating human waste and properly **disposing of** garbage, using alternative energy, and building in a manner that fits in with natural surroundings. The financial **benefits** from ecotourism are passed on to the community through conservation projects, employment, partnerships, and local participation in the development and management of local **resources**. Synonymous with "green" tourism, ecotourism promotes cultural sensitivity and respect for traditions and customs in order to avoid the kind of **exploitation** that has turned tribal ceremonies into sideshows and relics into souvenirs. Last but not least, ecotourism plays a political role in its support of human rights and democracy.

8   When it *adheres to* its principles, ecotourism can be a win-win situation for all involved. Ecuador's 15,000-acre Maquipucuna Reserve hosts an ecolodge, employs local staff and tour guides, and supports a project to protect local bears. Home to the rare and unique lemur, the island of Madagascar invests its tourist revenues in safeguarding its world-famous biodiversity and reducing poverty, while keeping tourist numbers small and manageable. The province of Palawan in the Philippines, where ecotourists can visit three bird sanctuaries, twelve national parks, six mangrove forest reserves, and twenty-four watershed forest reserves, has been

designated a fish and wildlife sanctuary and a UNESCO World Heritage Site. Visitors to Chitwan National Park, another UNESCO Natural Heritage Site in Nepal, can explore jungles on the backs of elephants that are raised in a scientific breeding center and cared for in a sanctuary.

9   A shining model of what can be achieved without *sacrificing* quality, comfort, and convenience for its guests is the Sí Como No resort near Manuel Antonio National Park in Costa Rica. Belonging to Greentique Hotels, Sí Como No runs on solar power, conserves water, and practices recycling and environmental gray-water management. The staff is trained in environmental awareness, and time and money are invested in programs that benefit the environment and the community.

10   There is another side, however, to the ecotourism success story. Because tourism is the least-regulated industry with no universal standards or formal accreditation programs, any company can slap a "green" label onto its operation and cash in on the trend. Developers and governments are particularly guilty of "greenwashing" projects that appear to be environmentally aware on the surface but destroy ecologically sensitive areas during large-scale construction. Although ecotourism has motivated governments to establish national parks and preserves, poorer countries cannot afford the costs of managing these areas and either neglect them or turn to private investors, who may be **committed** to conservation—or interested in getting their hands on valuable property for their own gain.

11   The popularity of ecotourism is a problem in itself. The original ecotourists were small in number, deeply committed to conservation and actively engaged in cultural exchange. At one time, they were willing to rough it and go off the beaten path, but now so-called ecotourists travel en masse and expect the comforts of home packaged in a pretty setting. In the process, nature, once an honored treasure, has become a **commodity** and a photo opportunity. Larger numbers of ecotourists consume more resources and leave a larger impact on the environment, and eco-operators require more land to **accommodate** demand. As ecotourism spreads to more sensitive corners of the earth, it could end up defeating its original purposes.

12   Ecotourism can be achieved only if steps are taken in the right direction. In 1993, British Airways led the way as the first airline to **implement** a systematic environmental policy. The International Hotels Environment Initiative (IHEI) has more than 8,000 members from 111 countries. In cooperation with the United Nations Environment Program and the International Hotel & Restaurant Association, the IHEI developed an "Environmental Action Pack for Hotels" in 1995 to promote environmental management, energy and water conservation, and waste and emission reduction. In 1996, the World Tourism Organization, the World Travel and Tourism Council, and the Earth Summit Council drafted *Agenda 21 for the Travel and Tourism Industry*, recognizing the interdependence of tourism, peace, development, and environmental protection. The year 2002 was declared the United Nations International Year of Ecotourism, with an ecotourism summit held in May.

13   Whether **initiated** by trade or intergovernmental organizations, blueprints and agreements can be meaningful only if governments are proactive. Belize and Costa Rica, for example, have established national policies and strategies to further ecotourism. Brazil, Indonesia, Namibia, and Nepal **integrate** small-scale, community-oriented approaches into their tourism programs. While progress continues to be made on many fronts and by many players, it is the individual traveler who will keep ecotourism on track. Tourists can make informed choices about travel destinations and tour operators, as well as conscious efforts to reduce their individual impact on the environment and to practice cultural sensitivity toward local peoples. They can participate in volunteer conservation projects and gain skills and knowledge in the process. They can pressure governments to pass and **enforce** laws that protect the environment. Ultimately, they can spend their money where it is put to green use. Nature is counting on them.

After reading

In the Pre-reading section, check to see if your predictions about the reading text were correct.

Vocabulary

EXERCISE
1·1

Thematic vocabulary *List 10 words or phrases related to tourism.*

_____   _____

_____   _____

_____   _____

_____   _____

_____   _____

EXERCISE
1·2

Academic vocabulary *Using a dictionary, complete the following chart with the correct forms and definitions of the **academic words** from the reading text.*

Noun	Adjective	Verb	Definition
1. *accommodation*	*un / nom*	accommodate	*space for (verb) willing to help sb fit in / wishes (adj) place where someone may live, stay.*
2. *converter / or*	*convertible*	convert	*change in form, turn about, to be able to be converted*
3. *disposer*	*disposed*	dispose of	*get rid of (verb)*
4. *enforcement*	*enforceable*	enforce	*make sure a law, rule, or duty is obeyed*
5. *Integration*	*integrative*	integrate	*combine, or be combined to form a whole.*
6. _____	_____	initiate	_____
7. _____	_____	minimize	_____
8. benefit	_____	_____	_____
9. diversification	_____	_____	_____
10. exploitation	_____	_____	_____
11. _____	committed	_____	_____
12. _____	sustainable	_____	_____
13. _____	X	implement	_____
14. _____	X	project	_____
15. _____	conventional	X	_____
16. impact	X	_____	_____

Noun	Adjective	Verb	Definition
17. environment	_____	X	_____
18. resource	_____	X	_____
19. commodity	X	X	_____
20. revenue	X	X	_____

EXERCISE
1·3

Using vocabulary *Complete each of the following sentences with the appropriate word(s) from the chart in Exercise 1-2. Be sure to use the correct form of each verb and to pluralize nouns, if necessary.*

1. At first, children from immigrant families find it difficult to _____ into their new school and to make friends.

2. The tour company is _____ to providing the best service to its customers now and in the future.

3. When people are not used to a foreign currency, they always _____ into their own and compare local prices with prices at home.

4. The manager plans to _____ the new regulations as soon as possible.

5. The airplane has become the _____ way for most people to travel to faraway places.

6. Laws will not be very effective if the police do not _____ them.

7. At the Shangri-la Hotel, our staff will do its best to _____ our guests' special needs and requests.

8. In order to save money, we have to _____ our expenses and stop buying things we don't really need.

9. Energy use will have a negative _____ on the environment if we don't change our consumption patterns.

10. The government _____ a 25-percent increase in health care spending in the coming years.

11. Shy people find it difficult to _____ a conversation with complete strangers.

12. Programs to protect the environment _____ both the local population and tourist businesses.

13. Developing countries need economic _____ so that they are not dependent on one source of _____.

14. Coffee is an important export _____ for many Latin American countries.

15. Unrestricted exploitation of natural resources is not a _____ practice.

16. Water is a precious _____ that most people take for granted.

17. If the _____ is destroyed or polluted, no tourists will want to visit the area.

18. When you go camping, you have to _____ your garbage and waste in the designated containers.

19. Using wild animals, such as elephants, to attract or entertain tourists is a form of

_____.

Nonacademic vocabulary *Match each* **nonacademic word or phrase** *in column 1 with its definition in column 2. Then, indicate each item's part of speech (n. for noun, v. for verb, or adj. for adjective).*

_____ 1. adhere to _____

_____ 2. compromise _____

_____ 3. conserve _____

_____ 4. designate _____

_____ 5. distinguish _____

_____ 6. immersion _____

_____ 7. pristine _____

_____ 8. sacrifice _____

_____ 9. surpass _____

_____ 10. affordable _____

a. deep involvement in an interest or activity
b. cheap or reasonable in price
c. follow or observe closely
d. in an original, unspoiled condition
e. be better or greater than expected
f. recognize as different
g. protect from harm or waste
h. an agreement in which each side meets the other halfway
i. offer or give up something for an important cause
j. officially give a status or name to something

Reading comprehension

Reading for main ideas *Identify the main idea in each of the following paragraphs by answering the questions below. Answer in one sentence, if possible, and summarize, rather than quote, details and figures by using an adjective or adverb; for example, use large, small, rapid(ly), significant(ly), or weak(ly). The main idea of paragraph 1 has been provided.*

Paragraph 1: What effect has tourism had on the world?
Tourism has made the world smaller and more accessible.

Paragraph 2: How fast is tourism expected to grow in the future?

_____

Paragraph 3: How important is tourism to the global economy?

_____

Paragraph 4: What is the effect of tourism on the environment?

_____

Paragraphs 5 and 6: What is the alternative to conventional mass tourism?

_____

Paragraph 7: What are the main aims of ecotourism?

_____

Paragraphs 8 and 9: Where has ecotourism been successful?

_____

Paragraph 10: What is the downside to ecotourism?

_____

Paragraph 11: What does the success of ecotourism depend on?

_____

EXERCISE

1·6

Reading for details *For each of the following sentences, choose the correct answer to fill in the blank.*

1. Tourism is expected to grow at an annual rate of _____.
   a. 4 percent
   b. 5 percent
   c. 6 percent

2. The world's most popular tourist destination is _____.
   a. South Asia
   b. North America
   c. Europe

3. Ecotourism has an annual growth rate of _____.
   a. 5 percent
   b. 10 percent
   c. 20 percent

4. Tourism is growing more rapidly in _____ countries.
   a. developed
   b. developing

5. Tourism is the _____-largest global export activity.
   a. second
   b. third
   c. fourth

6. Tourism makes up _____ of the world GDP.
   a. 11.4 percent
   b. 6 percent
   c. 40 percent

Indicate which of the following statements are true (T) and which are false (F).

7. _____ Ecotourism grew out of the environmental movement of the 1970s.

8. _____ Ecotourism is the fastest-growing sector in the tourist industry.

9. _____ Ecotourism has no negative impact on the environment.

10. _____ Ecotourism encourages recycling, energy conservation, alternative energy, and cultural sensitivity.

11. _____ Ecotourism involves a lack of luxury and comfort for travelers.

12. _____ Ecotourism, like tourism, is strictly regulated by one international organization.

Answer the following questions in complete sentences.

13. Give four examples of how tourism can negatively impact a community and its surroundings.

_____

_____

_____

_____

14. What four economic benefits of tourism do some countries depend heavily on?

_____

_____

_____

_____

15. What makes Sí Como No resort a successful example of ecotourism?

_____

_____

16. What is the difference between ecotourism and sustainable tourism?

_____

_____

17. What initiatives have hotels taken to reduce their impact on the environment?

_____

_____

Reading for interpretation and inference, part 1 *Choose the boldface word or phrase that correctly completes each of the following statements.*

1. "The number of tourists traveling every year has exploded from 25 million in 1950 to 939 million in 2010."

   The number of tourists has increased by nearly **200 percent** | **2,000 percent** | **4,000 percent**.

2. "For small Caribbean and Pacific islands, tourism can account for as much 40 percent of GDP."

   Small islands depend **heavily** | **somewhat** | **partly** on tourism.

3. "The future of the fourth-largest global export activity (after fuels, chemicals, and automotive products) looks bright for travelers, airlines, commercial tour operators, hotel chains, hospitality businesses, and governments."

   Tourism is a **major** | **minor** contributor to the global economy.

4. "The International Hotels Environment Initiative (IHEI) has more than 8,000 members from 111 countries. In cooperation with the United Nations Environment Program and the International Hotel & Restaurant Association, the IHEI developed an 'Environmental Action Pack for Hotels' in 1995 to promote environmental management, energy and water conservation, and waste and emission reduction."

   Efforts to minimize the impact of hotels on the environment are supported in **many** | **some** | **a few** countries.

Reading for interpretation and inference, part 2 *Choose the correct interpretation for each of the following statements from the reading text.*

1. "Exotic places that people used to only dream of or read about in books are as close as the nearest travel agency or online booking service."
   a. You can find exotic places in your own city.
   b. You can find exotic places in dreams and books.
   c. It's easy to book an exotic holiday.

2. "Developers and governments are particularly guilty of "greenwashing" projects that appear to be environmentally aware on the surface but destroy ecologically sensitive areas during large-scale construction."
   a. Developers and governments use the term "green" to make themselves appear environmental.
   b. Developers and governments are punished for destroying the environment.
   c. Developers and governments clean up the environment.

3. "The red flags are already appearing. . . ."
   a. There are many red flags to attract tourists.
   b. There are many warning signs about the negative impact of tourism.
   c. Red flags warn tourists of dangerous areas.

4. "At one time, they were willing to rough it and go off the beaten path, but now so-called ecotourists travel en masse and expect the comforts of home packaged in a pretty setting."
   a. Ecotourists used to be experience-seekers and to travel simply.
   b. Ecotourists are still experience-seekers and travel simply.
   c. Ecotourists don't exist anymore.

Reading strategies
Organizing information

To organize the information in a reading text, it is often useful to make an outline of the text, just as you would when you write an essay. Choose headings that reflect the main ideas of the text, then jot down important details and supporting statements under each heading.

Do not copy directly from the text; instead, use your own words to make your points. Use a dictionary or thesaurus to find other words that will help you express the ideas in the reading text.

Under the following headings, summarize the main points of paragraphs from the reading text.

Definition of ecotourism (Paragraph 6)

_____

_____

The principles of ecotourism (Paragraph 7)

_____

_____

_____

_____

Successful examples of ecotourism (Paragraphs 8 and 9)

_____

_____

_____

_____

The dangers of ecotourism (Paragraphs 10 and 11)

_____

_____

_____

_____

_____

_____

The industry's commitment to ecotourism (Paragraph 12)

_____

_____

_____

How governments support ecotourism (Paragraph 13)

_____

_____

What individual tourists can do to support ecotourism (Paragraph 13)

_____

_____

_____

_____

_____

_____

Critical thinking

**EXERCISE
1·9**

Making evaluations *Indicate which of the following activities conform (✓) or do not conform (X) to the concept of ecotourism.*

1. _____ Reusing towels and bed linens over several days

2. _____ Buying products made from wild and endangered animals

3. _____ Cleaning up the beach

4. _____ Renting bicycles at hotels

5. _____ Cutting down old-growth forest to build a road

6. _____ Using biodegradable soaps and detergents

7. _____ Hiring local people for jobs in tourism

8. _____ Paying local people low wages because they lack formal training

9. _____ Investing profits in conservation projects

10. _____ Learning useful phrases in the native language

EXERCISE
1·10

Making a case *Using the information in the reading text, make a case for or against the Royal Flush project proposed below. Do you think it should proceed or not, and why? Would you suggest any changes to the proposal?*

Royal Flush Developments has proposed construction of a casino-hotel-marina resort on a small island in the Pacific Northwest. The company plans to locate the development near Coral Beach, in an environmentally sensitive area that is home to a rare bird species.

In the past, island residents have made their living mostly from agriculture and fishing, but in the last few years, many young people have left the island to find work elsewhere. There are a couple of restaurants and bed-and-breakfast inns for the few tourists who come during the summer to enjoy the island's beautiful beaches and peaceful laid-back atmosphere.

While some residents welcome the idea of the resort, most of the people who have moved to the island to retire fear that Royal Flush's proposal will negatively impact their lifestyle. In addition, a group of residents has formed an environmental group to oppose the project. There are a lot of mixed feelings toward the development, and it has caused a major controversy among the island's 4,000 residents.

Bibliography

Lindsay, Heather E., "Ecotourism: the Promise and Perils of Environmentally-Oriented Travel" (ProQuest, February 2003), http://www.csa.com/discoveryguides/ecotour/overview.php.

Mastny, Lisa, "Traveling Light: New Paths for International Tourism" (Worldwatch Paper 159, December 2001), http://www.worldwatch.org/system/files/WP159.pdf.

Merg, Mike, "What is Ecotourism?" (Untamed Path, January 2005), http://www.untamedpath .com/Ecotourism/what_is_ecotourism.html#eco-links.

Neale, Greg, *The Green Travel Guide*, ed. 2 (London: Routledge, 1999).

The Human Genome Project
Writing the book of life

Pre-reading

Using the following questionnaire, interview your classmates, colleagues, family, and friends. Answers are provided in the answer key.

Questionnaire	A	B	C

1. What is a genome?
   a. A group of related genes
   b. The complete set of a species' genes
   c. Someone who studies genes

2. How many chromosomes does one human cell contain?
   a. 40
   b. 46
   c. 48

3. What do we call the genes that determine gender (male or female)?
   a. X/Y
   b. A/B
   c. M/F

4. About how many genes are there in the human genome?
   a. 2,500
   b. 20,500
   c. 205,000

5. How many nucleotides make up DNA?
   a. 2
   b. 4
   c. 6

6. Where do genes come from?
   a. The mother
   b. The father
   c. Both parents

Predicting content

Considering the title of the chapter, predict which of the following topics will *not* be mentioned in the reading text.

☐ What genetics is about

☐ The Human Genome Project's goals

☐ Only the benefits of the project

☐ What scientists and researchers were involved in the project

☐ The dangers of the project

☐ How much the project cost

Reading text

1   In 1990, the United States National Institutes of Health (NIH) and the Department of Energy, in collaboration with partners in 18 countries, *embarked* on the Human Genome Project (HGP), the most ambitious venture **undertaken** since the Manhattan Project to develop the atom bomb or the Apollo project to put a man on the moon. At an **estimated** cost of $3 billion to complete the task by 2005, leading scientists and researchers in the field of molecular biology set out to identify all 30,000 to 40,000 genes belonging to the human genome and to map the location of the three billion base pairs of DNA—in other words, to write the Book of Life. This **definitive** resource was intended to lead to the understanding of genetic diseases, the creation of effective pharmaceuticals and medical treatments, and the *alleviation* and prevention of human suffering due to genetically **transmitted** diseases. In order to serve all of humankind and prevent control by any scientific, corporate, or national interest, all information was to be stored in public electronic databases and made freely and readily accessible to anyone who required it.

Historical background

2   Throughout history, people have turned to mythology, folklore, and religion for explanations of life's origins, and to this day there are many who firmly believe what has been written in religious books and passed down from generation to generation. With the advent of the Age of Reason in the eighteenth century and scientific advances in the nineteenth century, however, the quest for deeper knowledge could be satisfied by digging for **empirical evidence** and putting it to empirical test.

3   In 1865, Gregor Mendel, an Austrian monk who had been experimenting for eight years with garden peas, announced to the scientific community that specific characteristics, or traits, were transmitted from parent to offspring in an organized and predictable manner. Along with Charles Darwin's theory of natural selection and evolution as stated in his 1859 publication, *On the Origin of Species,* Mendel's work set the stage for the science of genetics to become the *preeminent* explanation of where life comes from. With the help of improved microscopes, scientists discovered the existence and structure of cells containing chromosomes. In the early 1900s, experiments with fruit flies **revealed** that chromosomes located in the cell's nucleus were made up of genes. The *Drosophila,* commonly called the fruit fly, was the first living organism to be genetically mapped. In 1944, Oswald Avery identified genes in bacteria as genetic messengers made of deoxyribonucleic acid (DNA). In 1953, James Watson and Francis Crick discovered the double helix structure of DNA, for which they received the Nobel Prize nine years later.

4   With each groundbreaking discovery, molecular biologists were able to form an ever clearer picture of the mechanics of life. To crack the code of life, prominent scientists proposed compiling a comprehensive genetic map of a human being. Simpler organisms, such as the fruit fly and

bacteria, had already been genetically mapped, but due to technical limitations, attempts with human genes had produced crude versions lacking precise detail. To duplicate, analyze, and store human DNA on the scale that was being proposed, more *sophisticated* tools and advanced technology would have to be developed.

5   In the 1980s, technology was making great strides. The development of recombinant DNA technology enabled researchers to split long strands of DNA into fragments and to splice and copy specific genes for study. Rapid advances in the 1960s and 1970s had produced machines like the polymerase chain reaction (PCR) machine, or DNA amplifier, that could duplicate DNA faster and cheaper. Developments in computer technology, in particular the invention of the silicon semiconductor chip, had made it possible for huge amounts of data to be analyzed at greater speeds and stored on more compact, portable, and affordable personal computers. Finally, the Internet provided a means for institutions to share and distribute information quickly and widely.

6   At the same time, the world was becoming more genomic. The discovery of the gene that led to Huntington's disease and the Federal Drug Administration's approval of synthetic insulin, biotechnology's first pharmaceutical product, ignited hopes that once the genetic causes could be determined of such debilitating diseases as muscular dystrophy, cystic fibrosis, and sickle-cell anemia, effective drugs and treatments for cancer and heart disease would eventually follow. **Emerging** biotechnology companies were making headlines, and their stocks were soaring on Wall Street. In general, biologists agreed that the project could be *accomplished*, but not everyone believed that it should be done.

7   Despite **ethical** considerations and doubts that the project would bring about the desired results, **widespread** enthusiasm for the project's immense **potential** led to a series of meetings and conferences in 1986 and 1987 to set goals, to estimate the required outlay in money, time, and human resources, and to generate information for the government agencies and institutions that would provide the financial resources. When the U.S. Congress **allocated** funding to the NIH and the Department of Energy, the Human Genome Project was on its feet.

8   In September 1999, the Human Genome Project announced that 200 scientists working on three continents had assembled 25 percent of the entire genetic sequence. By February 2001, the HGP had published its first draft of 90 percent of the human genome in special issues of *Science* and *Nature*. In April 2003, two years ahead of schedule, the project succeeded in completing the sequencing of 99 percent of human genes to 99.99 percent accuracy, with 341 gaps. Even before its completion, the Human Genome Project and the information disseminating from it were opening doors in the fields of medicine, energy, the environment, agriculture, bioarchaeology, anthropology, and forensics.

Medical benefits

9   The Human Genome Project's ultimate goal was to provide **fundamental** genetic information that would lead to the treatment, and eventually the eradication, of many of the 4,000 genetic diseases and defects that afflict humans. As diagnostic genetic tests become more sophisticated and available, doctors will eventually put together genetic profiles for patients, determine their risk for disease, and make diagnoses before individuals become sick—or before they are even born. With the focus on preventing disease, doctors can begin to provide genetic counseling to families who want to understand their genetic background, as well as to couples who are planning a family. Advances in computer hardware and software will allow doctors to analyze biological samples more quickly and cost-effectively and to transfer the information to patients' computerized files, which they will then carry with them on computer chips. On the basis of this information, it will be possible to predict an individual's *susceptibility* to drugs and to environmental factors that are responsible for allergies.

10   The HGP will **revolutionize** not only how doctors treat patients but also how medical therapy is delivered, particularly in the emerging field of pharmacogenomics. An online article published on the Human Genome Project Information website predicts that up to 3,000 new drugs will have been developed, tested, and marketed by 2020. These products will generate sales in the billions of dollars for biotech and pharmaceutical companies, as researchers use genome targets to design and customize more effective drugs with fewer side effects, to **eliminate** adverse drug reactions in patients, and to make intervention more precise and successful. In addition, inexpensive vaccines will be *engineered* to activate the immune system without causing infections. In the long run, these improvements are expected to reduce the overall cost of health care. Although areas such as the cloning of organs for transplants have yet to be fully explored, the potential for life-saving and life-**enhancing** advances is vast and exciting.

Ethical, legal, and social issues

11   Although the Human Genome Project's picture of human health in the future appears rosy and immensely hopeful, it has its darker side. From the outset, the HGP **specified** as one of its goals the need to examine the ethical, legal, and social *issues* (ELSI) involved in making genetic information available. Between three and five percent of HGP's annual budget was allocated for this purpose. If the HGP is to serve humankind as intended, laws and regulations must prevent *abuse* and misuse of this information.

12   At the forefront of ELSI was the concern that employers and insurers could **discriminate** against employees and **deny** coverage on the basis of genetic test results. In May 2008, the Genetic Information Nondiscrimination Act (GINA) made it illegal for employers, insurers, courts, schools, and other entities in the United States to discriminate on the basis of genetic information. The potential for social *stigmatization* of individuals on the basis of their genetic makeup and the ensuing psychological suffering cannot be overlooked or minimized.

13   Sensitive issues of privacy, confidentiality, and ownership of genetic information that can only be dealt with through strict legislation are accompanied by philosophical and ethical issues. Scientists now know the location of genes on a chromosome, but it will take further research before they understand how genes work and how environmental factors come into play. This complexity makes it extremely difficult, if not impossible, for anyone to predict the outcome of what critics call tampering with nature or playing God. Although the idea of creating designer babies may seem attractive to some, the birth of a genetic elite brings to mind the practice of eugenics and the disastrous attempts of past regimes to create a superior race. Without clear ethical guidance, humankind's progress could end up in territory we should never have set foot in.

The Genomic Era

14   Regardless of the direction in which the Human Genome Project will take humans in the future, it has already ushered in the Genomic Era, and there is no turning back. One comfort lies in the fact that the completion of the Human Genome Project is really only the beginning of a long and uncertain journey of studying, **interpreting**, and applying the information it has amassed. How wisely that information is applied, or not applied, will determine the Human Genome Project's real value.

After reading

In the Pre-reading section, check to see if your predictions about the reading text were correct.

Vocabulary

Started 2021.04.02

Thematic vocabulary *List 10 words or phrases related to genetics.*

9. the genoma project... p.18

widespread

Academic vocabulary *Using a dictionary, complete the following chart with the correct forms and definitions of the **academic words** from the reading text.*

	Noun	Adjective	Verb	Definition
1.		X	allocate	
2.		X	deny	
3.			discriminate	
4.			emerge	
5.			interpret	
6.			reveal	
7.			revolutionize	
8.			specify	
9.			transmit	
10.		X	undertake	
11.		X	eliminate	
12.		X	enhance	
13.		X	estimate	
14.		empirical	X	
15.		ethical	X	
16.		fundamental	X	
17.	potential		X	

Noun	Adjective	Verb	Definition
18. evidence	_____	X	_____
19. X	definitive	X	_____
20. X	widespread	X	_____

EXERCISE 2·3

Using vocabulary, part 1 *Complete each of the following sentences with the appropriate word from the chart in Exercise 2-2. Be sure to use the correct form of each verb and to pluralize nouns, if necessary.*

1. The use of computers has become so _____ that it's impossible to think of the world without them.

2. Many governments have not passed laws that allow assisted suicide on _____ grounds.

3. In order to prove a theory, a scientist needs to provide _____ evidence.

4. The young girl has the _____ to become a great concert pianist.

5. We need to use our natural resources more wisely and try to _____ needless waste.

6. When the police searched the house where the break-in had occurred, they collected a lot of _____.

7. The students _____ a project to plant trees around the schoolyard.

8. I have read many books on the subject, but I have yet to find a _____ answer to the question of what happens to us after we die.

9. Malaria is _____ by mosquitoes.

10. A beginner's course in English teaches students the _____ grammar and vocabulary needed to communicate in everyday situations.

Using vocabulary, part 2 *For each of the following sentences, choose the correct form of the **academic word** to fill in the blank.*

1. It is against the law to _____ against people on the basis of their skin color, race, religion, sex, age, or sexual orientation.
   a. discrimination
   b. discriminatory
   c. discriminate

2. Olympic athletes are not allowed to compete if they have been taking performance-_____ drugs or substances.
   a. enhancement
   b. enhancing
   c. enhance

3. Your _____ of this poem is quite different from the way that I understand it.
   a. interpretation
   b. interpretative
   c. interpret

4. The pharmaceutical company is hoping to come up with a _____ drug for the treatment of breast cancer.
   a. revolution
   b. revolutionary
   c. revolutionize

5. The recipe _____ the ingredients and the exact amount that you are to use.
   a. specification
   b. specific
   c. specifies

6. Mendel's experiments were a _____ that changed the course of science.
   a. revelation
   b. revealing
   c. reveal

7. Many significant medical benefits have _____ from the research project.
   a. emergence
   b. emergent
   c. emerged

8. The research project was able to go ahead due to a generous _____ of funding from the government.
   a. allocation
   b. allocated
   c. allocate

9. The military government was criticized in the media for its _____ of basic human rights to its citizens.
   a. denial
   b. denied
   c. deny

10. What is the _____ number of students who will be attending college next year?
   a. estimation
   b. estimated
   c. estimate

Nonacademic vocabulary *Match each **nonacademic word or phrase** in column 1 with its definition in column 2. Then, indicate each item's part of speech (n., v., or adj.).*

_____ 1. abuse _____

_____ 2. accomplish _____

_____ 3. alleviation _____

_____ 4. embark _____

_____ 5. engineer _____

_____ 6. issue _____

_____ 7. preeminent _____

_____ 8. sophisticated _____

_____ 9. stigmatization _____

_____ 10. susceptibility _____

a. highly developed and complex
b. an important topic or problem to be resolved
c. the wrong use of something
d. the state of being easily harmed or affected
e. better than all others
f. achieve or complete something successfully
g. design and build
h. treatment of something as unworthy
i. begin a new project or course of action
j. the reduction of pain or severity

Reading comprehension

Reading for main ideas *Match each of the following headlines with the corresponding paragraph of the reading text. The answer for paragraph 1 has already been inserted.*

a. HGP associated with ethical, legal, and social issues
b. International meetings and conferences give birth to Human Genome Project
c. Molecular biologists succeed in mapping the genetic structure of simple organisms
d. Potential abuse of genetic information calls for clear ethical guidelines
e. Man seeks explanation to origins of life
f. HGP promises revolutionary new drugs and reduced health care costs
g. Rapid technological advances allow researchers to process and store more genetic information
h. International scientists to map the complete human genome and U.S. government to provide financial support
i. Human Genome Project completed ahead of schedule, opens doors to many fields
j. New field of biotechnology brings hopes of genetic cures for disease
k. Future value of HGP lies in further research and applications
l. HGP promises to revolutionize how doctors test and treat patients and diagnose disease
m. Lawmakers concerned with issues of discrimination based on genetic information
n. Scientific research leads to discovery of DNA and development of the science of genetics

__*h*__ Paragraph 1

_____ Paragraph 2

_____ Paragraph 3

_____ Paragraph 4

_____ Paragraph 5

_____ Paragraph 6

_____ Paragraph 7

_____ Paragraph 8

_____ Paragraph 9

_____ Paragraph 10

_____ Paragraph 11

_____ Paragraph 12

_____ Paragraph 13

_____ Paragraph 14

Reading for details *For each of the following sentences, choose the correct answer to fill in the blank.*

1. The Human Genome Project was completed in _____.
   a. September 1999
   b. February 2001
   c. April 2003

2. The discovery of recombinant DNA allowed researchers to _____.
   a. split, splice, and copy DNA
   b. duplicate DNA faster and cheaper
   c. store larger amounts of DNA

3. The Human Genome Project's greatest application lies in the field of _____.
   a. medicine
   b. anthropology
   c. environmental science

4. The structure of the DNA molecule was discovered by _____.
   a. Gregor Mendel
   b. Charles Darwin
   c. James Watson and Francis Crick

5. The first living organism to be genetically mapped was _____.
   a. bacteria
   b. the fruit fly
   c. the garden pea

6. The percentage of the human genome that had been mapped when the HGP announced its completion was _____.
   a. 90%
   b. 99.99%
   c. 100%

Indicate which of the following statements are true (T) and which are false (F).

7. _____ The Human Genome Project was more ambitious than the Manhattan Project to build the atom bomb.

8. _____ All information from the Human Genome Project is available to the public.

9. _____ Only American scientists and researchers worked on the Human Genome Project.

10. _____ Through the Human Genome Project, scientists now know everything about human genes and how they interact with each other and the environment.

11. _____ In the United States, it is illegal for companies and organizations to use genetic information to discriminate against people.

12. _____ There are no negative issues or concerns associated with the Human Genome Project.

Answer the following questions in complete sentences.

13. What were the three main goals of the Human Genome Project?

_____

_____

_____

14. What was the significance of the work of Gregor Mendel and Charles Darwin?

_____

_____

15. What four technological advances made the Human Genome Project possible?

_____

_____

_____

_____

16. What is the significance of the Genetic Information Nondiscrimination Act?

_____

_____

EXERCISE
2·8

Reading for interpretation and inference *Determine the amount of support the Human Genome Project received for each of the following statements from the reading text.*

1. "Emerging biotechnology companies were making headlines, and their stocks were soaring on Wall Street."
   a. Great
   b. Moderate
   c. Very little

2. "In general, biologists agreed that the project could be accomplished, but not everyone believed that it should be done."
   a. Great
   b. Moderate
   c. Very little

3. "When the U.S. Congress allocated funding to the NIH and the Department of Energy, the Human Genome Project was on its feet."
   a. Great
   b. Moderate
   c. Very little

4. "The potential for social stigmatization of individuals on the basis of their genetic makeup and the ensuing psychological suffering cannot be overlooked or minimized."
   a. Great
   b. Moderate
   c. Very little

5. "Even before its completion, the Human Genome Project and the information disseminating from it were opening doors in the fields of medicine, energy, the environment, agriculture, bioarchaeology, anthropology, and forensics."
   a. Great
   b. Moderate
   c. Very little

6. "Although the Human Genome Project's picture of human health in the future appears rosy and immensely hopeful, it has its darker side."
   a. Great
   b. Moderate
   c. Very little

7. "Without clear ethical guidance, humankind's progress could end up in territory we should never have set foot in."
   a. Great
   b. Moderate
   c. Very little

8. "Widespread enthusiasm for the project's immense potential led to a series of meetings and conferences in 1986 and 1987."
   a. Great
   b. Moderate
   c. Very little

9. "On the basis of this information, it will be possible to predict an individual's susceptibility to drugs and to environmental factors that are responsible for allergies."
   a. Great
   b. Moderate
   c. Very little

10. "This complexity makes it extremely difficult, if not impossible, for anyone to predict the outcome of what critics call tampering with nature or playing God."
    a. Great
    b. Moderate
    c. Very little

Reading strategies

A good summary contains the main ideas and supporting details of a reading text. Think of a main idea as the big picture: what the text or paragraph is about. You can usually find the main idea of a paragraph in its topic sentence. Supporting details provide the little picture, and they support, prove, or develop the main idea. Details can be facts, figures and statistics, or examples.

EXERCISE
2·9

Identifying main ideas and supporting details *Identify the main ideas of paragraphs 5, 9, and 10 of the reading text. For each of the main ideas, provide two supporting details from the text. As an example, this information has already been provided for paragraph 1. Note: You should write a summary in your own words, rather than copy directly from the text. In this exercise, however, it is necessary only to identify the supporting details.*

Paragraph 1—Main idea   *International scientists undertake to map the complete human genome and the U.S. government provides financial support.*

Supporting details

1.   *Goal: to identify all 30,000 to 40,000 genes belonging to the human genome and to map the location of the three billion base pairs of DNA*

2.   *Purpose: to lead to the understanding of genetic diseases, the creation of effective pharmaceuticals and medical treatments, and the alleviation and prevention of human suffering due to genetically transmitted diseases*

Paragraph 5—Main idea _____

_____

Supporting details

1. _____

_____

_____

2. _____

_____

_____

Paragraph 9—Main idea _____

_____

Supporting details

1. _____

_____

_____

2. _____

_____

_____

Paragraph 10—Main idea _____

_____

Supporting details

1. _____

_____

_____

2. _____

_____

_____

Next, skim each of the other paragraphs in the reading text and underline its main idea.

Finally, scan each of the paragraphs for supporting details and highlight them.

Critical thinking

Making evaluations *Indicate which of the following pursuits you think is a benefit (+) of the Human Genome Project and which is a potential danger (−). Give reasons to support your answers.*

1. _____ Developing customized drugs with fewer side effects

2. _____ Designing your children's appearance

3. _____ Treating and eliminating genetic diseases

4. _____ Selecting or rejecting employees on the basis of their genetic information

5. _____ Creating a race of superhumans

6. _____ Providing employers and insurance companies with private and confidential information

7. _____ Engineering new kinds of plants and animals

8. _____ Informing patients of their susceptibility to potential diseases or health problems

Making a case *Which of the following should or should not have access to your genetic information? Give reasons to support your choices.*

- Your doctor and other health care providers
- Your parents and family members
- Your school, university, or employer
- The police
- Health insurance companies

Bibliography

Boon, Kevin Alexander, *The Human Genome Project: What Does Decoding DNA Mean for Us?* (Berkeley Heights, NJ: Enslo Publishers, 2002).

Human Genome Project Information, "About the Human Genome Project," http://www.ornl.gov/sci/techresources/Human_Genome/project/about.shtml.

"An Overview of the Human Genome Project" (National Human Genome Research Institute, National Institutes of Health), http://www.genome.gov/12011239.

Near-death experiences
Fact or fantasy?

Pre-reading

Using the following questionnaire, interview your classmates, colleagues, family, and friends.

Questionnaire	A	B	C

Do you have strong religious beliefs about life and death?
Yes | No

Are you afraid of death? Yes | No

Have you ever been present when someone died? Yes | No

Has a friend or family member ever been so sick or injured that he or she almost died? Yes | No

Have you ever been so sick or injured that you almost died?
Yes | No

Do you believe in life after death? Yes | No

Do you believe that it is possible for people to die, then come back to life? Yes | No

What do you think happens to people after they die?
a. Nothing
b. They go to a better place.
c. They are born again and return to live a new life.
d. Other (specify: _____)

Predicting content

Considering the title of the chapter, predict which of the following topics will be covered in the reading text.

☐ What causes death

☐ What people experience when they die

☐ What family members go through when someone dies

☐ What doctors think about death and dying

☐ How people change after they have come close to death

Reading text

1   We know for certain what happens to our bodies when we die, but is physical death the end of our existence, or does some part of us—our spirit or our soul—go on living? What shape or form do we take, and how does our life continue? Are we **transported** to another place called heaven or hell, nirvana or paradise? Do we await *judgment* before we can return to an earthly life, or do we move on to a higher level of *consciousness*? Must we suffer for sins we have committed in the past, or are we rewarded for our good deeds? These questions have preoccupied human beings almost as long as we have been able to think and ponder the meaning of life and death. Religions have **evolved** to *relieve* people of their fear of death, and philosophers have contemplated the perplexing nature of our human existence. Regardless of the theories, beliefs, and explanations, death remains the greatest unsolved mystery.

2   Despite resurrections, the appearance of ghosts, and other reports of the dead returning to visit Earth, death is **irreversible**; that is, no one can physically die and come back to tell their tale. Throughout history, however, there have been numerous **incidents** in which people have been pronounced dead as the result of a serious illness, an accident, or a suicide attempt, but have not actually died. While they hovered between life and death, many claim to have left their bodies and caught a glimpse of what it is like on the other side. These near-death experiences (NDEs) have been *extensively* **documented**, and there is plenty of scientific proof to **conclude** that NDEs do in fact occur.

3   The **phenomenon** of NDEs goes as far back as ancient Greece and Rome, but it is only since the 1970s that these rare experiences have become the subject of scientific **research**. In his book *Life After Life,* published in 1975, Dr. Raymond Moody introduced 50 cases of individuals who described having vivid out-of-body experiences after almost dying. Dr. Moody coined the term *near-death experience,* defining it as "any conscious perceptual experience which takes place during . . . an event in which a person could very easily die or be killed (and even may be so close as to be believed or pronounced clinically dead) but nonetheless **survives** and continues physical life." Dr. Moody's best seller resulted in lively interest in the topic, and research-based books and publications in prestigious medical journals followed. In the early 1980s, reputable organizations such as the International Association for Near-Death Studies and the Near Death Experience Research Foundation were **established** to carry out clinical investigations into NDEs.

4   Death occurs when a person's breathing stops and the heart goes into cardiac arrest long enough to prevent blood from flowing to the brain. After 10 to 20 seconds, brain activity **ceases**, consciousness is lost, and the person is pronounced clinically dead. There are cases, however, of people who have been *revived*, and it is these survivors who have reported consistently similar experiences, regardless of age, gender, religion, race, marital status, education, occupation, cultural background, social class, geographic location, and medical condition. According to research, five percent of Americans have had an NDE, but because people will often not tell doctors out of fear of not being taken seriously, the percentage could be higher. A 1980 Gallup poll *determined* that eight million adults in the United States had had an NDE; by 1990, the number had increased to twenty million. It is also estimated that 35 percent of all people who have a close brush with death will have an NDE.

5   Although NDEs can differ in specific content and intensity, they follow a common pattern and contain any of 10 to 12 elements that have been **compiled** from historical reports, experiments, and extensive interviews and surveys. An NDE does not have to include all **elements** to be classified as an NDE.

1. **Out-of-body experience** The person leaves the physical body and hovers in the room or is transported to another location.
2. **Elevated sensual awareness** The person's senses are sharper, and the person experiences intense colors, sounds, feelings, and perceptions. Thinking is also clearer, and the person can experience three-dimensional **awareness**.

3. **Intensely positive feelings** Since the majority of NDEs are positive in nature, people experience extraordinary peace and joy.
4. **Entering or going through a tunnel** This and the experience in No. 5 are the most widely recognized elements of an NDE.
5. **Seeing a bright light** The person **encounters**, or is bathed in, brilliant light.
6. **Reunion with dead relatives or mystical beings** The person is surrounded or greeted by loved ones, who extend a feeling of welcome and security; these relatives appear younger and in perfect health. Sometimes, the person meets what are referred to as angels.
7. **An altered sense of time or space** The experience seems to last longer than the actual period in which the person is clinically dead, and the person may travel what seems to be a long distance.
8. **A life review** The person sees his or her life passing before their eyes as if in a movie. This review provides the opportunity to reevaluate actions and the impact they have had on others. Sometimes, the person is able to see into his or her future.
9. **Visiting unearthly places** These locations include beautiful natural environments or magnificent cities, all of which have otherworldly, supernatural features.
10. **Acquiring knowledge** The person gains **insight** or learns valuable lessons.
11. **Coming to a barrier** The person reaches a boundary where he or she must make a final choice between life and death.
12. **Returning to the body** During the NDE, most people wish to continue in death, but they come to understand the need to return to fulfill their life's purpose or they are told by relatives or mystical beings to go back.

6   As strange as these elements may seem, NDEs can be scientifically *verified*. The cases of children, including very young children, who have had NDEs provide strong supporting evidence. Because children have neither preconceived notions nor previous knowledge of death or an afterlife, they cannot *fake* an experience that shares so many elements with adult NDEs. Furthermore, people who have been blind from birth have described visual experiences of color, shape, and form during NDEs that they could never have "seen" if their experience had not been real. Although they were under anesthesia, NDEers have accurately described objects unknown to them and located them in a place they could not possibly have observed in an unconscious, immobile state. While on the operating table, one woman described a pair of running shoes lying on the roof of the hospital building; this was later confirmed. The *profound* life-changing effect that NDEers carry with them also testifies to the **validity** of their experience. After having an NDE, individuals are said to be changed people. They tend to be more religious, more aware of how short life is, more determined to live their life fully, and less afraid of death. They become more caring and show increased concern for others to the point of making personal sacrifices. Surely no one can be so deeply affected by an event that has never happened to them.

7   Seeing, or experiencing, is believing, and for anyone who has neither had an NDE nor encountered a person who has, accounts of NDEs sound unbelievable. Particularly where angels, mystical beings, cities of gold, and fantastic otherworldly aspects are involved, one is inclined to dismiss NDEs as figments of the imagination or wacky products of New Age wishful thinking. *Skeptics* call upon science to dispute NDEs as physiological and neurological anomalies that occur while the person is under the influence of anesthesia or lacks oxygen. Memories, mistaken for a life review, could be **triggered** by electrical discharges in the brain as it undergoes trauma. Rather than addressing the whole experience itself, skeptics and disbelievers have challenged only individual aspects of NDEs, and their arguments fail to explain how it is possible that so many people who have no connection to each other can fabricate the same story.

8   In the final analysis, whether we believe in NDEs or not depends on our **conception** of the human body and human life. Are we biological machines with finite life spans, or are we temporary manifestations of a greater spiritual life force? Regardless of our standpoints on this very

complex subject, NDEs can stimulate thought on the meaning of death and offer insights into the possibility of an afterlife. If NDEs can teach us to accept death without fear, then NDEs can do humanity a great service.

9   As for what really happens when or after we die, there is only one way we'll ever find out.

After reading

In the Pre-reading section, check to see if your predictions about the reading text were correct.

Vocabulary

EXERCISE
3·1

Thematic vocabulary *List 10 words or phrases related to death and dying.*

_____   _____

_____   _____

_____   _____

_____   _____

_____   _____

EXERCISE
3·2

Academic vocabulary *Using a dictionary, complete the following chart with the correct forms of the **academic words** from the reading text.*

Noun	Adjective	Verb
1. _____	_____	cease
2. _____	_____	conclude
3. _____	_____	document
4. _____	_____	establish
5. _____	_____	evolve
6. _____	_____	survive
7. _____	_____	transport
8. conception, _____	_____	_____
9. validity, _____	_____	_____
10. _____	(ir)reversible	_____
11. _____	X	alter
12. _____	X	compile

Noun	Adjective	Verb
13. _____	X	encounter
14. _____	X	trigger
15. awareness	_____	X
16. element	_____	X
17. incident	_____	X
18. insight	_____	X
19. phenomenon	_____	X
20. research, _____	X	_____

EXERCISE
3·3

Using vocabulary, part 1 *Replace the underlined word or phrase in each of the following sentences with the appropriate word from the chart in Exercise 3-2. Be sure to use the correct form of each verb and to pluralize nouns, if necessary.*

1. The documentary *An Inconvenient Truth* raised people's <u>consciousness</u> of the impact of global warming.

   _____

2. After he examined the evidence left at the crime scene, what did the detective <u>determine</u>?

   _____

3. Looking through the family photo album <u>set off</u> many happy memories of our vacations at the cottage on the lake.

   _____

4. Spending time in prison for a crime the man didn't commit completely <u>changed</u> his life.

   _____

5. You can gain a lot of <u>clear understanding</u> into famous people's lives by reading their memoirs.

   _____

6. In his journal, the explorer <u>recorded</u> the weather conditions and the team's experiences in the Antarctic.

   _____

7. On its journey across the ocean, the ship <u>unexpectedly experienced</u> a violent storm and sank.

   _____

8. The journalist has <u>gathered</u> shocking case studies on victims of violent crime.

   _____

9. The university is carrying out <u>a systematic study to establish facts</u> in the field of genetics.

   _____

10. The appearance of ghosts is one <u>rare occurrence</u> that science cannot rationally explain.

   _____

EXERCISE
3·4

Using vocabulary, part 2 *For each of the following sentences, choose the correct form of the **academic word** to fill in the blank.*

1. The student's claim that he failed his course because the teacher didn't like him is not
   _____.
   a. validity
   b. valid
   c. validate

2. Every religion has a different _____ of what happens to a person after he dies.
   a. conception
   b. conceptual
   c. conceive

3. As the result of a motorcycle accident, the young driver suffered _____ brain damage.
   a. irreversibility
   b. irreversible

4. Every day, airplanes _____ passengers and cargo from continent to continent.
   a. transportation
   b. transported
   c. transport

5. The _____ of a credible theory depends on solid evidence.
   a. establishment
   b. established
   c. establish

6. After we found that someone had broken into our car, we reported the _____ to the police.
   a. incident
   b. incidental

7. Computer technology is constantly _____.
   a. evolution
   b. evolved
   c. evolving

8. A person is considered clinically dead when all brain function _____.
   a. cessation
   b. ceaseless
   c. ceases

9. Our _____ depends on a healthy environment.
   a. survival
   b. surviving
   c. survive

10. What are the main _____ of a short story?
    a. elements
    b. elemental

Nonacademic vocabulary *Using a dictionary, complete the following chart with the correct part of speech and definition of each of the **nonacademic words** in the reading text.*

Word	Part of speech	Definition
1. consciousness	_____	_____
2. determine	_____	_____
3. extensive	_____	_____
4. fake	_____	_____
5. judgment	_____	_____
6. profound	_____	_____
7. relieve	_____	_____
8. revive	_____	_____
9. skeptic	_____	_____
10. verify	_____	_____

Reading comprehension

Reading for main ideas *Choose the boldface word or phrase that correctly completes each of the following statements.*

1. Near-death experiences **are** | **are not** a recent phenomenon.

2. NDEs **have been** | **have not been** scientifically proven to have occurred.

3. NDEs occur when people **die** | **nearly die**.

4. NDEs follow **a very similar pattern, regardless of** | **a very different pattern, depending on** a person's age, gender, religion, culture, geographic location, and medical condition.

5. NDEs are the subject of **scientific research** | **rumor and speculation**.

6. The majority of NDEs are generally **unpleasant** | **pleasant** experiences.

7. An NDE **has to** | **does not have to** include all 12 elements to be classified as an NDE.

8. Skeptics **have successfully proven** | **have not successfully proven** that NDEs are just stories that people have made up.

9. NDEs have a **positive** | **negative** impact on people's lives.

10. NDEs **can** | **cannot** provide insight into the death process.

EXERCISE
3·7

Reading for details *For each of the following sentences, choose the correct answer to fill in the blank.*

1. According to research, _____ of Americans have had an NDE.
   a. 0.5%
   b. 5%
   c. 15%

2. Between 1980 and 1990, the number of reports of NDEs in the United States _____.
   a. decreased
   b. stayed the same
   c. increased

3. NDEs consist of _____ common elements.
   a. 2
   b. 8
   c. 12

4. _____ percent of people who have come close to death have had an NDE.
   a. Thirty-five
   b. Fifty
   c. Five

5. The term *near-death experience* was first used by _____.
   a. the Greeks and Romans
   b. Dr. Raymond Moody
   c. the International Association for Near-Death Studies

Indicate which of the following statements are true (T) and which are false (F).

6. _____ Children have very different NDEs than adults.

7. _____ Most people who have NDEs do not wish to return to their bodies and their earthly life.

8. _____ During an NDE, a person often encounters loved ones who have already died.

9. _____ After having an NDE, people are more afraid of death than they were previously.

10. _____ Entering a tunnel and seeing a bright light are the most commonly reported elements of an NDE.

11. _____ NDEs have never been scientifically studied.

Answer the following questions in complete sentences.

12. What does the term *near-death experience* mean?

_____

_____

13. Why do some people not tell their doctor that they have had an NDE?

_____

_____

14. What organizations were established to carry out research into NDEs?

_____

_____

15. What is the first thing that happens to a person who loses consciousness and has an NDE?

_____

_____

16. When is a person pronounced "clinically dead"?

_____

_____

17. What is a "life review"?

_____

_____

EXERCISE
3·8

Reading for interpretation and inference *Choose the correct interpretation for each of the following statements from the reading text. Pay special attention to the boldface words and phrases.*

1. "These questions have **preoccupied** human beings almost as long as we have been able to think and ponder the meaning of life and death."
   a. For many centuries, people have thought a lot about what death means.
   b. For many centuries, people have lived with the fear of death.

2. "While they hovered between life and death, many claim to have left their bodies and **caught a glimpse of what it is like on the other side**."
   a. People have watched themselves die.
   b. People have seen where we go when we die and what it looks like.

3. "The experience seems to last longer than the actual period in which the person is **clinically dead**. . . ."
   a. The experience seems to last longer than when the person is in the hospital.
   b. The experience seems to last longer than when the person is considered dead.

4. "It is also estimated that 35 percent of all people who **have a close brush with death** will have an NDE."
   a. Thirty-five percent of all people who have almost died have an NDE.
   b. Thirty-five percent of all people who are sick have had an NDE.

5. ". . . one is inclined to dismiss NDEs as **figments of the imagination or wacky products of New Age wishful thinking**."
   a. Some people think NDEs are make-believe.
   b. Some people think NDEs are supernatural.

6. "As for what really happens when or after we die, **there is only one way we'll ever find out**."
   a. We have to do more research to understand what happens when we die.
   b. We have to die in order to know what happens when we die.

Reading strategies
Organizing information

One useful way to organize information in a reading text is to create a chart with headings to represent the main ideas. Complete the following chart with the most important details from the reading text. Summarize the details in note form, not in complete sentences.

Definition of an NDE	
The effects of NDEs on people's lives	
Common elements of NDEs	

Arguments for the existence of NDEs	
Arguments against the existence of NDEs	

Critical thinking

EXERCISE 3·9

Making evaluations *Indicate which of the following experiences conform (✓) or do not conform (X) to a near-death experience.*

1. _____ I entered a room full of famous people. There I met Dr. Martin Luther King, Jr., and Mother Teresa, and talked to them for what seemed to be a long time.

2. _____ I could hear beautiful, harmonious music coming from all directions. It was almost angelic, like something I'd never heard before.

3. _____ I could feel myself floating above the operating table, and as I hovered, I could look down on the doctors as they tried to revive me.

4. _____ All of a sudden, I woke up on another planet, like Mars, or the moon. It was like I was in a science-fiction movie, and there were all these strange creatures, like robots, looking down at me.

5. _____ I felt a deep peace and happiness, like I had come home, and I had no sensation of pain, only joy and calm.

6. _____ I was very confused and terrified, and all I wanted was to return to my body and get out of this cold place that felt like a grave.

7. _____ Suddenly, everything went black, and when I woke up, I could remember nothing.

8. _____ At first, I entered a dark tunnel, but the light got much brighter as I moved up and into it. In the light, I could see my grandmother and my little sister, who died when she was a small child. They were holding hands and smiling at me.

9. _____ I had the feeling that I had to make a choice. I wanted to stay in this peaceful, loving place, but I knew that I was too young to die and that I had to go back and finish my life and be with my family, who were sad that I had tried to kill myself.

10. _____ I walked down this golden street, and at the end was a beautiful castle covered in jewels. When I entered the gate, everyone standing there bowed to me and led me to a great throne, where they put a crown on my head and made me king.

EXERCISE
3·10

Making a case *A family member or a good friend is hit by a car and almost dies. After the person recovers from the accident, you make a hospital visit and the person tells you the following story. Do you believe the person or not? Why? Which details would you believe, and which would you doubt or question?*

I was crossing the street, when suddenly this car came toward me and there was a loud crash and I flew through the air. It all happened so fast. I must have landed on the ground, because I felt this terrible pain, but then I could feel myself rising up, and when I looked down, there were people trying to help me. It was like I was floating and I could see them attach tubes and stuff to me and carry me to an ambulance.

Then I looked up, where I could see this light—a bright, shining, white light all around me, and it was like something was lifting me up into the light. At the end of the light, there was this beautiful, peaceful place, sort of like a meadow with mountains in the background. I could hear a voice, a soft voice calling me, and I recognized the voice of my grandmother, who died last summer.

When she held out her hand, I ran to her, but I wasn't really running—I was floating, like in slow motion or in water. She held out her arms to hug me, and I started to cry, I was so happy to see her. Then she said that she loved me and was glad to see me, but that I had to go back. I wanted to stay with her in that peaceful place, but she said it wasn't my time, and that my parents were very sad and worried and I had to go back to them.

_____

_____

_____

_____

_____

_____

Bibliography

Kellehear, Allan, "Near-Death Experiences" (*Macmillan Encyclopedia of Death and Dying*, 2002), http://www.encyclopedia.com/topic/near-death_experience.aspx.

Long, Jeffrey, with Paul Perry, *Evidence of the Afterlife: The Science of Near-Death Experiences* (New York: HarperCollins, 2010).

Lundahl, Craig R., and Harold A. Widdison, *The Eternal Journey: How Near-Death Experiences Illuminate Our Earthly Lives* (New York: Warner Books, 1997).

Genetically modified organisms

Breadbasket or Pandora's box?

Pre-reading

Using the following questionnaire, interview your classmates, colleagues, family, and friends.

Questionnaire   A   B   C

Where do you buy your food?
a. At a large supermarket
b. At a small grocery store
c. At a farmer's market
d. Other (specify: _____)

Do you buy locally grown food? Yes | No

Do you buy food that is imported from other countries?
Yes | No

What kind of food do you buy?
a. Organic food and natural products
b. Processed foods that are easy to prepare
c. Both

How would you rate the quality of food that is produced
and sold in your area?
a. Very good
b. Good
c. Average
d. Poor

Do you like to try new foods? Yes | No

Predicting content

Considering the title of the chapter, predict which of the following topics will
not be mentioned in the reading text.

☐ How cooks prepare food

☐ How farmers grow food

☐ How biotechnology alters food

☐ How companies sell food

☐ How government regulates food

Reading text

1   Imagine a tomato that doesn't lose its flavor when it's refrigerated, a potato that doesn't absorb oil when it's deep-fried, or a peanut that doesn't cause fatal allergic reactions. And what if plants and animals could deliver vaccines and pharmaceuticals in addition to *vital* nutrients? Are these foods just the product of someone's wild imagination, or can biotechnology create tastier, more appealing, and more nutritious foods? And if so, are genetically engineered superfoods all that they're cracked up to be?

2   For thousands of years, farmers have been using low-tech forms of genetic **manipulation** to **modify** plants and animals. From experience, farmers understood that plants and animals with desirable qualities produced offspring with the same traits. By mating superior animals or collecting seed from the best plants, farmers could improve their livestock and increase crop yields. In the mid-nineteenth century, Gregor Mendel's experiments with garden peas transformed traditional breeding practice into the science of genetics and sowed the seeds of an agricultural revolution.

3   The first of many scientists to *apply* Mendel's findings to commercial crop development was Dr. John Garton, who invented the process of multiple cross-fertilization of crop plants in England. Gartons Agricultural Plant Breeders became the first plant-breeding business; its first commercial product was Abundance Oat, *bred* from a controlled cross in 1892. Between 1904 and World War II, Nazareno Strampelli experimented with wheat hybrids in order to **significantly** reduce Italy's dependence on grain imports. In 1943, Norman Borlaug, an American agronomist, humanitarian, and Nobel laureate, conducted agricultural research in Mexico to develop high-yielding varieties of cereal grains. His efforts led to the "Green Revolution," which increased world food production into the 1970s through the distribution of hybridized seeds, the expansion of irrigation, the modernization of agricultural management, the development of more efficient farm machinery, and the introduction of synthetic fertilizers and pesticides.

4   At the same time, government institutions, universities, crop science industry associations, and private companies were competing to come up with hardier, higher-yielding hybrids that were resistant to disease, pests, and harsh climate conditions. In the 1970s and 1980s, breakthrough research in molecular biology provided scientists with the necessary tools to alter organisms at the cellular level. In 1972, scientists discovered the ability of restriction enzymes to identify genes and cut them out of a chromosome. That same year, researchers at Stanford University succeeded in splicing DNA fragments from different organisms. Three years later, the discovery of another group of enzymes, or ligases, made splicing genes easier. Further research into restriction enzymes revealed that once an **inserted** gene was accepted by its host organism, it could also be replicated when cells divided.

5   Genetic engineering, or recombinant DNA technology, was able to achieve with **precision** and efficiency what traditional breeding could never have accomplished: the creation of a transgenic organism that contained genes from another organism. The first to make it onto the cover of a magazine (the December 1982 issue of *Nature*) was a rat-sized transgenic mouse engineered with a rat gene for growth. The food industry, of course, had a strong interest in biotechnology, and the U.S. government gave genetic engineering technology the green light by providing grants for research into genetic manipulation of food crops. The early 1980s saw a proliferation of biotechnology companies in the fields of agriculture and pharmaceuticals, where the potential successes of recombinant DNA promised to be as *lucrative* as they were **innovative**.

6   By the mid-1980s, recombinant DNA technology moved from the laboratory into fields and markets. In 1986, the first transgenic tobacco crops were grown in the United States and France, and by 1997, 10 percent of corn and 14 percent of soybeans in the U.S. were grown from genetically engineered seeds. The next crops to be modified were herbicide- and insect-resistant canola, cotton, potatoes, squash, and tomatoes. Chymosin, the first genetically engineered food to receive, in 1990, Food and Drug Administration (FDA) *approval*, began to replace rennet in the production

of cheese. Three years after being approved for sale in 1994, the genetically engineered hormone bovine somatotropin (BST) was given to about 30 percent of dairy cows in the United States to increase milk production. In 2006, 10.3 million farmers in 22 countries planted 252 million acres of transgenic crops. The main producers of genetically engineered (GE) crops are the United States, Argentina, Brazil, Canada, India, China, Paraguay, and South Africa. In the future, the cultivation of GE crops is expected to increase dramatically in developing countries.

7   At first glance, the benefits of genetic engineering speak overwhelmingly in its favor, particularly when one considers that the United Nations predicts that, in 2050, there will be 9.2 to 10.5 billion mouths to feed on a planet with **finite** agricultural land. Supporters of biotechnology argue that genetic engineering can **ensure** an **adequate** food supply from crops that will mature earlier, contain more *nutrients*, resist pesticides and herbicides used to control insects and weeds, and produce higher yields. Researchers have had less success with animals due to the **complexity** of animal genes, the high cost of working with livestock, and the slow rate of animal reproduction, but genetic engineering has succeeded, for example, in improving the wool production of merino sheep in Australia. The birth of Dolly, the first cloned sheep, in 1997 showed that remarkable progress can be made.

8   The most serious issue surrounding genetically engineered foods is their safety. GE crops are grown in monocultures and require heavy use of pesticides and herbicides. Despite recommended safety limits, pesticides and herbicides leave residues on plants harvested and processed for human consumption. **Exposure** to organophosphorus, glufosinate ammonium, and glysophate has been proven to cause neurotoxicity, disruption of the endocrine system, immune system suppression, cancer, and other serious health problems. GE foods themselves have not been around long enough for their health effects to be thoroughly studied, let alone scientifically determined. Scientists may be able to turn genes off or to **transfer** them from one organism to another, but no one knows exactly how genes **interact** or what long-term effects these interactions could have. To date, very few studies have been published on the safety of GE foods, and since tests are **conducted** by the companies who develop and sell the products, the **reliability** of their findings is questionable.

9   In the meantime, governments have done little to **regulate** GE products and the companies who develop and market them. Shortly after BST was approved in the U.S., the Pure Food Campaign and some producers of milk products opposed it as *detrimental* to human and animal health, but their protests failed to bring about changes in the law. Food safety comes under the jurisdiction of the Department of Agriculture and the FDA, who evaluate the final product rather than the process that creates it. Since genes are considered to occur naturally and genetic modification is regarded as an extension of traditional agricultural breeding methods, GE foods are not subject to the same degree of regulation as either artificial additives and preservatives or potentially allergenic substances. Despite activist campaigns for stricter controls and labeling laws in the U.S. and a growing public resistance to GE products, the regulatory system tends to side with powerful food and pharmaceutical companies. In Europe, on the other hand, public opinion views genetically engineered organisms with skepticism and caution. In addition to the European Union's strict labeling laws, France and five other European countries proceeded in 2011 to ban genetically modified organisms on their soil.

10   Another sensitive issue in the debate is the long-term impact of GE crops on the environment. Heavy use of herbicides and pesticides leads to the emergence of more resistant weeds and pests. In addition to being *toxic* to humans, these chemicals harm or kill birds, insects, butterflies, bees, and other animals and threaten biodiversity, which is essential to maintaining balance in nature. Monocultures that employ industrial farming methods result in *contamination* of soil and groundwater, as well as depletion of soil nutrients, while large-scale irrigation depletes water resources.

11   **So-called** terminator crops that have been engineered for male sterility threaten both the environment and family farms. Sterile crops cannot produce seed, which means that farmers who used to save and replant seed are forced to buy new seed each planting season. Because plants reproduce through cross-pollination, the danger of transgenic contamination of non-GE crops and wild species can be neither avoided nor controlled, and the spread of sterile genes could be devastating. In 2011, 60 family farmers, seed businesses, and organic agricultural organizations filed a lawsuit against Monsanto, turning the tables on a multinational giant that has been in the habit of bringing patent infringement suits against farmers. These plaintiffs claimed that their crops had been contaminated by Monsanto's seeds. The number of lawsuits against companies like Monsanto has been growing.

12   Healthy crops can grow only in healthy environments. A significant number of farmers all over the world have been turning to sustainable agriculture in the form of organic, ecological, and biological agriculture as an economic, environmental, and socially *viable* means of boosting food production and protecting their livelihood. Contrary to the argument that organic farming produces low yields, studies have shown that agroecological practices not only increase yields, but also improve soil quality, reduce pests and diseases, **restore** traditional breeds and varieties, and result in better-tasting, more nutritious foods.

13   Of all the applications that genetic research has come up with, biotechnology and genetic engineering will likely remain the most **controversial**. The amount of time, energy, and money that has already been invested **indicates** that genetic engineering is here to stay, but the associated health and environmental risks coupled with social, philosophical, and ethical issues will continue to fuel the debate. Battles between companies claiming their right to do business and small farmers and producers defending their right to reject GE products will be lost and won in court. Biotechnological research will produce successes and failures, and studies will show positive and negative findings on both sides. In the end, the future will be decided by everyday consumers, who will choose what kind of food they put on their tables and into their mouths.

After reading

In the Pre-reading section, check to see if your predictions about the reading text were correct.

Vocabulary

EXERCISE
4·1

Thematic vocabulary *List 10 words or phrases related to agriculture.*

_____   _____

_____   _____

_____   _____

_____   _____

_____   _____

Academic vocabulary *Using a dictionary, complete the following chart with the correct part of speech and definition of each of the **academic words** in the reading text. If a word has multiple meanings, match the definition to the context in which the word is used in the text.*

Word	Part of speech	Definition
1. adequate	_____	_____
2. complexity	_____	_____
3. conduct	_____	_____
4. controversial	_____	_____
5. ensure	_____	_____
6. exposure	_____	_____
7. finite	_____	_____
8. innovative	_____	_____
9. indicate	_____	_____
10. insert	_____	_____
11. interact	_____	_____
12. manipulation	_____	_____
13. modify	_____	_____
14. precision	_____	_____
15. regulate	_____	_____
16. reliability	_____	_____
17. restore	_____	_____
18. significant	_____	_____
19. so-called	_____	_____
20. transfer	_____	_____

Using vocabulary, part 1 *Complete each of the following sentences with the appropriate word from the chart in Exercise 4-2. Be sure to use the correct tense and form of each verb and to pluralize nouns, if necessary.*

1. Genetic research has raised many _____ issues concerning the proper use of genetic information.

2. One way to _____ that no one can gain access to your e-mail or online bank accounts is to change your password every six months.

3. Not everyone can understand physics because of the subject's _____.

4. When you use an ATM, you must first _____ your bank card and then enter your PIN.

5. Brain and heart surgery require _____ and expertise on the part of the surgical team.

6. After the earthquake, the residents didn't have a(n) _____ supply of food and clean water.

7. Over the last decade, there has been _____ growth in the popularity of ecotourism and green tour operators.

8. The _____ expert turned out to be an impostor who pretended to have a medical degree.

9. The students are _____ a survey to find out how well the other classes manage their time and studies.

10. Because the supply of fossil fuels is _____, it is necessary to conserve energy and develop alternative renewable sources.

Using vocabulary, part 2 *For each of the following sentences, choose the correct form of the **academic word** to fill in the blank.*

1. _____ to toxic substances can have a long-term effect on a person's health.
   a. Exposure
   b. Exposed
   c. Expose

2. The arrows on the sign _____ the direction in which you must go.
   a. indication
   b. indicative
   c. indicate

3. Inventors and artists are very _____ people who come up with revolutionary ideas.
   a. innovation
   b. innovative
   c. innovate

4. It is interesting to observe how people _____ when they are required to solve a problem in a group.
   a. interaction
   b. interactive
   c. interact

5. The leader of the religious sect was accused of _____ and mind control in the case of the members who committed mass suicide.
   a. manipulation
   b. manipulative
   c. manipulate

6. Paralympic athletes use specially _____ equipment in order to compete in sports events.
   a. modification
   b. modified
   c. modify

7. The politician expressed his opposition to strict government _____ of businesses.
   a. regulation
   b. regulatory
   c. regulate

8. Cochlear implants can _____ a person's hearing.
   a. restoration
   b. restorative
   c. restore

9. Most Americans _____ on a car for transportation.
   a. reliability
   b. reliable
   c. rely

10. Money is _____ from one account to another.
    a. transference
    b. transferable
    c. transfer

Nonacademic vocabulary *Match each **nonacademic word** in column 1 with its definition in column 2. Then, indicate each word's part of speech (n., v., or adj.).*

_____ 1. apply _____
_____ 2. approval _____
_____ 3. contamination _____
_____ 4. detrimental _____
_____ 5. lucrative _____
_____ 6. nutrient _____
_____ 7. breed _____
_____ 8. toxic _____
_____ 9. viable _____
_____ 10. vital _____

a. nourishment, food
b. profitable, rewarding
c. use, employ
d. necessary, essential
e. poisonous, deadly
f. pollution, infection
g. possible, feasible
h. harmful, damaging
i. reproduce, mate
j. acceptance, permission

Reading comprehension

Reading for main ideas *Match each of the following headlines with the corresponding paragraph of the reading text. The answer for paragraph 1 has already been inserted.*

a. GE foods pose potential health threats
b. U.S. government supports biotechnology through minimal regulation; European countries take a more cautious position
c. Genetically engineered transgenic organisms lead to boom in biotechnology
d. Increasing numbers of farmers turn to organic farming and sustainable agriculture
e. GE technology promised to increase world food supply and improve livestock
f. Genetic modification used in traditional breeding practices
g. Government-approved transgenic products are grown and sold for mass consumption
h. Future of GE products to be determined by the consumer
i. Environmentalists and family farmers oppose multinational producers of terminator crops in court
j. Cultivation of GE crops has negative impacts on the environment
k. Discoveries in molecular biology provide scientists with technological tools to alter organisms
l. Science of genetics revolutionizes agriculture and crop breeding
m. Can science produce superfoods?

_m_ Paragraph 1

_____ Paragraph 2

_____ Paragraph 3

_____ Paragraph 4

_____ Paragraph 5

_____ Paragraph 6

_____ Paragraph 7

_____ Paragraph 8

_____ Paragraph 9

_____ Paragraph 10

_____ Paragraph 11

_____ Paragraph 12

_____ Paragraph 13

EXERCISE 4·7

Reading for details *For each of the following sentences, choose the correct answer to fill in the blank.*

1. The development of high-yielding cereal hybrids led to a period of advancement and modernization in agriculture known as the _____ Revolution.
   a. Industrial
   b. Green
   c. Agricultural

2. Organisms that can identify genes and cut them out of a chromosome are called _____.
   a. restriction enzymes
   b. ligases
   c. transgenic organisms

3. The first transgenic crops were grown in _____.
   a. Canada
   b. Brazil and Argentina
   c. the United States and France

4. Beginning in the 1990s, the genetically engineered hormone BST was given to _____ of dairy cows in the U.S.
   a. 10 percent
   b. 30 percent
   c. 50 percent

5. In 2006, transgenic crops were grown in _____ countries.
   a. 12
   b. 22
   c. 200

6. The first animal to be cloned was _____.
   a. a sheep
   b. a mouse
   c. a chicken

Indicate which of the following statements are true (T) and which are false (F).

7. _____ Traditional breeding practices are a form of genetic modification.

8. _____ Norman Borlaug invented cross-fertilization.

9. _____ Genetic engineering takes genes from one organism and transfers them into another.

10. _____ It is more difficult to genetically engineer animals than plants.

11. _____ The United States has stricter labeling laws for GE foods than the European Union.

12. _____ Studies show that organic farming produces lower yields than conventional farming.

Answer the following questions in complete sentences.

13. What are "terminator" crops?

_____

14. What are the two most serious issues regarding GE crops and foods?

_____

_____

15. According to supporters of biotechnology, what are four reasons that GE crops will be able to feed more people in the future?

_____

_____

_____

_____

16. Why are studies on the safety of GE products unreliable?

_____

_____

17. What are five benefits of organic farming?

_____

_____

_____

_____

_____

Reading for interpretation and inference, part 1 *Indicate which of the following statements in the reading text support (✓) or do not support (X) genetically engineered products.*

1. _____ "Genetic engineering, or recombinant DNA technology, was able to achieve with precision and efficiency what traditional breeding could never have accomplished: the creation of a transgenic organism that contained genes from another organism."

2. _____ "The early 1980s saw a proliferation of biotechnology companies in the fields of agriculture and pharmaceuticals, where the potential successes of recombinant DNA promised to be as lucrative as they were innovative."

3. _____ "France and five other European countries proceeded in 2011 to ban genetically modified organisms on their soil."

4. _____ "The birth of Dolly, the first cloned sheep, in 1997 showed that remarkable progress can be made."

5. _____ "GE foods themselves have not been around long enough for their health effects to be thoroughly studied, let alone scientifically determined."

6. _____ "Healthy crops can grow only in healthy environments."

EXERCISE

4·9

Reading for interpretation and inference, part 2 *Choose the correct interpretation for each of the following statements from the reading text. Pay special attention to the boldface words and phrases.*

1. "And if so, are genetically engineered superfoods all that **they're cracked up to be**?"
   a. Are genetically engineered superfoods defective?
   b. Are genetically engineered superfoods as good as people say they are?

2. "In the mid-nineteenth century, Gregor Mendel's experiments with garden peas transformed traditional breeding practice into the science of genetics and **sowed the seeds of an agricultural revolution**."
   a. In his experiments, Gregor Mendel planted a new kind of seed.
   b. Gregor Mendel's experiments were the beginning of great changes in agriculture.

3. "...the U.S. government **gave** genetic engineering technology **the green light** by providing grants for research into genetic manipulation of food crops."
   a. GE technology was able to go ahead with research.
   b. GE technology had to protect the environment.

4. "...but the associated health and environmental risks coupled with social, philosophical, and ethical issues will continue **to fuel the debate**."
   a. People will disagree about the value of genetic engineering.
   b. People will eventually agree about the value of genetic engineering.

5. "In 2011, 60 family farmers, seed businesses, and organic agricultural organizations filed a lawsuit against Monsanto, **turning the tables on** a multinational giant that has been in the habit of bringing patent infringement suits against farmers. These plaintiffs claimed that their crops had been contaminated by Monsanto's seeds."
   a. Family farmers, seed businesses, and organic agricultural organizations damaged Monsanto's offices.
   b. Family farmers, seed businesses, and organic agricultural organizations did to Monsanto what Monsanto had been doing to them.

Reading strategies

To summarize a text, particularly one that is long and contains lots of facts and details, it is necessary to differentiate between essential details, which support the main idea, and nonessential details, which the author has added for effect or interest's sake. An example of each type of detail follows:

ESSENTIAL DETAIL   "[Borlaug's] efforts led to the "Green Revolution," which increased world food production into the 1970s through the distribution of hybridized seeds, the expansion of irrigation, the modernization of agricultural management, the development of more efficient farm machinery, and the introduction of synthetic fertilizers and pesticides."

NONESSENTIAL DETAIL   Borlaug won a Nobel Prize for his research.

Imagine that you are an assistant to a political candidate who doesn't have time to read everything about genetically engineered food, but who has to decide whether to support it or not in an election campaign. It is your job to review articles on the subject and provide the candidate with only the most essential information. Remember that your candidate has to think about a lot of other important issues, but he or she needs to be informed enough to put forward a solid position on this issue.

EXERCISE
4·10

Essential and nonessential ideas and details *Indicate which detail in each of the following pairs of details from the reading text you consider essential (✓) and would include in a summary, and which you would consider nonessential (X) and leave out.*

1. Paragraph 2

   a. _____ Farmers bred plants and animals with desirable traits to produce better offspring.

   b. _____ Gregor Mendel experimented with garden peas.

2. Paragraph 3

   a. _____ Wheat and cereal grain hybrids were developed after World War II to increase food production.

   b. _____ Nazareno Strampelli experimented with hybrids to reduce Italy's dependency on grain imports.

3. Paragraph 4

    a. _____ Researchers at Stanford University succeeded in splicing DNA fragments in 1972.

    b. _____ Research in molecular biology made it possible for scientists to identify, splice, and duplicate DNA.

4. Paragraph 5

    a. _____ The first transgenic mouse appeared on the cover of *Nature* magazine in 1982.

    b. _____ The U.S. government supported genetic engineering by providing funding for research.

5. Paragraph 8

    a. _____ Herbicides and pesticides cause serious health problems, such as neurotoxicity, disruption of the endocrine system, immune system suppression, and cancer.

    b. _____ GE crops are grown in monocultures.

6. Paragraph 9

    a. _____ In 2011, France and five other countries banned genetically modified organisms on their soil.

    b. _____ GE foods are not as strictly regulated or controlled as additives and preservatives.

Now, scan the rest of the reading text and highlight the essential details.

Critical thinking

Making evaluations *Indicate which of the following uses of genetic engineering you support (✓) and which you do not support (X). Give reasons to support your answers.*

1. _____ Creating a peanut that doesn't cause an allergic reaction

2. _____ Creating larger fruits and vegetables in different colors and shapes

3. _____ Creating fruits, such as peaches or cherries, that don't have stones or pits

4. _____ Improving or changing the taste of unpopular foods, such as spinach

5. _____ Producing animals, such as pigs, with less fat

6. _____ Producing animals and plants that carry vaccines and drugs

7. _____ Creating giant animals that produce more meat

8. _____ Injecting seeds with pesticides and herbicides so that crops do not have to be sprayed

Making a case *Who do you think should win the court case in the following scenario? Give reasons to support your answer.*

Dream Ice Cream, a small natural foods company, makes organic ice cream products. To ensure its image as a "natural" food company, Dream Ice Cream advertises that it does not use milk containing genetically engineered hormones, and it includes this information on its labels.

The government passes a law forbidding advertising that directly or indirectly opposes GE products, and Dream Ice Cream is ordered to remove all labels from its products or pay a heavy fine.

Dream Ice Cream decides to take its case to court and argues that it has the right to advertise that its products are safe. The government's regulatory agency argues that GE products have not been proven unsafe and that Dream Ice Cream is guilty of unfair advertising.

_____

_____

_____

_____

_____

_____

_____

_____

_____

_____

_____

_____

_____

_____

_____

Bibliography

Ho, Mae-Wan, and Lim Li Ching, *GMO Free: Exposing the Hazards of Biotechnology to Ensure the Integrity of Our Food Supply* (Ridgefield, CT: Vital Health Publishing, 2004).

Huff, Ethan A., "Organic groups, farmers file preemptive lawsuit against Monsanto to protect themselves from inevitable destruction by GMOs" (Natural News.com, 2011), http://www.naturalnews.com/031922_Monsanto_lawsuit.html.

Human Genome Project Information, "Genetically Modified Foods and Organisms," http://www.ornl.gov/sci/techresources/Human_Genome/elsi/gmfood.shtml.

Marshall, Elizabeth, *High-Tech Harvest: A Look at Genetically Engineered Foods* (New York: Franklin Watts, 1999).

Men and women
Long live the difference

Pre-reading

Using the following questionnaire, interview your classmates, colleagues, family, and friends. Answers are provided in the answer key.

Questionnaire	A	B	C

1. Who is more likely to die in a car accident?
   Men | Women

2. Who has a greater chance of becoming blind?
   Men | Women

3. Who is more likely to subscribe to an Internet dating website? Men | Women

4. Who is more likely to commit suicide? Men | Women

5. Who is more likely to die within a year of having a heart attack? Men | Women

6. Who is more likely to die of a heart attack?
   Men | Women

7. Whose body has less water? Men | Women

8. Who is less likely to become a victim of online fraud?
   Men | Women

9. Who is more likely to go on a diet? Men | Women

10. Whose computer is more likely to be attacked by a virus? Men | Women

SOURCE http://socyberty.com/psychology/20-statistical-differences-between-men-and-women/.

Predicting content

Considering the title of the chapter, predict which of the following topics will be mentioned in the reading text.

☐ The biological differences between men and women

☐ The different jobs that men and women do

☐ How women's brains differ from men's brains

☐ Typical things that men and women say

☐ The reasons men and women behave the way they do

Reading text

1   The *relationship* between men and women has been the subject of lively discussion and countless jokes for who knows how long. More poems, stories, and songs have been written about the love between a man and woman than about any other **theme**. Some of literature's most memorable characters are lovers; take, for example, Romeo and Juliet, Antony and Cleopatra, Tristan and Isolde, Lancelot and Guinevere, Salim and Anarkali, and Scarlett O'Hara and Rhett Butler. It would seem that men and women simply cannot live without each other. Yet, despite their passionate and irresistible attraction to each other, men and women have a hard time figuring each other out.

2   Men and women have been regarded throughout human history as opposites. In Eastern philosophy, this **dichotomy** is characterized as *yin*, **representing** feminine energy, and *yang*, representing masculine energy. *Yin* stands for slowness, softness, coldness, wetness, tranquility, and night, while *yang* **symbolizes** dryness, heat, aggression, hardiness, and daylight. For every typically female characteristic, the opposite is **attributed** to males. Women are emotional; men are rational. Women are intuitive; men are logical. Women tend to be **passive** and submissive; men tend to be aggressive and dominant. Women need to **communicate**; men clam up and withdraw. Women seek relationships and community; men seek independence and power.

3   No one can dispute the universal biological difference between males and females, without which none of us would be around, as well as the distinct anatomical variations in height, weight, build, physical strength, and so on. On a cellular level, all that **differentiates** one gender from the other is the combination of two single chromosomes. A fertilized egg that contains two X chromosomes will develop into a female; if it has one X and one Y chromosome, it will become a male. Sex hormones—specifically estrogen and progesterone produced by a female's ovaries and testosterone secreted by the testes in males—are responsible for girls **maturing** at puberty into women and boys into men. Oxytocin, another important hormone that is released during stress, induces strong emotional **attachments** in females, while in males high levels of testosterone minimize the effects of this "relationship drug." Women are designed by nature to become pregnant, to give birth, and to nurture. Men, on the other hand, are built to protect their dependents and to provide for them.

4   In addition to playing a **role** in sexual development, hormones present in the mother's uterus during pregnancy *influence* the sexual differentiation of the brain. Men's brains are 11 percent larger, because they require more neurons to control their larger bodies and muscles. Men predominantly use the logical, rational left side of the brain, which makes them more skilled at mathematics and problem-solving. Their larger inferior parietal lobule **accounts for** their superior ability to **orient** and visualize three-dimensional shapes and to perform mechanical tasks. Women's more compact and efficient brains contain 4 percent more cells and cellular connections, a larger corpus callosum, and more developed Broca's and Wernicke's areas, which are

related to language. Women use both hemispheres of the brain to **process** information, and they are more communicative and creative in their thinking. Women are able to multitask, to carry out preplanned tasks, and to tune into specific stimuli, such as a baby crying at night.

5   Until recently, boys and girls were usually raised from early childhood to fullfil distinct roles in many cultures. These traditional gender roles of leader/hunter/protector and nurturer/caretaker/homemaker have their roots in tribal, agrarian, or nomadic societies where survival depended on the specific **functions** that men and women performed. Human society, however, is not static, and as everyday living became less survival-oriented through economic, social, and technological progress, strictly defined **gender** roles that worked in the past were no longer necessary or appropriate. In the Western world, feminism and the women's liberation movement of the 1960s and 1970s, coupled with universally accessible birth control and legalized abortion, gave women the choice to reproduce or not and freed them from the *stereotypes* a largely male-**dominated** society had **imposed** on them.

6   Social roles can change; biological roles cannot. As a result, men, who were generally comfortable with the status quo, and women, who began demanding more *autonomy*, equality, and opportunity, were finding themselves at odds. In the 1960s, the "battle of the sexes" began, and as divorce rates of around 50 percent in some countries would indicate, it is still raging.

7   In his best-selling book published in 1992, *Men Are from Mars, Women Are from Venus*, relationship therapist John Gray accounts for the conflicts between men and women by suggesting that they come from different planets,[1] speak completely different languages, and require different kinds of emotional nourishment. In addition to how they think and feel, men and women "**perceive**, react, respond, love, need, and appreciate differently." Gray identifies 12 areas in which men and women differ: *values*, *coping* with stress, **motivation**, improving relationships, language, need for *intimacy*, loving attitudes and feelings, love, arguments, keeping score, communication, and asking for support. Seven of these are summarized as follows:

- **Values** Men (Mr. Fix-It) offer solutions to problems; women (Mrs. Home Improvement Committee) volunteer advice. When a woman talks about a problem, she wants a man to listen and sympathize. Because she wants to help, a woman offers a man unsolicited advice, which he takes as disapproval or a lack of trust in his competence. Women complain that men never listen. Men object to women always trying to change them.

- **Coping with stress** Under stress, men focus and "go into their caves," where they work things out for themselves. Women feel emotionally overwhelmed and need to talk about their feelings. When a man goes into his cave, the woman feels shut out, because she senses that something is wrong and wants to be included. When a woman complains about a problem, she is getting things off her chest, but a man will think that she is either looking for advice or blaming him for the problem.

- **Motivation** Men are motivated when they feel needed, whereas women are motivated when they feel cherished. Because success is important to men, they want to make their partners happy. If a man doesn't feel needed, trusted, or appreciated, he shuts off. Because a woman values empathy, compassion, and attention more than solutions, she needs a man to show that he cares. When men can overcome their fear of not being good enough, they can give love. When women overcome their fear of being abandoned, they can receive love.

- **Language** Even though men and women may use the same words, they do not mean the same thing. Women are given to exaggeration ("I can't do *anything*" or "We *never* go out"), and they use superlatives, generalizations, and **metaphors** that men, who are more direct, factual, and concise, will take literally ("That's ridiculous" or "We went out last Friday"). As a result, women complain that they are not being heard, when in fact men are hearing them but not decoding their messages properly. A man misunderstands a woman's words; she misinterprets

---

[1] The planets Mars and Venus were named, respectively, for the Roman god of war and goddess of love.

his silence. Because men are taught never to say that they don't know the answer, they go into their caves to think in silence—something that women who think out loud absolutely do not understand.

- **Need for intimacy** Men are like rubber bands, alternating between autonomy, or pulling away, and intimacy. Women are like waves that rise and fall between feeling loving and good about themselves and feeling depressed, inadequate, and vulnerable.
- **Love** To feel loved, women need caring, understanding, respect, devotion, validation, and reassurance. Men's love priorities are trust, acceptance, appreciation, admiration, approval, and encouragement. If they are not aware of these different **primary** needs, men and women give only what they want rather than what their partner needs. The result is dissatisfaction, resentment, and hurt.
- **Arguments** When two people are emotionally and sexually involved, arguments end up being more about the way the couple is arguing than the issue that started the argument. The woman will disapprove of how the man is talking to her and he will feel that she disapproves of his point of view. When men are unable to say they are sorry because they believe it is a sign of weakness, and when women do not share their feelings in a clear and direct way, arguments can kill love.

8   In his book, Gray compares love to a garden that has to endure four seasons in order to flourish. To avoid the false expectations, bitter resentments, and deep disappointments that can damage a relationship irreparably, men and women have to recognize and accept their **intrinsic** differences. This requires ongoing effort and attention, but the rewards of a lasting relationship are worth everything one puts into it.

9   Just as we learn to use revolutionary new technology in our modern lives, we have the opportunity in the twenty-first century to transcend the *patterns* of the past and to redefine the way we interact. We cannot change our chromosomes, our hormones, or our brain structure, but we can change our habits, our behavior, and our attitudes toward the opposite sex. Instead of competing against each other, we can cooperate. Instead of showing disdain or ridicule, we can practice respect. Instead of striving for dominance, we can seek balance. We need not only to value the qualities that distinguish us as men and women, but also to maximize the resources that we share as human beings.

10   Maybe men and women can't always live with each other, but they can't live without each other either.

After reading

In the Pre-reading section, check to see if your predictions about the reading text were correct.

Vocabulary

EXERCISE

5·1

Thematic vocabulary *List 10 words or phrases related to men and women.*

_____	_____
_____	_____
_____	_____
_____	_____
_____	_____

EXERCISE

5·2

Academic vocabulary *Using a dictionary, complete the following chart with the correct part of speech and definition of each of the **academic words** in the reading text. If a word has multiple meanings, match the definition to the context in which the word is used in the text.*

Word	Part of speech	Definition
1. attachment	_____	_____
2. attribute	_____	_____
3. communicate	_____	_____
4. differentiate	_____	_____
5. dominate	_____	_____
6. function	_____	_____
7. gender	_____	_____
8. impose	_____	_____
9. intrinsic	_____	_____
10. mature	_____	_____
11. metaphor	_____	_____
12. motivation	_____	_____
13. orient	_____	_____
14. passive	_____	_____
15. perceive	_____	_____
16. primary	_____	_____
17. process	_____	_____

Word	Part of speech	Definition
18. role	_____	_____
19. symbolize	_____	_____
20. theme	_____	_____

EXERCISE 5·3

Using vocabulary, part 1 *Complete each of the following sentences with the appropriate **academic word** from the chart in Exercise 5-2. Be sure to use the correct form of each verb and to pluralize nouns, if necessary.*

1. How long will it take to _____ my passport application?

2. Katie Melua's song *If I Were a Sailboat* is full of powerful _____ for feelings of love.

3. This cell phone can _____ as a camera as well as a telephone.

4. The group's _____ focus is to come to a decision that everyone can accept.

5. _____ motivation, such as the desire to learn and do better, is more important than the promise of rewards or money.

6. When Jason came home from his first year at the university, everyone noticed how much he had _____.

7. An ultrasound examination can determine the _____ of the baby a pregnant woman is carrying.

8. The _____ for our Halloween party this year is the graveyard.

9. Our drama class is going put on Shakespeare's *Romeo and Juliet,* and I'm going to try out for the _____ of Juliet.

10. If you are too _____, other people will think that you don't care or that you're afraid to speak out and voice your opinion.

EXERCISE 5·4

Using vocabulary, part 2 *For each of the following sentences, choose the correct form of the **academic word** to fill in the blank.*

1. Small children have a very strong _____ to their mothers.
   a. attachment
   b. attachable
   c. attach

2. The young man's shyness is _____ to his lack of self-confidence.
   a. attribution
   b. attributed
   c. attribute

3. In order to work well together, the members of a group must be able to _____ clearly and effectively.
   a. communication
   b. communicative
   c. communicate

4. Because Sharon and Karen are identical twins, anyone who doesn't know them well can't _____ between the two of them, especially when they are wearing the same clothes and hairstyles.
   a. differentiation
   b. different
   c. differentiate

5. In any group, there is usually one person who tends to _____ the discussion.
   a. domination
   b. dominant
   c. dominate

6. Due to the riots, the government has _____ a 7 P.M. curfew to prevent people from going out into the streets at night.
   a. imposition
   b. imposing
   c. imposed

7. Despite his physical handicaps, Nick Vujocic has become an amazing _____ speaker.
   a. motivation
   b. motivational
   c. motivate

8. On the first day of classes, students are invited to attend an _____ session to acquaint them with the different services the university offers.
   a. orientation
   b. oriented
   c. orient

9. James Thurber's short story "The Secret Life of Walter Mitty" is witty and _____ in its analysis of how a man tries to escape an unhappy marriage.
   a. perception
   b. perceptive
   c. perceive

10. The white dove and the olive branch _____ peace.
    a. symbol
    b. symbolic
    c. symbolize

Nonacademic vocabulary *Match each **nonacademic word or phrase** in column 1 with its definition in column 2. Then, indicate each item's part of speech (n., v., or adj.).*

_____ 1. account for _____
_____ 2. cope _____
_____ 3. dichotomy _____
_____ 4. influence _____
_____ 5. intimacy _____
_____ 6. pattern _____
_____ 7. relationship _____
_____ 8. represent _____
_____ 9. stereotype _____
_____ 10. value _____

a. deal effectively with something
b. close familiarity or friendship
c. oversimplified idea of a person's characteristics
d. be the primary factor in
e. a form, design, or order that repeats itself
f. have a strong effect on someone or something
g. a belief about what is important
h. a connection between people or things
i. a separation between two things that are opposite
j. be an example of something

Reading comprehension

Reading for main ideas *Indicate which of the following areas are a main difference (✓) between men and women and which are not (X).*

1. _____ Biological functions and physical build

2. _____ Jobs and career choice

3. _____ Character traits

4. _____ Intelligence

5. _____ Ways of communicating and use of language

6. _____ Brain structure and functions

7. _____ Upbringing and roles in society

8. _____ Love and the need for intimacy

9. _____ Political opinions

10. _____ Motivation

11. _____ The importance of family

12. _____ Values

Reading for details *For each of the following sentences, choose the correct answer to fill in the blank.*

1. Females have _____ X chromosome(s).
   a. one
   b. two
   c. no

2. Males have _____ X chromosome(s).
   a. one
   b. two
   c. no

3. Men's brains are _____ women's brains.
   a. smaller than
   b. larger than
   c. the same size as

4. Women's brains contain _____ brain cells and cellular connections _____ men's brains.
   a. more . . . than
   b. fewer . . . than
   c. as many . . . as

5. Women produce only small amounts of _____.
   a. estrogen
   b. progesterone
   c. testosterone

6. Oxytocin produces strong emotional attachments in _____.
   a. men
   b. women
   c. both men and women

Indicate which of the following statements are true (T) and which are false (F).

7. _____ *Yin* stands for masculine energy and *yang* for feminine energy.

8. _____ Women have a stronger need to talk and communicate than men.

9. _____ Men predominantly use the right side of the brain.

10. _____ Women use both sides of their brain to process information.

11. _____ The divorce rate in many countries is 50 percent.

12. _____ Men and women use language in the same ways and mean the same things.

Answer the following questions in complete sentences.

13. In his book *Men Are from Mars, Women Are from Venus*, how does John Gray account for the differences between men and women?

   _____

   _____

14. What happened in the 1960s and 1970s to change the traditional roles that men and women had filled in the past?

_____

_____

Answer the following question.

15. Indicate which of the following characteristics or habits can be attributed to men (M) and which to women (W).

    a. _____ The ability to multitask

    b. _____ Rational, logical thinking

    c. _____ The need to talk about things

    d. _____ The role of breadwinner and leader

    e. _____ The role of caregiver and homemaker

    f. _____ Creative thinking

    g. _____ The tendency to offer solutions

    h. _____ The tendency to offer advice

    i. _____ The need to be appreciated

    j. _____ The need to be cherished

    k. _____ The need to think alone in silence

    l. _____ The ability to perform mechanical tasks

EXERCISE
5·8

Reading for interpretation and inference *Express the meaning of each of the following sentences by correctly interpreting the simile or metaphor it contains.*

1. Love is like a garden.

_____

2. Men are like rubber bands.

_____

3. Women are like waves.

_____

4. Men go into their caves.

_____

5. Men are Mr. Fix-It.

_____

6. Women are Mrs. Home Improvement Committee.

_____

7. Men are from Mars.

_____

8. Women are from Venus.

_____

Reading strategies

Organizing information *Outline the differences between men and women in the following chart. Enter the eight main ideas in Exercise 5-6 as categories, then scan the reading text for details and enter them in the appropriate columns.*

Category	Men	Women
1. _____	_____	_____
	_____	_____
2. _____	_____	_____
	_____	_____
3. _____	_____	_____
	_____	_____
4. _____	_____	_____
	_____	_____
5. _____	_____	_____
	_____	_____
6. _____	_____	_____
	_____	_____
7. _____	_____	_____
	_____	_____
8. _____	_____	_____
	_____	_____

Critical thinking

Making evaluations *Indicate who is likely to make each of the following statements: a man (M) or a woman (W).*

1. _____ "The house is always a mess."

2. _____ "Are you saying I'm not romantic?"

3. _____ "If you don't like your job, then quit."

4. _____ "You don't love me anymore."

5. _____ "Nothing is working."

6. _____ "I'm all right."

7. _____ "I think we should talk."

8. _____ "I can't do everything myself."

9. _____ "That's ridiculous."

10. _____ "Why didn't you call?"

EXERCISE
5·11

Making a case *American comedian George Carlin once said, "Women are crazy. Men are stupid. The main reason women are crazy is that men are stupid." Do you agree or disagree with this statement? Why?*

_____

_____

_____

Indicate whether you believe a man (M) or a woman (W) would be the better choice for each of the following positions, or whether both (B) would be suitable. Support your beliefs with facts and examples.

1. _____ The leader of a country

_____

_____

2. _____ An officer in the army

_____

_____

3. _____ A negotiator in a labor dispute

_____

_____

4. _____ The CEO of a multinational company

_____

_____

5. _____ A family counselor

_____

_____

6. _____ An astronaut

_____

_____

7. _____ An organizer of a citizen action group

_____

_____

8. _____ A language teacher

_____

_____

9. _____ A police officer

_____

_____

10. _____ A homecare worker for elderly people

_____

_____

Bibliography

Gray, John, *Men Are from Mars, Women Are from Venus: A Practical Guide for Improving Communication and Getting What You Want in Your Relationships* (New York: HarperCollins, 1992).

Hensley, Amber, "10 Big Differences Between Men's and Women's Brains" (*Masters of Healthcare*, June 16, 2009), http://www.mastersofhealthcare.com/blog/2009/10-big-differences-between-mens-and-womens-brains/.

Sabbatini, Renato, "Are There Differences Between the Brain of Males and Females?" (*Brain and Mind: Mind and Behavior*, No. 11), http://www.cerebromente.org.br/n11/mente/eisntein/cerebro-homens.html.

Electric cars
Greener, cleaner driving

Pre-reading

Using the following questionnaire, interview your classmates, colleagues, family, and friends.

Questionnaire	A	B	C

Do you or your family have a car? Yes | No

What kind of car do you have?
a. Compact or economy car
b. Full-size sedan
c. Luxury sedan
d. SUV
e. Minivan
f. Other (specify: _____)

How is your car powered?
a. Gas engine
b. Hybrid gas engine and electric motor
c. Electric motor

How often do you use your car?
a. Every day
b. One to two times a week
c. Only when necessary
d. Other (specify: _____)

How important is it to you to own a car?
a. Very important
b. Somewhat important
c. Slightly important
d. Not important at all

What is the most important feature of a car?
a. Fuel efficiency
b. Style and design
c. Speed
d. Size and comfort
e. Environmentally friendly
f. Other (specify: _____)

Predicting content

Read only the first paragraph of the reading text, then make three predictions about the content of the entire text.

_____

_____

_____

Reading text

1   Humans and their cars constituted the greatest love affair of the past century. Cars represent freedom, *mobility*, power, and status. Most people who don't have a car want one, and those who already own one would like a newer, bigger, faster, and fancier model. When one **considers** that in the United States the number of **vehicles** is increasing faster than the population, it looks like the love affair with the automobile has turned into an addiction.

U.S. household and vehicle statistics

Year	No. of households (thousands)	No. of registered vehicles (thousands)	Total vehicle miles (millions)
1950	43,554	43,501	458,246
1980	80,776	139,831	1,527,295
2000	104,705	213,300	2,746,925
2010	117,538	239,812	2,966,494

SOURCE *Transportation Energy Data Book: Edition 31,* Chapter 8, Office of Energy Efficiency and Renewable Energy, U.S. Department of Energy, 2010.

2   Statistics on car ownership are staggering. Between 1950 and 2010, the number of U.S. households nearly tripled, but the number of **registered** vehicles per household increased by 551 percent and the total miles driven by nearly 650 percent. Even though car sales **declined** almost 28 percent between 2007 and 2009 due to the **global** financial crisis, a total of 5.7 million new passenger cars were purchased in 2010. According to the U.S. Department of Energy's *Transportation Energy Data Book,* in 2010 there was nearly one vehicle (0.77) per capita, and nearly two vehicles (1.79) per household. In 1960, 2.5 percent of American households owned three or more cars; in 2010, that number had mushroomed to 19.5 percent. Data from the International Organization of Motor Vehicle Manufacturers reports that Japan, the United States, China, and Germany produced a total of 35,654,551 vehicles in 2008, with Japan in the lead at over 11.5 million units. In China, where an estimated 1.6 million cars were sold in 2000, car sales are projected to reach 100 million by 2015. As India and other Asian countries experience increasing economic **stability**, car ownership is expected to rise on a global scale.

3   Car manufacturing is responsible for one in ten manufacturing jobs, but along with car driving it is one of the biggest **contributors** to air pollution and global warming. Car manufacturing **consumes** one half of the world's oil, and for every gallon of gas burned in an automobile engine, 20 pounds of carbon dioxide (CO_2) are released into the atmosphere. Up to the 1960s, when the federal Clean Air Act gave governments in the United States the power to set air quality controls, cars had no pollution control **devices** whatsoever. Between 1975 and 2011, the carbon footprint for cars shrank by 51.5 percent, but the total output of CO_2 continued to grow. In 2008, the U.S. was responsible for 19.34 percent of global CO_2 emissions, **exceeded** only by China, which produced 6,801 million metric tons, and in 2010, CO_2 emissions from the U.S. transportation sector was 15

percent higher than 1990 levels. In addition to air pollution and greenhouse gases, automobiles have resulted in traffic gridlock, urban *sprawl*, and the paving of land for highways, roads, and parking lots. If there are one billion cars on the roads by 2030, as predicted, cars will have to change.

4   The *quest* for cleaner, greener cars in the U.S. has been slow going, and industry efforts have **fluctuated** with the price and supply of oil. Led by the Big Three—General Motors (GM), Ford, and Chrysler—the American car industry resisted pollution control, shoulder belts and headrests, unleaded gasoline, catalytic converters, and air bags until **legislation** made them *mandatory*. However, a mightier impetus for change came with the 1973–74 OPEC oil embargo, when within a few months the price of gasoline skyrocketed from 25 cents a gallon to a dollar and Americans started buying smaller, fuel-efficient Japanese and European cars. The Big Three reacted by turning out lighter economy cars—at least until oil supplies started flowing again and prices stabilized.

5   In 1989, the U.S. Congress banned leaded gasoline, but the state of California, where cities like Los Angeles were choking on automobile *exhaust* and smog, took an aggressive lead in the battle against air pollution. In 1990, the California Air Resources Board (CARB) *stipulated* that two percent of all cars sold in California must be zero-emission in 1998, and ten percent in 2003. Only electric cars would meet these requirements.[1]

6   While the automobile industry waged an all-out war against CARB's mandate, GM announced in 1990 that it would build an electric car. In December 1996, the lightweight, aerodynamic, snappy EV1 was introduced for lease only in test markets in California and Arizona. Powered by nickel–metal hydride batteries, EV1s had a driving **range** of 100 to 120 miles. To recharge the batteries at home, the lessee could use a safe and easy paddle charging system. Between 1996 and 1999, GM built 1,117 electric cars in three generations. Drivers, many of whom were celebrities, were enthusiastic about their EV1s and the car's fast *acceleration* and smooth ride. In fact, many would not have been deterred by the EV1's retail price of $34,995 or the $20,000 to $30,000 replacement cost for the battery pack, but GM decided in 2003 to withdraw the car and crush all but a few, which the company kept or donated to museums. Although GM justified ending the program due to high production costs and lack of economic viability, there is some speculation that GM caved in to pressure from the automobile and oil industries and that the electric car was doomed from the get-go.

7   While GM was developing the EV1, competing carmakers were coming out with their own **versions**. Their limited driving range, a long recharging time, and the shortage of charging stations made electric vehicles better suited to city driving. The Ford Electric Ranger and the Chevrolet S-10 electric trucks were produced in limited numbers and leased to urban delivery fleets, but a few years later, both models were **terminated** and destroyed. Consumer-oriented vehicles, like Toyota's RAV4 EV, Honda's EV Plus, and the Nissan Altra, also ended up as scrap. In Europe, towns and cities were turning their busy centers into internal combustion engine–free zones, where electric vehicles turned out to be more successful as taxis, small delivery vehicles, buses, rental cars, and city cars.

8   In North America, electric cars just could not make it on the market despite the clear benefits of zero emissions, cheaper operating costs, 90 percent efficiency, and an overall reduced dependency on oil. Naysayers might argue that since the electric car relies on fossil fuel–burning power plants for electricity, they are not so environmentally friendly after all. On the other hand, the Union of Concerned Scientists **maintains** that it would take 1,440 EVs to produce the CO_2 emitted by one conventional automobile. Nevertheless, as long as gas remained cheap and plenti-

---

[1] From the late 1880s to the turn of the century, electric vehicles had enjoyed popularity in American cities, but after 1910, the internal combustion automobile emerged as the nation's vehicle of choice, and electric car manufacturers disappeared.

ful, drivers who were used to a convenient fill-up at the nearest service station were not ready to trust a car powered by a battery that might run out of juice in the middle of the highway. As a result, the electric car died a premature death.

9   When Toyota *launched* the Prius in 1997 in Japan, the breakthrough hybrid gas-electric car looked like a best-of-both-worlds solution. There are two types of hybrids: series hybrids, which use a small gasoline or diesel engine to **generate** the power that drives an electric motor and recharges the battery pack, and parallel hybrids, which can switch between a gasoline engine and an electric motor, depending on the power needed for driving. Electric motors work best for acceleration, while gasoline engines produce a steady speed on the highway. Hybrid cars are light, compact, quiet, and fuel- and energy-efficient, and some shut off automatically when the car is stopped at a traffic light. **Conversely**, hybrids are more expensive to purchase, service, and maintain, and their high-voltage battery can be dangerous in an accident or fail to *charge* fully in colder climate conditions. Although hybrids are low in *emissions,* they still give off greenhouse gases.

10   The Prius has been the front-runner in the hybrid race for market share, and its sales in 70 countries suggest that car buyers are more tuned in to the hybrid's benefits than its drawbacks. Of course, every other carmaker has been following on Toyota's heels with its own hybrid sedan, coupe, SUV, pickup, van, and luxury models. Judging by the variety of series and parallel hybrids, including diesel, plug-in, mild, and full hybrids on the market, the hybrid seems to be well on the road to replacing the conventional internal combustion–powered automobile.

11   Ever since Karl Benz built the first modern gasoline-powered automobile in Mannheim, Germany, in 1885, the car has undergone constant metamorphosis. To see how cars keep up with the times, all anyone has to do is attend an **annual** automobile show or subscribe to an automobile publication. Whereas car manufacturers have been more concerned in the past with styling and performance, they are beginning to focus more on making cleaner and greener cars, which makes one wonder what cars will look like down the road. In 10 or 20 years, will we be driving a new generation of hybrids, or will the electric models make a comeback? Will people be cruising down the highways in cars powered by hydrogen fuel cells, or motoring around town in mini Smart cars? Will cars, at some point, be able to fly?

12   In any case, people are not likely to **abandon** their cars, even if cities build more efficient, affordable, and environmentally friendly public transportation systems. People's love affair with the car is still going strong, and if car manufacturers have their way, it will not cool down any time soon.

After reading

In the Pre-reading section, check to see if your predictions about the reading text were correct.

Vocabulary

EXERCISE
6·1

Thematic vocabulary *List 10 words or phrases related to cars and driving.*

_____   _____

_____   _____

_____   _____

_____   _____

EXERCISE
6·2

Academic vocabulary *Using a dictionary, complete the following chart with the correct forms and definitions of the **academic words** from the reading text. If a word has multiple meanings, match the definition to the context in which the word is used in the text.*

Noun	Adjective	Verb	Definition
1. stability	_____	_____	_____
2. legislation	_____	_____	_____
3. _____	global	_____	_____
4. _____	X	abandon	_____
5. _____		consider	_____
6. _____	_____	consume	_____
7. _____	_____	exceed	_____
8. _____	_____	generate	_____
9. _____	_____	maintain	_____
10. _____	X	register	_____
11. _____	_____	terminate	_____
12. contributor, _____	_____	_____	_____
13. _____	X	decline	_____
14. _____	X	fluctuate	_____
15. range	X	_____	_____
16. vehicle	_____	X	_____

Noun	Adjective	Verb	Definition
17. device	X	X	_____
18. version	X	X	_____
19. X	annual	X	_____
20. _____	converse(ly)	X	_____

EXERCISE
6·3

Using vocabulary, part 1 _Complete each of the following sentences with the appropriate **academic word** from the chart in Exercise 6-2. Be sure to use the correct form of each verb and to pluralize nouns, if necessary._

1. We _____ our candidate to be the best-qualified person for the position of party leader.

2. I have to make an appointment with my doctor for my _____ checkup.

3. The Internet can be a very useful tool for research. _____, because there is so much information out there, you have to differentiate between unreliable and trustworthy websites.

4. When there was no hope of recovery from his illness, the patient decided to

   _____ his treatment.

5. The birthrate in industrialized countries has been _____ in recent years.

6. A large number of _____ prepared traditional foods and participated in this year's multicultural festival.

7. When you drive a car regularly, you have to _____ it in order to keep it in good running condition.

8. This store has a wide _____ of excellent digital cameras.

9. All countries should be concerned about _____ warming.

10. The newly elected president promises to restore economic _____ and create jobs.

11. Industrialized countries _____ a large share of the world's resources.

12. Every year, cell phone companies bring out new _____ of their most popular models to stay competitive.

13. There are too many _____ on the road during rush hour.

14. Hydroelectric dams _____ most of British Columbia's electricity.

15. Our blood pressure and heart rate _____, depending on our level of physical activity.

16. The passengers had to _____ the sinking ship.

17. The government has just passed new _____ making it illegal to use cell phones while driving.

18. During takeoff and landing, all passengers on the airplane must turn off their electronic _____.

19. Prices rise when demand for goods and commodities _____ the supply.

20. When you check into the hotel, you have to _____ at the front desk.

EXERCISE
6·4

Nonacademic vocabulary *Match each **nonacademic word or phrase** in column 1 with its definition in column 2. Then, indicate each item's part of speech (n., v., or adj.).*

_____ 1. acceleration _____

_____ 2. charge _____

_____ 3. emission _____

_____ 4. exhaust _____

_____ 5. launch _____

_____ 6. mandatory _____

_____ 7. mobility _____

_____ 8. quest _____

_____ 9. sprawl _____

_____ 10. stipulate _____

a. specify, require
b. start, initiate
c. speeding up
d. flexibility, movement
e. spreading out
f. gases, waste
g. top up, replenish
h. compulsory, obligatory
i. search, mission
j. discharge, outflow

Reading comprehension

EXERCISE
6·5

Reading for main ideas *Choose the boldface word or phrase that correctly completes each of the following statements. Some statements include two sets of choices.*

1. In the United States, car ownership is **increasing | decreasing** at a **slower | faster** rate than the population.

2. Car manufacturing and driving are **minor | major** sources of air pollution, greenhouse gases, and environmental destruction.

3. The American car industry **has been | has not been** a leader in developing cleaner, greener cars.

4. **The price of oil | Government regulation** has had a greater effect on the car industry than the price of oil | government regulation.

5. Electric cars, such as the EV1, **were | were not** commercial successes in the United States largely due to **technical problems | pressure from the automotive and oil industries.**

6. Electric cars **are | are not** more environmentally friendly than internal combustion–powered cars.

7. The electric-gasoline hybrid car **has proven | has not proven** to be a successful alternative to the internal combustion–powered car.

8. Car manufacturers are becoming more focused on **improving performance and styling | making cars more energy-efficient and environmentally friendly.**

9. The car is **likely | unlikely** to disappear from streets and roads in the future.

EXERCISE
6·6

Reading for details *For each of the following sentences, choose the correct answer to fill in the blank.*

1. In 2010, the average household in the United States owned nearly _____ cars.
    a. one
    b. two
    c. three

2. _____ produced the greatest number of cars in 2008.
    a. The United States
    b. Germany
    c. Japan

3. _____ in ten people work(s) in the car manufacturing industry.
    a. One
    b. Three
    c. Five

4. _____ developed the EV1.
    a. Ford
    b. GM
    c. Chrysler

5. "The Big Three" refers to _____.
    a. the three most popular car models
    b. Ford, GM, and Chrysler
    c. three anti-pollution laws passed by governments in the United States

6. The Prius was developed by _____.
    a. GM
    b. Daimler-Benz
    c. Toyota

Indicate which of the following statements are true (T) and which are false (F).

7. _____ Before the 1960s, there were no pollution control devices of any kind in cars.

8. _____ The state of California has been a leader in fighting air pollution caused by cars.

9. _____ During the 1973–74 oil embargo, American carmakers continued to make big cars that consumed a lot of gasoline.

10. _____ GM decided to destroy its fleet of EV1s, because no one was interested in buying or driving them.

11. _____ Electric cars have been more popular in Europe than in North America.

12. _____ Hybrid cars are cheaper to produce and maintain than conventional automobiles.

Answer the following questions in complete sentences.

13. What effect did the 1973–74 oil embargo have on American carmakers?

_____

_____

14. What was the 1990 CARB mandate, and what was its effect?

_____

_____

15. What is the difference between a series hybrid and a parallel hybrid?

_____

_____

16. What are four advantages of electric cars?

_____

_____

_____

_____

17. What are five advantages of hybrid cars?

_____

_____

_____

_____

_____

Reading for interpretation and inference *Choose the correct interpretation for each of the following statements from the reading text. Pay special attention to the boldface words and phrases.*

1. "... it looks like the love affair with the automobile **has turned into an addiction**."
   a. People can live without their cars.
   b. People can't live without their cars.

2. "... there is some speculation that GM **caved in to pressure** from the automobile and oil industries...."
   a. GM lost the most money in the automobile and oil industry.
   b. GM stopped its EV1 program, because the automobile and oil industry didn't support electric cars.

3. "... the electric car was **doomed from the get-go**."
   a. There was no hope of success for the electric car from the beginning.
   b. The electric car project got off to a bad start.

4. "Statistics on car ownership are **staggering**."
   a. Statistics fluctuate.
   b. Statistics are shocking.

5. "... cities like Los Angeles were **choking** on automobile exhaust and smog...."
   a. Los Angeles had a serious air pollution problem.
   b. Los Angeles couldn't solve its air pollution problem.

6. "While the automobile industry **waged an all-out war against** the CARB mandate, GM announced in 1990 that it would build an electric car."
   a. The automobile industry did everything in its power to fight the CARB mandate.
   b. The automobile industry protested the CARB mandate.

7. "In North America, electric cars **just could not make it on the market** despite the clear benefits of zero emissions, cheaper operating costs, 90 percent efficiency, and an overall reduced dependency on oil."
   a. Electric cars were not produced in North America.
   b. Electric cars did not sell well in North America.

8. "As a result, the electric car **died a premature death**."
   a. The electric car was an immediate failure.
   b. The electric car was stopped before it had a chance to develop.

9. "When Toyota launched the Prius in 1997 in Japan, the breakthrough hybrid gas-electric car looked like a **best-of-both-worlds solution**."
   a. The hybrid car was an ideal compromise.
   b. The hybrid car was popular in both North America and Japan.

10. "... car buyers are **more tuned in to** the hybrid's benefits than its drawbacks."
    a. Car buyers prefer hybrids to other cars.
    b. Car buyers are more aware of the advantages.

Reading strategies
Paraphrasing

To summarize a reading text, you don't have to quote all the facts and figures. Instead, to show that you understand what these numbers mean, you can restate them; that is, you can get the general idea across without referring to the actual numbers. You can do this by

- converting percentages to fractions, and vice versa
- using the descriptive verbs, adjectives, and adverbs in the following chart to describe a trend

Verbs that indicate an increase

grow, rise, increase, climb, surge, swell, explode, skyrocket

Verbs that indicate a decrease

fall, decline, decrease, lower, drop, dwindle, sink, plummet, plunge

Verbs that indicate stability

remain, stay, hold steady, stagnate, linger, show no change, level off, freeze

Verbs that indicate a combination of increases and decreases

fluctuate, change, vary, shift, waver, go up and down, seesaw

Adjectives and adverbs that indicate a mathematical change

by ½	*half*
by 2	*double / two times*
by 3	*triple / three times*
by 4	*quadruple / four times*
by more	*five/ten/twenty times*
	fivefold / tenfold

Adjectives and adverbs that indicate a large change

sharp(ly), steep(ly), dramatic(ally), significant(ly), measurable (measurably), exponential(ly), sudden(ly), major

Adjectives and adverbs that indicate stability

steady (steadily), constant(ly), consistent(ly), continuous(ly), progressive(ly), regular(ly)

Adjectives and adverbs that indicate a small change

gradual(ly), slow(ly), incremental(ly), little by little, minor, limited

Adjectives and adverbs that indicate very little change

minimal(ly), marginal(ly), nominal(ly), negligible (negligibly), barely, hardly

Here are some examples:

QUOTATION	"Costs have risen by 98 percent."
CONVERSION	Costs have **almost doubled.**
USING DESCRIPTIVE WORDS	Costs have **risen dramatically/significantly.**

Restating facts and figures *Paraphrase each of the following statements from the reading text, restating the facts and figures.*

1. "Between 1950 and 2010, the number of U.S. households nearly tripled, but the number of registered vehicles per household increased by 551 percent and the total miles driven by nearly 650 percent."

_____

_____

_____

2. "In 1960, 2.5 percent of American households owned three or more cars; in 2010, that number had mushroomed to 19.5 percent."

_____

_____

3. "Data from the International Organization of Motor Vehicle Manufacturers reports that Japan, the United States, China, and Germany produced a total of 35,654,551 vehicles in 2008, with Japan in the lead at over 11.5 million units. In China, where an estimated 1.6 million cars were sold in 2000, car sales are projected to reach 100 million by 2015."

_____

_____

_____

_____

4. "... in 2010, CO_2 emissions from the U.S. transportation sector was 15 percent higher than 1990 levels."

_____

_____

5. "... within a few months the price of gasoline skyrocketed from 25 cents a gallon to a dollar. ..."

_____

_____

6. "In 1990, the California Air Resources Board (CARB) stipulated that two percent of all cars sold in California must be zero-emission in 1998, and ten percent in 2003."

_____

_____

7. "Powered by nickel–metal hydride batteries, EV1s had a driving range of 100 to 120 miles."

_____

_____

8. "On the other hand, the Union of Concerned Scientists maintains that it would take 1,440 EVs to produce the CO_2 emitted by one conventional automobile."

_____

_____

Now, scan other reading texts for facts and figures, and apply what you have learned in this exercise to restate them.

Critical thinking

EXERCISE
6·9

Making evaluations *Paragraph 6 of the reading text states that many of the people, or lessors, who leased the EV1 would have bought one. Indicate which of the following statements would have been a reason to buy (✓) or not to buy (X) an EV1. Give reasons to support your answers.*

1. _____ The EV1 was cute and stylish.

2. _____ The EV1 was different from other cars.

3. _____ The EV1 drove and handled well.

4. _____ The EV1 was environmentally friendly.

5. _____ The EV1 was safe, reliable, and cheaper to run.

6. _____ The lessors were rich and could afford the price.

7. _____ The lessors preferred a small car.

8. _____ The lessors didn't have to do a lot of long-distance driving.

EXERCISE
6·10

Making a case *For each of the following types of cars, list the pros and cons regarding the car's popularity ten years from now.*

Type of car	Pros	Cons
Gasoline-powered	_____	_____
	_____	_____
	_____	_____
	_____	_____

Gasoline-electric hybrid _____ _____

_____ _____

_____ _____

_____ _____

Electric _____ _____

_____ _____

_____ _____

_____ _____

Hydrogen fuel cell–powered _____ _____

_____ _____

_____ _____

_____ _____

Bibliography

Brain, Marshall, "How Electric Cars Work" (How Stuff Works), http://auto.howstuffworks.com/electric-car.htm.

Cogan, Ron, "20 Truths about the GM EV1 Electric Car" (Green Car, 2008), http://www.greencar.com/articles/20-truths-gm-ev1-electric-car.php.

Davis, Stacy C., Susan W. Diegel, and Robert G. Boundy, *Transportation Energy Data Book: Edition 31* (Office of Energy Efficiency and Renewable Energy, U.S. Department of Energy, July 2012), http://cta.ornl.gov/data/index.shtml.

Motavalli, Jim, *Forward Drive: The Race to Build "Clean" Cars for the Future* (San Francisco: Sierra Club Books, 2000).

DNA fingerprinting
Condemning evidence

Pre-reading

Using the following questionnaire, interview your classmates, colleagues, family, and friends.

Questionnaire	A	B	C

Do you like to watch television shows or movies about crime? Yes | No

If your answer to No. 1 is "yes," which shows or movies do you watch?

Is crime a problem in your city or county? Yes | No

What is the most serious crime in your city or county?

Do you think the police do a good job of solving crimes and protecting people from criminals? Yes | No

Do you know of any famous cases in which DNA evidence was used to identify a criminal? Yes | No

Do you know of any famous cases in which DNA evidence was used to free someone who was sent to prison by mistake? Yes | No

Predicting content

Considering the title of the chapter, predict which of the following topics will be mentioned in the reading text.

☐ The types of crimes people commit

☐ How DNA can identify a criminal

☐ How long DNA has been used to solve crimes

☐ The first case in which DNA evidence identified a criminal

☐ What DNA is

Reading text

1   Anyone who watches television shows like *CSI: Crime Scene Investigation* will be familiar with DNA fingerprinting's importance in modern crime-solving. The day-to-day work of police detectives, crime scene **investigators**, and *forensic* technicians may not be as glamorous as it appears on television; nor can blood, saliva, hair, or skin samples be collected, **analyzed**, and *matched* to a *suspect* in 45 minutes. In any case, without DNA evidence and the technology that has evolved around its **detection**, many **violent** offenders would still be on the loose and innocent people would be executed or imprisoned for crimes they did not commit.

2   Before DNA arrived on the scene, digital fingerprints were the key to determining an individual's identity. The ridges and loops of fingerprints were first discovered in 1686 by an Italian anatomy professor, but it was not until 1892 that an Argentine police official **identified** a woman as the murderer of her two sons from a bloody fingerprint left on a doorpost. Fingerprints soon made their way into the criminal justice systems of England and the United States, where they were used to keep a record of convicted criminals. Although fingerprints are an *infallible* means of identification, careful criminals can avoid leaving them at a crime scene. On the other hand, DNA, which is present in every human cell even though invisible to the naked eye, is nearly impossible to **remove** completely, particularly in cases involving violent, unpremeditated crimes.

3   DNA testing would not be where it is today without the discoveries of British geneticist Alec Jeffreys and American biochemist Kary Mullis. In the early 1980s, Jeffreys developed the process of restriction fragment length polymorphism (RFLP) to **locate** polymorphic **regions** of a DNA strand where the greatest variation from person to person occurs. In 1984, he succeeded in photographing radioactive DNA fragments with X-ray film. The resulting image resembled a bar code, and the genetic **sequence** was unique to an individual, the only *exception* being identical twins.

4   In 1987, RFLP was used for the first time in the investigation into the rape and murder of two young girls. The first suspect, who had confessed to the earlier murder but denied the second, was released after his DNA failed to match the semen stains left on the *victims'* clothing. From January to July 1987, police collected saliva *samples* from 4,582 males between the ages of 17 and 34, but they could not catch the killer until a woman reported that she had overheard a man in a tavern tell his friends how he had been *intimidated* into giving a sample under the killer's name. The perpetrator was arrested, tested, and convicted.

5   While Alec Jeffreys was carrying out his lengthy research, Kary Mullis worked out, one night in 1983, an *ingenious* method to increase the amount of DNA **available** for testing. Polymerase chain reaction (PCR) analysis, for which Mullis received the Nobel Prize in chemistry in 1993, made it possible to create billions of copies of DNA in a matter of seconds and at low cost. Whereas RFLP tests produced more conclusive matches and a more complete picture of a DNA fingerprint, PCR could generate far more material from minute samples. Together, the two techniques would revolutionize forensic science.

6   Before DNA testing became a standard feature of the criminal justice system, **legal** hurdles had to be cleared. The same year that DNA fingerprinting solved its first criminal case in England, an accused rapist in the United States was also convicted on the basis of DNA evidence. This seemingly foolproof tool quickly made a stir in the media and the courts, where it went largely uncontested by defense lawyers, judges, and juries. The right to a fair trial regardless of a defendant's guilt or innocence is a fundamental right in any democratic society that operates under the rule of law. DNA evidence, however, was making it difficult for lawyers to defend their clients and for the courts to guarantee a fair trial to anyone **implicated** in a crime on the basis of DNA fingerprinting. Faced with such powerful physical evidence, defense lawyers could prove reasonable doubt only by questioning how the DNA evidence had been collected, handled, and analyzed.

7   At the time, private DNA testing laboratories were springing up in the United States. Without standardization or scientific **evaluation** of their methods, these companies were engaged

more in competing for dominance in a very profitable field than in ensuring the quality of their services. In the case of *People v. Castro,* defense lawyers Barry Scheck and Peter Neufeld **challenged** Lifecodes' analysis of the dried blood found on their client's watchband and sought to have the results **excluded** from testimony. A Frye hearing[1] determined that Lifecodes had done a sloppy job of **obtaining** the evidence and had misinterpreted the results. **Consequently,** the evidence was excluded and the case against Jose Castro was dismissed. Later, Castro admitted to the two murders for which he had stood trial, which proved that the testing laboratory and its methods, and not DNA evidence, were unreliable.

8 In the late 1980s, DNA testing achieved *legitimacy* with the involvement of governmental agencies. The Federal Bureau of Investigation (FBI), in collaboration with the National Institutes of Health, had been doing its own research, and in 1988, the FBI Crime Lab, established in the 1920s, included DNA evidence techniques in its services and provided analysis to law enforcement agencies free of charge. The Royal Canadian Mounted Police (RCMP) had also set up its own DNA testing facilities, and joint American-Canadian efforts brought about much-needed standards.

9 In the meantime, the controversy over DNA testing was still raging in the media, and lawyers Scheck and Neufeld were fighting for a moratorium on DNA evidence. In 1992, a two-year federally funded National Research Council study recommended that DNA evidence continue to be used in courts, and in 1994, the scientific and law enforcement communities agreed that DNA evidence should be considered legitimate and admissible in court. With further support for DNA fingerprinting in Great Britain, the controversy was defused, standards were implemented, research was stimulated, and a program was introduced in the United States to educate court judges about genetics and DNA testing.

10 The widespread acceptance of DNA fingerprinting led to the establishment of DNA databases, beginning in Great Britain, where DNA evidence had been more widely embraced from the start. Since the mid-1980s, the British government had been investing funds in a nationwide computerized database of DNA evidence from crime scenes and convicted criminals. Most violent offenders are repeat offenders, and by comparing DNA samples to available data, police investigators were able to solve both cold cases and recent crimes.

11 In the United States, a law passed in 1994 laid the groundwork for the formation of a nationwide database. Another three years passed, however, before eight states combined their databases into the National DNA Index System (NDIS). Within a few months, 300 previously unsolved violent crimes were cleared up. Further advances in DNA fingerprinting technology and its success rate culminated in the formation of the Combined DNA Index System (CODIS), and DNA profiles were **assembled** from federal, state, and local systems. By 1998, CODIS housed DNA fingerprints from 250,000 convicted criminals and evidence from the scenes of 4,600 violent crimes. In addition to computerized databases, DNA fingerprinting technology reduced the probability that someone other than the suspect had the same fingerprint from 1 in 1,000 to 1 in 26 billion.

12 DNA fingerprinting was not only bringing criminals to justice, but was also freeing wrongly convicted persons from long prison sentences. Predominantly poor African-American males in their mid-twenties (at the time of conviction) are frequently accused and found guilty, particularly in cases involving sexual assault, as a result of mistaken identity, police misconduct, careless forensics, an incompetent defense, or a false confession made under pressure. DNA evidence has been used by the Innocence Project, founded in 1992 at the Benjamin N. Cardozo School of Law at Yeshiva University by Barry Scheck and Peter Neufeld, to exonerate hundreds of wrongfully

---

[1] The Frye standard, established in 1923 to set standards for scientific evidence, states that scientific evidence must be based on a valid theory and must be obtained through a valid technique, which must be properly carried out.

convicted people. From 1989 to 2012, DNA evidence freed 292 men, 17 of whom were facing execution. Another 15 had been sentenced to life. DNA testing gave these men their lives back, and in 142 of these cases, the real perpetrator was found.

13   Despite DNA fingerprinting's usefulness, significant issues temper its success. Over the years, massive amounts of DNA evidence have been collected, but a lack of funding, qualified staff, and time has created huge backlogs of unprocessed information. DNA fingerprinting requires a high level of **expertise** and **accuracy**, and when testing is not properly carried out, violent offenders can go free to commit more crimes. The mishandling and possible contamination of evidence can still present a major problem, as was evident in the controversial 1994 double-murder case against O. J. Simpson[2] in Los Angeles. DNA evidence and DNA databases have become so vital to the criminal justice systems that politicians and police authorities have proposed requiring all persons who have been arrested and charged to give DNA samples, regardless of their guilt or innocence. Civil liberties organizations vigorously oppose such measures as an invasion of privacy and warn of the dangers should such private information ever be released to employers or insurance companies.

14   While lawmakers debate the legal uses of DNA fingerprinting, the science will continue to prove itself outside the crime lab and court of law. Already, DNA fingerprinting has been used to establish paternity and family relationships, to identify the remains of soldiers reported missing in action, to match organ donors with potential recipients, and to protect endangered animal and plant species. Population geneticists working with the Human Genome Diversity Project have been using DNA testing to study genetic differences within the human population in hopes of reconstructing human history. In the future, DNA fingerprinting will trace not only what we have done, but more importantly, where we come from and who we are.

After reading

In the Pre-reading section, check to see if your predictions about the reading text were correct.

Vocabulary

EXERCISE
7·1

Thematic vocabulary *List 10 words or phrases related to criminal justice.*

_____   _____

_____   _____

_____   _____

_____   _____

_____   _____

---

[2] O. J. Simpson, a former American football star and celebrity, was acquitted of the brutal murders of his estranged wife and a friend of hers after his lawyers argued that the police had mishandled and planted blood evidence in order to frame him; further, they argued that Simpson, an African-American, was the victim of racial discrimination on the part of the lead homicide detective.

Academic vocabulary *Using a dictionary, complete the following chart with the correct forms and definitions of the **academic words** from the reading text. If a word has multiple meanings, match the definition to the context in which the word is used in the text.*

Noun	Adjective	Verb	Definition
1. detection	_____	_____	_____
2. evaluation	_____	_____	_____
3. investigator, _____	_____	_____	_____
4. sequence	_____	_____	_____
5. _____	legal	_____	_____
6. _____	violent	_____	_____
7. _____	_____	analyze	_____
8. _____	X	assemble	_____
9. _____	_____	challenge	_____
10. _____	_____	exclude	_____
11. _____	_____	identify	_____
12. _____	X	locate	_____
13. _____	_____	implicate	_____
14. _____	_____	remove	_____
15. accuracy	_____	X	_____
16. expertise, _____	_____	X	_____
17. region	_____	X	_____
18. _____	available	_____	_____
19. _____	consequent(ly)	X	_____
20. X	_____	obtain	_____

Using vocabulary, part 1 *Complete each of the following sentences with the appropriate **academic word** from the chart in Exercise 7-2. Be sure to use the correct form of each verb and to pluralize nouns, if necessary.*

1. Processing DNA evidence requires considerable _____ on the part of trained forensic technicians.

2. Cars used to be _____ entirely by humans until the introduction of industrial robots.

3. To participate in the contest, you must enter the numbers in the same _____ in which they appear on your ticket.

4. Before scientists can come to a conclusion, they have to _____ their data to see if there are any patterns.

5. Family members are usually the first suspects to be _____ in a murder case.

6. The defense lawyer _____ the evidence gathered by police investigators.

7. Every month, the teachers write an _____ of each student's progress.

8. Last week, I _____ an application form from the passport office.

9. Because the witness has lied before, we have reason to doubt the _____ of his statement.

10. Red wine stains on a white tablecloth are very difficult to _____.

Using vocabulary, part 2 *For each of the following sentences, choose the correct form of the **academic word** to fill in the blank.*

1. The police investigators have promised to use all _____ resources to track down the murderer.
   a. availability
   b. available

2. DNA evidence, such as skin cells or body fluids, can be so small that it escapes _____.
   a. detection
   b. detectable
   c. detect

3. The _____ of people from clubs or organizations based on race or skin color is discriminatory and unacceptable in a democratic society.
   a. exclusion
   b. exclusive
   c. exclude

4. The special police team was called in to _____ the disappearance of two young children from a shopping mall.
   a. investigation
   b. investigative
   c. investigate

5. The research team has collected statistics on crime and organized its findings according to different _____ of the country.
   a. regions
   b. regional

6. Under interrogation, the suspect revealed the exact _____ of the victim's body.
   a. location
   b. local
   c. locate

7. Fewer _____ crimes occur in countries that have strict gun control laws.
   a. violence
   b. violent
   c. violate

8. The _____ of marijuana is a controversial subject.
   a. legalization
   b. legal
   c. legalize

9. When the police showed the woman photographs of known criminals, she was able to _____ the man who assaulted her and stole her purse.
   a. identification
   b. identifiable
   c. identify

10. Our actions can sometimes have serious _____.
    a. consequences
    b. consequently

EXERCISE 7·5

Nonacademic vocabulary *Match each **nonacademic word or phrase** in column 1 with its definition in column 2. Then, indicate each item's part of speech (n., v., or adj.).*

_____ 1. exception _____
_____ 2. forensic _____
_____ 3. infallible _____
_____ 4. ingenious _____
_____ 5. intimidate _____
_____ 6. legitimacy _____
_____ 7. match _____
_____ 8. sample _____
_____ 9. suspect _____
_____ 10. victim _____

a. relating to the use of science to investigate crime
b. a person believed to be guilty of a crime
c. frighten or force someone into doing something
d. something that does not follow a rule
e. a specimen taken for scientific analysis
f. a person harmed or killed in a crime or accident
g. being in accordance with the law
h. clever and inventive
i. never failing
j. correspond in appearance or likeness

Reading comprehension

Every paragraph has a topic sentence. A topic sentence contains the controlling idea for the paragraph and is usually the first sentence of the paragraph. Skimming only the topic sentences in a reading text can give the reader a general idea or overview of the text.

EXERCISE 7·6

Reading for main ideas *Write the topic sentence of each of the paragraphs of the reading text. The topic sentence of paragraph 1 has already been provided.*

Paragraph 1 _Anyone who watches television shows like CSI: Crime Scene Investigation will be familiar with DNA fingerprinting's importance in modern crime-solving._

Paragraph 2 _____

_____

Paragraph 3 _____

_____

Paragraph 4 _____

_____

Paragraph 5 _____

_____

Paragraph 6 _____

_____

Paragraph 7 _____

_____

Paragraph 8 _____

_____

Paragraph 9 _____

_____

Paragraph 10 _____

_____

Paragraph 11 _____

_____

Paragraph 12 _____

_____

Paragraph 13 _____

_____

Paragraph 14 _____

_____

Reading for details *For each of the following sentences, choose the correct answer to fill in the blank.*

1. Restriction fragment length polymorphism, or RFLP, was developed by a(n) _____.
   a. Italian anatomy professor
   b. British geneticist
   c. American biochemist

2. DNA testing was first used to solve a crime in _____.
   a. Argentina
   b. the United States
   c. England

3. The FBI Crime Lab was established in the _____.
   a. 1920s
   b. 1980s
   c. 1990s

4. The mishandling of DNA evidence played a major role in the defense of the accused in the
   _____.
   a. Jose Castro case
   b. O. J. Simpson case
   c. rape and murder of two young girls

5. From 1989 to 2012, DNA evidence cleared _____ wrongfully convicted people.
   a. 292
   b. 15
   c. 142

6. CODIS is a(n) _____.
   a. method for duplicating DNA in large amounts
   b. nationwide DNA database in the United States
   c. organization that helps wrongly accused prisoners

Indicate which of the following statements are true (T) and which are false (F).

7. _____ Digital fingerprints are more reliable than DNA fingerprints.

8. _____ DNA evidence can make it difficult for lawyers to defend their clients.

9. _____ RFLP and PCR analyses revolutionized forensic science.

10. _____ The first DNA database was established in the United States.

11. _____ Lawyers Scheck and Neufeld won their fight for a moratorium on DNA evidence.

12. _____ The FBI and the Royal Canadian Mounted Police were responsible for establishing
    scientific standards for processing DNA evidence.

Answer the following questions in complete sentences.

13. What two major advantages does DNA evidence have over digital fingerprints?

    _____

    _____

14. State five common reasons that innocent people are accused and convicted of crimes
    they didn't commit.

    _____

    _____

    _____

    _____

    _____

15. What was Kary Mullis's contribution to improving DNA testing?

    _____

    _____

16. State two reasons why civil liberties organizations object to mandatory DNA testing.

_____

_____

17. State five ways in which DNA testing can be useful outside of police work.

_____

_____

_____

_____

_____

_____

EXERCISE
7·8

Reading for interpretation and inference, part 1 *For each of the following statements from the reading text, choose the answer that more closely indicates the amount of support it provides for the use of DNA evidence.*

1. "DNA, which is present in every human cell even though invisible to the naked eye, is nearly impossible to remove completely, particularly in cases involving violent, unpremeditated crimes."
   a. Strong support
   b. Weak or no support

2. "The resulting [RFLP] image resembled a bar code, and the genetic sequence was unique to an individual, the only exception being identical twins."
   a. Strong support
   b. Weak or no support

3. "DNA evidence, however, was making it difficult for lawyers to defend their clients and for the courts to guarantee a fair trial to anyone implicated in a crime on the basis of DNA fingerprinting."
   a. Strong support
   b. Weak or no support

4. "A Frye hearing determined that Lifecodes had done a sloppy job of obtaining the evidence and had misinterpreted the results."
   a. Strong support
   b. Weak or no support

5. "In addition to computerized databases, DNA fingerprinting technology reduced the probability that someone other than the suspect had the same fingerprint from 1 in 1,000 to 1 in 26 billion."
   a. Strong support
   b. Weak or no support

6. "Civil liberties organizations vigorously oppose such measures as an invasion of privacy and warn of the dangers should such private information ever be released to employers or insurance companies."
   a. Strong support
   b. Weak or no support

EXERCISE
7·9

Reading for interpretation and inference, part 2 *Choose the correct interpretation for each of the following statements from the reading text. Pay special attention to the boldface words and phrases.*

1. "In any case, without DNA evidence and the technology that has evolved around its detection, many violent offenders would **still be on the loose**. . . ."
   a. Many violent offenders would not win their case.
   b. Many violent offenders would not be caught.

2. "Faced with such powerful physical evidence, defense lawyers could **prove reasonable doubt** only by questioning how the DNA evidence had been collected, handled, and analyzed."
   a. Defense lawyers could show that there is reason to believe their client is innocent.
   b. Defense lawyers could not believe in their client's innocence.

3. "A Frye hearing determined that Lifecodes had **done a sloppy job** of obtaining the evidence. . . ."
   a. Lifecodes had mishandled the evidence.
   b. Lifecodes had lost the evidence.

4. "Most violent offenders are repeat offenders, and by comparing DNA samples to available data, police investigators were able to solve both **cold cases** and recent crimes."
   a. Police investigators could solve previously unsolved cases.
   b. Police investigators could solve difficult cases.

5. "DNA testing **gave these men their lives back**, and in 142 of these cases, the real perpetrator was found."
   a. DNA testing improved the prisoners' health.
   b. DNA testing allowed these men to go free and resume their lives outside of prison.

Reading strategies
Paraphrasing: Using synonyms and definitions

When you paraphrase a reading text, it is important to use *your own words* to demonstrate that you understand the text. Copying directly from a text, especially if you claim the material as your own without crediting the original author, is plagiarism. Not only is plagiarism theft (and can land you in trouble), but it shows a lack of thought, effort, and originality.

The first paraphrasing technique is to substitute one of the following for a key word in the text:

- A different form of the word (noun, adjective, or verb)
- A synonym
- A definition

It is not enough to simply plug in other words; you also have to change the sentence structure. When choosing words, avoid making the text longer and wordier. Of course, some words cannot be changed, for example, proper nouns, scientific terms, and words that simply do not have an equivalent.

As an exercise, let's paraphrase the first topic sentence of the reading text.

> Anyone who watches television shows like *CSI: Crime Scene Investigation* will be familiar with DNA fingerprinting's importance in modern crime-solving.

First, identify the most important, or key, words.

> <u>Anyone</u> who watches television shows like *CSI: Crime Scene Investigation* will be <u>familiar</u> with DNA fingerprinting's <u>importance</u> in <u>modern</u> <u>crime-solving</u>.

Second, find a suitable synonym or short definition for the key words.

> anyone: most people
> familiar: to know about something
> importance: essential, necessary
> modern: today's, contemporary
> crime-solving: police work

Third, set the original topic sentence aside, think about its meaning, and rewrite the sentence *in your own words.*

> Most people who watch crime shows on television know how essential DNA fingerprinting is in today's police work.

Paraphrasing the topic sentences in the reading text *Paraphrase each of the topic sentences that you identified in Exercise 7-6: identify the key words, write a synonym or definition for each, and rewrite the sentence in your own words. For the topic sentences from paragraphs 2 and 3, the key words and their synonyms or definitions have been provided.*

Paragraph 2   "Before DNA <u>arrived on the scene</u>, digital fingerprints <u>were the key to determining</u> an individual's identity."

arrived on the scene: appeared

were the key to determining: identified

_____

_____

Paragraph 3   "DNA testing <u>would not be where it is today</u> without the <u>discoveries</u> of British geneticist Alec Jeffreys and American biochemist Kary Mullis."

would not be where it is today: wouldn't exist

discoveries: work

_____

_____

Paragraph 4   "In 1987, RFLP was used for the first time in the investigation into the rape and murder of two young girls."

_____

_____

_____

Paragraph 5   "While Alec Jeffreys was carrying out his lengthy research, Kary Mullis worked out, one night in 1983, an ingenious method to increase the amount of DNA available for testing."

_____

_____

_____

Paragraph 6   "Before DNA testing became a standard feature of the criminal justice system, legal hurdles had to be cleared."

_____

_____

_____

Paragraph 7   "Without standardization or scientific evaluation of their methods, these companies were engaged more in competing for dominance in a very profitable field than in ensuring the quality of their services."

_____

_____

_____

_____

Paragraph 8   "In the late 1980s, DNA testing achieved legitimacy with the involvement of governmental agencies."

_____

_____

_____

_____

Paragraph 9   "In 1992, a two-year federally funded National Research Council study recommended that DNA evidence continue to be used in courts, and in 1994, the scientific and law enforcement communities agreed that DNA evidence should be considered legitimate and admissible in court."

_____

_____

_____

_____

Paragraph 10   "The widespread acceptance of DNA fingerprinting led to the establishment of DNA databases, beginning in Great Britain, where DNA evidence had been more widely embraced from the start."

_____

_____

_____

_____

Paragraph 11   "In the United States, a law passed in 1994 laid the groundwork for the formation of a nationwide database."

_____

_____

_____

_____

Paragraph 12   "DNA fingerprinting was not only bringing criminals to justice, but was also freeing wrongly convicted persons from long prison sentences."

_____

_____

_____

_____

Critical thinking

EXERCISE
7·11

Making evaluations *Indicate which of the following uses of a DNA database are acceptable (✓) and which are not (X). Give reasons or examples to support your answers.*

1. _____ Keeping a record of known criminals

2. _____ Keeping a record of known criminals' family members

3. _____ Keeping a record of the entire population of a country

4. _____ Helping clear people convicted of crimes they didn't commit

5. _____ Identifying the remains of victims of crimes and of soldiers missing in action

6. _____ Categorizing the population in terms of race or ethnic background

7. _____ Finding potential organ donors for patients who require organ transplants

8. _____ Determining whether couples should have children

EXERCISE 7·12

Making a case *As part of its crime-fighting program, the government proposes a law that will require all citizens of all ages, including children and infants at birth, to provide DNA samples. These samples will then be registered in a nationwide database. Do you agree with this proposed law or not? Give reasons and examples to support your answer.*

_____

_____

_____

_____

_____

_____

_____

_____

_____

_____

_____

_____

_____

_____

_____

_____

_____

_____

_____

_____

_____

_____

Bibliography

"CODIS—Crime" (Federal Bureau of Investigation), http://www.fbi.gov/about-us/lab/codis/codis_crime.

"DNA Forensics" (Human Genome Project Information, June 2009), http://www.ornl.gov/sci/techresources/Human_Genome/elsi/forensics.shtml.

Fridell, Ron, *DNA Fingerprinting: The Ultimate Identity* (New York: Grolier Publishing, 2001).

"How many people have been exonerated through DNA testing?" (The Innocence Project), http://www.innocenceproject.org/Content/How_many_people_have_been_exonerated_through_DNA_testing.php.

"What are the causes of wrongful convictions?" (The Innocence Project), http://www.innocenceproject.org/Content/What_are_the_causes_of_wrongful_convictions.php.

Eco-cities
Building sustainable urban communities

Pre-reading

Using the following questionnaire, interview your classmates, colleagues, family, and friends.

Questionnaire	A	B	C

Where do you live?
a. In a large city (over 1 million people)
b. In a small city (under 1 million people)
c. In a suburb
d. In a town or village
e. In the country

What is the best thing about city living?
a. Shopping and restaurants
b. Culture and entertainment
c. Schools, colleges, and universities
d. Medical facilities
e. Job opportunities
f. Other (specify: _____)

What is the worst thing about city living?
a. Pollution
b. Crime
c. Traffic congestion
d. Unfriendly people
e. High cost of living
f. Other (specify: _____)

Do you think cities in your country have enough parks and green spaces? Yes | No

Do you think cities in your country have good public transportation? Yes | No

What do cities in your country need more of?
a. Parks and green spaces
b. Public transportation
c. Affordable housing
d. Clean and renewable energy
e. Better waste and sewage disposal
f. Other (specify: _____)

Predicting content

Considering the title of the chapter, make three predictions about the content of the reading text.

_____

_____

_____

Reading text

1   Cities are where all roads lead, and where commerce and culture flourish. The United States without New York, France without Paris, England without London, or Japan without Tokyo, would be like a body without a heart.

2   Up until the turn of the twentieth century, most people lived in rural areas, but they have always formed **communities** to protect themselves from hostile tribes, or to establish places where they could trade products and goods. The Industrial Revolution, which started in Great Britain in the 1800s and spread from Europe to North America, contributed significantly to the growth of cities, as people flocked to rapidly evolving manufacturing centers in search of jobs and business *opportunities*.

3   Urbanization—the *demographic* **shift** from country to city—began with industrialization, and it has not let up. In 1900, fewer than 15 percent of the world's population lived in cities. Fifty years later, that number had doubled to 30 percent, or a total population of 750 million. By 2000, 2.9 billion people, or 47 percent of the world's population, were living in urban areas, with the greatest growth occurring in Africa, Asia, and Latin America. In 2007, for the first time in history, the urban population exceeded 50 percent, and by 2050, according to the World Health Organization (WHO), seven out of ten people will call urban areas home. At a growth rate of 1.5 percent, or 60 million people per year, the number of urban inhabitants is expected to almost double to 6.4 billion by 2050. By then, developing countries, where the growth rate averages 1.2 million people per week, will see their urban population reach 5.2 billion.

4   Contrary to common belief, fewer than 10 percent of urban dwellers are **residents** of megacities with populations of over ten million. A megacity **consists of** the city proper and its adjoining suburban centers. An example is the New York–Newark **aggregation**, which in 1950 was the world's only megacity; by 2001, it was the fourth largest of 16 megacities, and by 2011, it was the sixth largest of 21 megacities. The population of Greater Tokyo, the world's largest urban area and home to 36.7 million residents, is forecast to exceed 37 million by 2020. Megacities Mumbai, Delhi, Dhaka, and Lagos, which do not yet appear on the Top Ten list, are steadily moving up the ladder. About half of the world's urban dwellers live in cities of under half a million people, and these cities continue to outpace megacities in growth.

World's largest cities		World's fastest-growing cities	
City	Population (millions)	City	Total growth* (percent)
1. Tokyo, Japan	36.7	1. Yamoussoukro, Côte d'Ivoire	43.8
2. Delhi, India	22.1	2. Ouagadougou, Burkina Faso	38.5
3. São Paolo, Brazil	20.3	3. Lilongwe, Malawi	28.9
4. Mumbai, India	20.0	4. Blantyre, Malawi	28.8
5. Mexico City, Mexico	19.5	5. Abuja, Nigeria	28.4
6. New York, United States	19.4	6. Huambo, Angola	26.1
7. Shanghai, China	16.6	7. Luanda, Angola	26.0
8. Kolkata, India	15.6	8. Jinjiang, China	25.9
9. Dhaka, Bangladesh	14.7	9. Sana'a, Yemen	25.3
10. Buenos Aires, Argentina	13.1	10. Hanoi, Vietnam	24.9
Karachi, Pakistan	13.1	Katmandu, Nepal	24.9

*2010–15.

SOURCE *The Economist Pocket World in Figures,* 2011 edition.

5   While the benefits of a developed infrastructure, public transportation system, employment opportunities, better health care, and education, plus a wide range of services, make cities *the* place to live, work, and enjoy, they are plagued with enormous problems. As engines of growth, cities have also become engines of pollution, traffic congestion, waste production, and environmental destruction. Besides producing tons of garbage and carbon dioxide emissions, North American cities, in particular, consume huge amounts of energy and leave a massive ecological footprint.[1] Compared with an ideal ecological footprint of 1, Canada's largest city, Toronto, with a population of 5.4 million, covers 240 square miles and requires 200 times the area to meet its resource requirements and absorb its waste. Vancouver's ecological footprint is 180 times its size, and London's is 125 times.

6   Poor pollution control and substandard water and waste management have a devastating impact on human health. Between 1664 and 1666, poorly managed water led for the second time in history to the spread of the bubonic plague in London and the death of one in every five citizens. Cholera epidemics, which claimed thousands of victims in cities all over the world in the 1800s and early 1900s, are by no means a thing of the past, as recent WHO reports verify in Africa today. In developing countries, cities with a high **concentration** of poor families housed in slums and substandard living conditions have no sewage system or toilets. In Dhaka, Bangladesh, people dispose of paper bags containing human waste by throwing them into the Buriganga River. When cities like Nairobi, Johannesburg, and São Paulo ignore the urgent need for proper *sanitation* and decent housing for the poor, violent crime and social unrest are the result.

7   The responsibility for city management lies with municipal governments that *derive* revenue from service fees and property taxes. To build and maintain infrastructure, cities also depend on federal and state or provincial government payment transfers. For several years, federal and state governments with high debt loads have offloaded more responsibilities onto already cash-strapped municipalities without providing the necessary financial support. In addition to **funding**, city governments need a clear **vision** for the future and innovative public administrators who can see that vision through. Unfortunately, elected public officials are more often bogged down in crisis

---

[1] A city's ecological footprint is the total area of productive land that a city requires to provide resources and absorb wastes divided by its geographical area.

management and Band-Aid solutions, which they hope will get them reelected. In the end, demands on failing services increase, an outdated **infrastructure** deteriorates, and poverty spirals downward into crime and despair.

8   So, are cities doomed to spread like cancers, devouring more agricultural land, wetlands, and sensitive natural habitats, or to *stagnate* like gigantic pools lacking the oxygen required to renew themselves? Or can our cities be saved, and even turned around, before it is too late? Can sustainable development meet "the needs of the present without compromising the ability of future generations to meet their own needs," as stated in the Brundtland Commission's 1987 report, *Our Common Future*, and create sustainable and vibrant cities?

9   In the 1960s, the concept of urban ecology emerged from the growing awareness of cities' impact on the environment. In 1975, the nonprofit organization Urban Ecology was founded in Berkeley, California, with the purpose of rebuilding cities in balance with nature. The 1992 Earth Summit in Rio de Janeiro established Agenda 21, a plan for the sustainable development of cities, and in 2002, 1,200 representatives (including 200 slum dwellers) from 80 countries participated in the first World Urban Forum, making urban ecology and sustainable eco-cities based on environment, economy, education, and equity more than just a nice idea.

10   Ideally, ecological cities should provide a high quality of life for their citizens while using minimal resources and reducing waste. Ten Ecopolis Development **Principles** identify how greener, safer, and healthier cities can be **achieved**.

1. **Restore degraded land** As stewards of the earth, people must clean up contaminated land, reestablish natural vegetation, designate green spaces, and encourage urban agriculture.
2. **Fit the bioregion** Urban settlements should conform to natural cycles and climate conditions, conserve and recycle resources, and use local materials to construct buildings that fit in with the landscape.
3. **Balance development** Urban expansion should occur within the limitations set by nature and leave a minimal ecological footprint on surrounding rural areas.
4. **Create compact cities** Cities can end urban sprawl by expanding vertically and creating high-density, walkable, and bikeable cities with an integrated public transportation network.
5. **Optimize energy performance** This means not only conserving energy and decreasing overall consumption, but also using efficient and locally generated renewable energy sources and **incorporating** energy-saving technology into building design.
6. **Contribute to the economy** Ecologically responsible industries and enterprises can provide stable employment, attract **investment**, and keep money in the local community.
7. **Provide health and security** A safe, healthy environment ensures a safe, healthy community.
8. **Encourage community** Since every resident has a vested interest, active citizen participation in decision-making and planning is key to a city's future.
9. **Promote social justice** Citizens must have equal rights and equal access to affordable housing; public services, facilities, and spaces; and local government information. They must be included in the democratic process.
10. **Enrich history and culture** As cultural meccas, cities should function as cultural caretakers and encourage diversity, creativity, and celebration.

These ten principles sound like a pretty tall order, but as Curibita and Hammerby Sjöstad **demonstrate**, sustainable cities are doable.

Curitiba, Brazil

11   The capital of the agricultural and resource-rich southernmost state of Paraná, Curitiba attracted waves of **immigrants** in the 1940s. Twenty years later, its population had exploded to 430,000. To manage the increasing demand for housing, services, and transportation, a team of architects and planners led by Jamie Lerner *devised* a redevelopment plan for the city. Adopted in 1968, when the population had increased to 600,000, the Curitiba Master Plan succeeded in

* establishing parks and increasing green areas, which are protected from future development
* reducing car traffic by 30 percent, creating the world's largest pedestrian shopping district, and building an affordable and easily accessible bus rapid transit system
* initiating a recycling system in which citizens receive bus vouchers, and children receive school supplies, toys, and chocolate as *rewards* for their participation
* preserving the city's historic core

Curitiba's recycling rate of 70 percent is the highest in the world, and 99 percent of its 1.8 million residents are happy living there. Despite economic recession, growing poverty, and increasing deforestation in Brazil, Curitiba's success in implementing eco-friendly programs has earned the city international *acclaim*.

Hammarby Sjöstad, Stockholm, Sweden

12   In the 1960s, a wave of residents moved out of Stockholm and into rural areas in search of a more environmentally harmonious lifestyle. When the **trend** reversed in the 1990s, the city found itself short of housing. After Stockholm lost its bid for the 2004 Olympic Games, the city **administration** used its plans for the most sustainable games ever by initiating a pilot housing project on the former industrial site of Hammarby Sjöstad. After purchasing and *rehabilitating* the land, the city implemented a master plan in **phases** for 11,000 residential apartments, which included

* closed-loop systems for water, waste, and energy to reduce consumption and increase efficient resource use
* incorporation of solar panels and solar cells into apartment blocks
* walkways and bike paths **linked** to public transportation that runs on alternative energy
* a neighborhood car-sharing program
* solid waste composting
* linear green spaces connecting housing with nature reserves
* retail space for shops, cafés, and restaurants on the ground floor of innovatively designed apartment buildings

13   Contrary to the city's expectations that, for the most part, retired people would move into the area, Hammarby Sjöstad became popular with young families. An education center called the *Glashus Ett* exhibits environmental technology and encourages environmental consciousness.

14   Curitiba and Hammarby Sjöstad are just two of many exciting examples of how cities can change for the better. It doesn't take much more than materials to build a city, but it takes commitment, foresight, and caring to make an eco-city a home for future generations.

After reading

In the Pre-reading section, check to see if your predictions about the reading text were correct.

Vocabulary

Thematic vocabulary *List 10 words or phrases related to cities and city living.*

_____   _____

_____   _____

_____   _____

_____   _____

_____   _____

Academic vocabulary *Using a dictionary, complete the following chart with the correct forms and definitions of the **academic words** from the reading text. If a word has multiple meanings, match the definition to the context in which the word is used in the text.*

Noun	Adjective	Verb	Definition
1. administration	_____	_____	_____
2. aggregation	_____	_____	_____
3. community	_____	_____	_____
4. immigrant, _____	_____	_____	_____
5. investment	X	_____	_____
6. resident, _____	_____	_____	_____
7. security	_____	_____	_____
8. trend	_____	_____	_____
9. vision	_____	_____	_____
10. _____	_____	demonstrate	_____
11. _____	X	incorporate	_____
12. _____	_____	achieve	_____
13. _____	X	link	_____
14. concentration	X	_____	_____

Noun	Adjective	Verb	Definition
15. funding, _____	X	_____	_____
16. phase	X	_____	_____
17. shift	X	_____	_____
18. principle	_____	X	_____
19. infrastructure	X	X	_____
20. X	X	consist of	_____

EXERCISE 8·3

Using vocabulary, part 1 *Complete each of the following sentences with the appropriate **academic word** from the chart in Exercise 8-2. Be sure to use the correct form of each verb and to pluralize nouns, if necessary.*

1. The new business, shopping, and residential complex is going to be built in five

   _____.

2. This neighborhood _____ mostly single-family dwellings and smaller apartment buildings.

3. The federal government will provide the city with _____ to build a new bridge.

4. There is a higher _____ of people living in the city core than in the suburbs.

5. We would rather live in a small, quiet _____ than a big bustling city.

6. Over the next several years, the city will need to upgrade its _____, and this

   work will require a large financial _____.

7. The city's transit system _____ buses with a light rail service so that people can travel from downtown to the airport.

8. An earthquake occurs when tectonic plates _____ and move against each other.

9. A city built on ecological _____ offers its citizens a higher quality of life.

Using vocabulary, part 2 *Complete each of the following sentences with the appropriate **academic word** from the pair of words listed. Be sure to use the correct form of each verb and to pluralize nouns, if necessary.*

1. administration, administrative

   a. The city _____ has its offices in Centennial Square.

   b. The city staff is responsible for all _____ work.

2. demonstration, demonstrate

   a. Curitiba and Hammarby Sjöstad _____ that it is possible to create sustainable communities where people like to live.

   b. Curitiba and Hammarby Sjöstad are _____ of successful eco-cities.

3. immigrant, immigrate

   a. My ancestors _____ to the United States from Germany and Sweden in the mid-1800s.

   b. In the mid-1880s, there was a large wave of European _____ settling in North America.

4. investment, invest

   a. The construction of a new bridge requires a major _____.

   b. It is necessary to _____ in upgrading the city's infrastructure.

5. achievement, achieve

   a. The newly elected city council hopes to _____ a higher quality of life for its downtown residents.

   b. Revitalizing the downtown area was a major _____.

6. resident, reside

   a. I am a _____ of James Bay.

   b. I _____ in James Bay.

7. incorporation, incorporate

   a. The building design should _____ passive solar energy.

   b. The architect recommended the _____ of passive solar heating into the building design.

8. vision, envision

   a. We need leaders who have a _____ for the future of our community.

   b. The planning committee _____ a greener community that includes parks, pedestrian trails, and bicycle paths.

9. security, secure

   a. A residential alarm system can give the homeowners a sense of _____.

   b. Deadbolt door locks and steel doors are more _____ than old-fashioned locks and wooden doors.

10. trend, trendy

   a. Condominiums in Yaletown are very _____ and popular with young professionals.

   b. The _____ among young professionals is to buy a condominium in Yaletown.

EXERCISE 8·5

Nonacademic vocabulary *Using a dictionary, complete the following chart with the correct part of speech and definition of each of the **nonacademic words** in the reading text.*

Word	Part of speech	Definition
1. acclaim	_____	_____
2. demographic	_____	_____
3. derive	_____	_____
4. devise	_____	_____
5. opportunity	_____	_____
6. optimize	_____	_____
7. rehabilitate	_____	_____
8. reward	_____	_____
9. sanitation	_____	_____
10. stagnate	_____	_____

Reading comprehension

EXERCISE 8·6

Reading for main ideas *Indicate which of the two statements in the following pairs contains a main idea (M) and which contains a supporting detail (SD)?*

1. a. _____ Throughout history, cities have functioned as commercial and cultural centers.

   b. _____ Cities began to grow because of the Industrial Revolution in England in the 1800s.

Eco-cities: Building sustainable urban communities **107**

2. a. _____ The greatest urban growth has occurred in Asia, Africa, and Latin America.

  b. _____ Since the 1900s, the urban population has more than tripled.

3. a. _____ Tokyo is the world's largest megacity.

  b. _____ Megacities are growing, but not as rapidly as smaller cities.

4. a. _____ Despite the benefits of an established infrastructure, cities have a negative ecological footprint.

  b. _____ Toronto needs an area 200 times the size of the actual city to meet its needs for resources and waste absorption.

5. a. _____ Poorly managed cities experience serious human health and social problems.

  b. _____ Cities in developing countries are characterized by overpopulated slums, poor sanitation, high crime rates, and social unrest.

6. a. _____ City officials are often more concerned with getting elected than with solving problems.

  b. _____ City governments have difficulty dealing with problems due to a lack of funding and vision.

7. a. _____ Urban ecology and sustainable cities can offer a higher quality of life based on ecological principles.

  b. _____ Agenda 21 specifies a plan for the sustainable development of cities.

8. a. _____ Curitiba and Hammarby Sjöstad were affected by trends in population growth.

  b. _____ Curitiba and Hammarby Sjöstad are examples of successful eco-cities built on environmental principles.

**EXERCISE
8·7**

Reading for details *For each of the following sentences, choose the correct answer to fill in the blank.*

1. The number of people living in urban communities exceeded 50 percent in the year _____.
   a. 1950
   b. 2000
   c. 2007

2. Megacities are classified according to _____.
   a. population
   b. total area
   c. their ecological footprint

3. The world's largest megacity is _____.
   a. New York
   b. Mumbai
   c. Tokyo

4. The urban ecology movement began in the _____.
   a. 1960s
   b. 1970s
   c. 1990s

5. Agenda 21 grew out of the _____.
   a. 1987 Brundtland Commission
   b. 1992 Rio Earth Summit
   c. ten Ecopolis Development Principles

6. Curitiba's recycling rate is _____.
   a. 30 percent
   b. 70 percent
   c. 99 percent

Indicate which of the following statements are true (T) and which are false (F).

7. _____ The ideal ecological footprint for a city is 10.

8. _____ Cities produce vast amounts of garbage and carbon dioxide emissions.

9. _____ Cities depend on service fees and property taxes for revenue.

10. _____ Sustainable development means maintaining cities as they are.

11. _____ Ecological cities use fewer resources and produce less waste.

12. _____ Megacities are growing at a faster rate than smaller cities.

Answer the following questions in complete sentences.

13. What is the definition of *urbanization*?

_____

14. Name five reasons that people are attracted to cities.

_____

_____

_____

_____

_____

15. How do you calculate the ecological footprint of a city?

_____

16. What are the four major problems facing modern cities?

_____

_____

_____

_____

17. What population trend was responsible for the development of Curitiba?

_____

_____

18. What population trend was responsible for the development of Hammarby Sjöstad?

_____

_____

EXERCISE
8·8

Reading for interpretation and inference *Match each of the following meanings with the corresponding underlined phrase in the numbered items below.*

a. reaching a higher position
b. something not very practical
c. seriously suffering from
d. very short of money
e. the absolute best
f. not being alive
g. answers that only temporarily hide a problem
h. entangled
i. no longer possible
j. passed on

_____ 1. "The United States without New York, France without Paris, England without London, or Japan without Tokyo, would be like a body without a heart."

_____ 2. "Megacities Mumbai, Delhi, Dhaka, and Lagos, which do not yet appear on the Top Ten list, are steadily moving up the ladder."

_____ 3. "... the benefits of a developed infrastructure, public transportation system, employment opportunities, better health care, and education, plus a wide range of services, make cities *the* place to live, work, and enjoy...."

_____ 4. "... they are plagued with enormous problems."

_____ 5. "Cholera epidemics, which claimed thousands of victims in cities all over the world in the 1800s and early 1900s, are by no means a thing of the past...."

_____ 6. "For several years, federal and state governments with high debt loads have offloaded more responsibilities...."

_____ 7. "... onto already cash-strapped municipalities without providing the necessary financial support."

_____ 8. "Unfortunately, elected public officials are more often bogged down in crisis management...."

_____ 9. "... and Band-Aid solutions, which they hope will get them reelected."

_____ 10. "... making urban ecology and sustainable eco-cities based on environment, economy, education, and equity more than just a nice idea."

Reading strategies

EXERCISE 8·9

Paraphrasing *Using the paraphrasing techniques in Chapter 7, paraphrase the ten Ecopolis Development Principles on page 102. The paraphrase of the first principle has already been provided.*

Principle 1 *Return land to its natural state by planting native species and creating parks and gardens.*

Principle 2 _____

_____

Principle 3 _____

_____

Principle 4 _____

_____

Principle 5 _____

_____

Principle 6 _____

_____

Principle 7 _____

_____

Principle 8 _____

_____

Principle 9 _____

_____

Principle 10 _____

_____

Organizing information

Summarize the features of Curitiba and Hammarby Sjöstad in the following chart.

Features	Curitiba	Hammarby Sjöstad
Location	_____	_____
Date plan was adopted	_____	_____
Green spaces	_____	_____

Features	Curitiba	Hammarby Sjöstad
Traffic and transportation	_____	_____
Energy	_____	_____
Handling of waste	_____	_____

Critical thinking

EXERCISE 8·10

Making evaluations *Indicate which of the following activities contribute to a sustainable eco-city (✓) and which do not (X). Give reasons to support your answers.*

1. _____ Growing lawns that require heavy watering in the summer

2. _____ Building neighborhoods of luxury single-family dwellings on a mountainside where all the trees have been removed

3. _____ Making the downtown core of the city a pedestrian zone

4. _____ Recycling organic household waste as compost for municipal parks and community gardens

5. _____ Tearing down a historic building and replacing it with multilevel parking

6. _____ Increasing fares for public transportation on a yearly basis

7. _____ Establishing rock gardens of native plants in a city that has a hot, dry climate and a limited water supply

8. _____ Incorporating solar energy into all public buildings

9. _____ Building more garbage landfills on the edge of the city

10. _____ Consulting residents when major construction projects are being planned

EXERCISE 8·11

Making a case *Make a case for or against the proposal for building a new bridge below. Do you think the city should build a new bridge or upgrade the old one and spend money on other projects? Give reasons to support your position.*

The city council has decided to borrow a large sum of money to replace a 90-year-old bridge with a modern structure. The old bridge is one of two of its kind in North America and is considered a heritage landmark by many citizens, who want to see it restored rather than torn down.

The city argues that it is too late to save the bridge, which has not been well maintained over the years, and that it would not be safe in the event of an earthquake. The new bridge design will include a separate bike lane and a separate pedestrian crossing.

The supporters of the old bridge argue that the city has purposefully neglected the bridge so that companies can make money building the new bridge, and that the city has misinformed the public and excluded citizens from the decision-making process. The new bridge would also use up money that is badly needed for more necessary projects, such as improving public transportation, renovating public buildings, and maintaining parks. In addition, city taxpayers will end up paying higher property taxes to finance the bridge when construction turns out to cost much more than estimated.

Bibliography

Bowden, Rob, *Cities* (Farmington Hills, MI: KidHaven Press, 2004).

"Building a 'Green' City Extension" (Future Communities), http://www.futurecommunities.net/case-studies/hammarby-sjostad-stockholm-sweden-1995-2015.

"The Development of Brazil's City of the Future" (PBS Frontline World), http://www.pbs.org/frontlineworld/fellows/brazil1203/master-plan.html.

The Economist Pocket World in Figures (London: Profile Books, Ltd., 2011).

Global Health Observatory, "Urban Population Growth (World Health Organization), http://www.who.int/gho/urban_health/situation_trends/urban_population_growth_text/en/index.html.

Hallsmith, Gwendolyn, *The Key to Sustainable Cities: Meeting Human Needs, Transforming Community Systems* (Gabriola Island, B.C.: New Society Publishers, 2003).

Just, Tobias, and Christian Thater, "Megacities: Boundless Growth?" (Frankfurt: Deutsche Bank Research, 2008), http://www.dbresearch.com/PROD/CIB_INTERNET_EN-PROD/PROD0000000000222116.pdf.

"What Is an Ecocity?" (Urban Ecology Australia, Ltd.), http://www.urbanecology.org.au/eco-cities/what-is-an-ecocity/.

·9· Solar energy
Power for the future

Pre-reading

Using the following questionnaire, interview your classmates, colleagues, family, and friends.

Questionnaire	A	B	C

What does the sun represent to you?
a. Power
b. Life
c. Happiness
d. Other (specify: _____)

Where does the energy that heats your home come from?
a. Oil
b. Coal
c. Natural gas
d. Hydroelectric power
e. Wood
f. Solar power
g. Other (specify: _____)

Does your city use solar energy? Yes | No

If "yes," how does your city use solar energy?
a. To heat and cool buildings
b. To heat water and swimming pools
c. To provide interior lighting
d. To provide street and garden lighting
e. Other (specify: _____)

What uses of solar energy are you familiar with?
a. Water heaters
b. Solar cells for calculators and electronic devices
c. Radios and emergency phone systems
d. Power for space satellites and telescopes
e. Other (specify: _____)

What kind of energy do you think is best for the environment?
a. Solar energy
b. Wind energy
c. Wave energy
d. Geothermal energy
e. Hydroelectric energy
f. Other (specify: _____)

114

Predicting content

Considering the title of the chapter, predict which of the following topics will *not* be mentioned in the reading text.

☐ The pros and cons of solar energy

☐ How much it costs to use solar energy

☐ The history of solar energy

☐ The pros and cons of fossil fuels

☐ The first developer of solar energy

Reading text

1   Throughout human history, the sun has been worshipped as a symbol of life and power. The ancient Egyptians, Romans, Greeks, Hittites, Persians, Aztecs, and Incas held annual celebrations, performed rituals, and made sacrifices to sun gods and goddesses. Kings and rulers, such as the "Sun King," Louis XIV of France, and the Japanese imperial family, claimed to be direct descendants or incarnations of the sun. Fifteen countries, notably Japan, Argentina, and Taiwan, display the sun on their national flags.

2   The sun is the most abundant **source** of energy in the solar system. Every day, 173,000 terawatts[1] of energy—100,000 times more energy than humans use—strike the earth in the form of sunlight. Sunlight consists of visible light; ultraviolet light, which is responsible for the production of Vitamin D in our skin; and infrared radiation, which heats the air, water, and ground, and **constitutes** nearly 50 percent of the total solar radiation reaching the earth. Without the sun, life on Earth would not exist. One would think that all that free, available energy would have been *harnessed* long ago, but only in recent decades have people taken a serious interest in the sun as a source of **alternative** *renewable* energy.

3   So far, the world has relied on wood, oil, coal, and natural gas to produce energy for heating, lighting, transportation, and manufacturing. Since the 1950s, world consumption has been increasing *relentlessly*. In the year 2000, 80 percent of commercial energy was generated from the *combustion* of fossil fuels, and every day, 50 million barrels of oil are **refined** and converted to gasoline and other fuels. In addition to the rapid *depletion* of fossil fuels, the consequences of high consumption rates are pollution and global warming.

4   Increasing **concentrations** of carbon dioxide (CO_2) in the atmosphere have been causing global temperatures to rise, with the greatest increase occurring in the last decade. In the 1990s, global CO_2 emissions rose by 1.3 percent per year. Between 2000 and 2006, annual CO_2 emissions increased to 3.3 percent, and since then they have been accelerating. To meet the 50–60 percent increase in energy demand by 2030, as predicted by the International Energy Agency, and to prevent the disastrous effects of global warming, people have been looking to the sun.

5   The most practical form of solar energy is passive solar energy, which occurs when natural light floods in through windows or is *absorbed* by stone or concrete walls. In 1956, the world's first commercial solar building was constructed in Albuquerque, New Mexico, by engineers Frank Bridgers and Don Paxton. Considered ahead of its time, architect Francis Stanley's design provided for large sloping south-facing windows to capture infrared radiation, following the same principles used by the ancient Romans to heat their bathhouses. Passive solar energy is now being incorporated into environmentally friendly building designs, which include double- or triple-glazed windows and insulated walls and ceilings to trap heat, Trombe walls painted black to

---

[1] One terawatt is **equivalent** to one billion watts.

maximize the absorption of infrared radiation, and mirrors or fiber optics to enhance natural lighting.

6   The most recognizable solar technology, photovoltaic (PV) cells, convert direct sunlight into electricity. Developed in 1941, the modern silicon PV cell, or solar cell, is a wafer made of two layers of crystalline silicon, a semiconducting material derived from sand or quartz. When sunlight strikes a PV cell's surface, electrons are knocked out of place, creating an electrical current. Solar cells are soldered together to form modules, which are combined into panels sandwiched between sheets of glass within an aluminum frame. PV panels, which work best in direct sunlight, can be mounted on tracking devices to follow the sun's movement. Solar panels are assembled into solar arrays; the larger the array, the greater the energy **output**.

7   In the late 1950s, solar cells were adopted by NASA to power satellites. The space industry's *pioneering* of solar technology for use in spacecraft has contributed to the *advancement*, reliability, and cost effectiveness of solar technology. PV panels are most commonly seen on rooftops and walls, but nowadays, anything from clocks, watches, calculators, road signs, and bus shelters to houses and commercial buildings can run on power generated by PV systems. Areas of PV arrays known as solar farms produce electricity on a scale large enough to be **distributed** through a power grid to thousands of homes. The world's largest solar farm, Waldpolenz Solarpark near Leipzig, Germany, covers 110 hectares[2] and uses state-of-the-art thin-film photovoltaic technology to produce 40,000 megawatts (MW) of electricity.

8   Concentrating solar power (CSP) uses large mirrors or receiving collectors to concentrate the sun's radiation on pipes, tubes, or cylinders filled with fluid or gas. An **intense** heat of 160° to 540°C (300° to 1,000°F) creates steam or expands gas to drive a turbine or electric generator. High-temperature collectors, such as giant parabolic dishes covered with mirrors, generate large amounts of electricity that is fed into a power grid. In the 1980s, nine thermal solar power plants with a combined **capacity** of 354 MW were built in the Mojave Desert. The Ivanpah Solar Power Facility, which is still under construction in the southwestern United States, will have a combined capacity of 392 MW.

9   Another form of collector technology is solar thermal energy, which heats swimming pools and household water. The first solar water heater was patented in the United States in 1891, and by 1897, nearly a third of the homes in Pasadena, California, had *installed* a solar water heating system. Interest in these systems revived in the late 1970s, but in the mid-1980s, their popularity declined with energy prices and the expiration of a federal tax credit.

10   Solar power has been the subject of intense debate. The **principal** issues are the following:

- **Fuel supply** Sunlight is free, renewable, and available to everyone, **albeit** more plentiful in areas closest to the equator, such as the Sahara Desert, which receives in excess of 4,000 hours of sunlight per year. Of course, the sun shines only during the day and its intensity depends on its position in a cloudless sky.
- **Environmental impact** Essentially, solar power releases zero emissions, and no or very few polluting chemicals or gases into the environment. The manufacture of solar equipment, however, occurs in factories that burn fossil fuels and emit CO_2. Solar cells are also made of chemicals that can end up as toxic waste.
- **Costs** Processing silicon for PV cells is expensive and consumes time and energy. Although silicon is abundant, prices are subject to demand and are expected to rise in the future. Nevertheless, solar cell manufacturing has become more efficient and cheaper, and prices have been falling steadily since the 1970s. Engineers continue to explore nonsilicon technology and to develop generations of thinner, cheaper, more flexible, more efficient, and more cost-effective solar cells for diverse applications. Microphotovoltaic substances can be printed on surfaces or

---

[2] One hectare is the equivalent of 2.47 acres.

woven into fabric for carrying cases, backpacks, and bags that can recharge electrical equipment, cell phones, and MP3 players.

- ◆ **Energy payback** Naysayers claim that solar energy is **prohibitively** expensive. At 20 cents per kilowatt hour, energy produced by PV plants costs ten times more than energy generated by fossil fuel–burning plants. Calculating the "payback," or time required to **offset** the carbon emissions from manufacturing, depends on many **variables**. The average payback of a residential or commercial PV system is estimated at four years, and technological advances are expected to reduce that timeframe. Because of additional construction and infrastructure costs, PV solar farms have a payback of 20 years or more. When focusing on costs, one must also consider that the scarcer fossil fuels become, the more expensive they will become.

- ◆ **Long-term energy savings** Not all individuals or businesses can afford a solar system. A two-kilowatt off-grid private system can cost $20,800, and a ten-kilowatt system can cost up to $104,000. A zero-energy home that feeds surplus power into a grid during the summer and draws electricity back on cloudy days or in winter adds an extra 10 to 20 percent to building costs, but over a period of 20 to 30 years, these additional expenses are **recovered** in energy savings. By reducing overall energy consumption and incorporating further energy-saving features into homes and buildings, a return on investment can be realized much sooner. Buildings that take advantage of passive solar heating can cut their heating costs in half. Through net metering, individuals can sell surplus electricity back to utility companies, as is done in Germany, Italy, and Spain.

11 Despite the safety, efficiency, and numerous environmentally friendly applications of solar energy, commitment to its development has fluctuated with the price of oil, particularly in North America, where government energy **policy** is strongly influenced by oil companies. During the 1973–74 OPEC oil embargo and the ensuing energy crisis, President Carter had solar panels installed on the White House, and the U.S. Department of Energy initiated the Federal Photovoltaic Utilization Program to install and test PV systems, many of which are still in operation. When the embargo was lifted six months later, oil prices stabilized and solar energy as a national energy policy ended up on the back burner.

12 In the meantime, solar energy has fared better in energy-conscious Europe and Japan, where the solar industry is **promoted** through government **subsidies** and tax **incentives**. Since 1990, Germany has become a world leader in thermal solar technology and the foremost installer of photovoltaic systems, having spent billions so far to promote solar energy. In Spain, all new buildings are required to include solar power, and Japanese researchers have developed a solar cell that can store electricity as well as generate it. Solar power is the cheapest, most practical solution for developing nations and remote areas without access to a national power grid, such as Antarctica and rural areas in China.

13 The onset of global warming and warnings from reputable organizations such as the United Nations' Intergovernmental Panel on Climate Change, have revived the solar market in North America and *spurred* government support of solar technology. In the United States, consumer demand and government tax credits are giving sales of solar systems a boost. In the first quarter of 2012, solar panel installations increased 85 percent over the previous year's first quarter, and total installations are expected to reach 3,300 megawatts, making the United States the fourth largest solar market.

14 If the upward trend continues and the global solar industry grows to a predicted $51 billion by 2014, it could very well be said that the world is beginning to see the light.

After reading

In the Pre-reading section, check to see if your predictions about the reading text were correct.

Vocabulary

Thematic vocabulary *List 10 words related to energy.*

_____   _____

_____   _____

_____   _____

_____   _____

_____   _____

Academic vocabulary *Using a dictionary, complete the following chart with the correct part of speech and definition of each of the **academic words** in the reading text. If a word has multiple meanings, match the definition to the context in which the word is used in the text.*

Word	Part of speech	Definition
1. albeit	_____	_____
2. alternative	_____	_____
3. capacity	_____	_____
4. concentration	_____	_____
5. constitute	_____	_____
6. distribute	_____	_____
7. equivalent	_____	_____
8. incentive	_____	_____
9. intense	_____	_____
10. offset	_____	_____
11. output	_____	_____
12. policy	_____	_____
13. principal	_____	_____
14. prohibitive	_____	_____
15. promote	_____	_____
16. recover	_____	_____

Word	Part of speech	Definition
17. refine	_____	_____
18. source	_____	_____
19. subsidy	_____	_____
20. variable	_____	_____

EXERCISE 9·3

Using vocabulary, part 1 *Complete each of the following sentences with the appropriate word from the chart in Exercise 9-2. Be sure to use the correct form of each verb and to pluralize nouns, if necessary.*

1. The government offers _____ to students who wish to study overseas at an English-language college or university.

2. Planting trees can _____ carbon emissions by absorbing CO_2.

3. During rush hour, the bus is full to _____.

4. Getting a good job is an _____ for going to college.

5. When you are traveling during the tourist season, it's always good to know an

   _____ hotel in case the one you want to stay at is fully booked.

6. What is the electrical _____ of this generator?

7. The economy is growing, _____ at a slower pace than economists anticipated.

8. Citrus fruits are a good _____ of Vitamin C.

9. The language school has an English-only _____.

10. The _____ ingredients of bread are flour and yeast.

EXERCISE 9·4

Using vocabulary, part 2 *For each of the following sentences, choose the correct form of the academic word to fill in the blank.*

1. constitution, constituent, constitutes

   Currently, solar energy _____ less than 0.1 percent of the electricity produced in the United States.

2. distribution, distributional, distributed

   The Internet has contributed to the rapid _____ of information.

3. intensity, intense, intensify

   Sunlight is most _____ at the equator.

4. recovery, recoverable, recover

   Economists expect to see a _____ in the global economy by the end of the year.

5. Refinement, Refined, Refine

   _____ flour is not as healthy as whole wheat flour.

6. variation, variable, vary

   Tastes and preferences in music _____ greatly with age.

7. equivalence, equivalent

   One mile is _____ to 1.6 kilometers.

8. prohibition, prohibitive, prohibits

   The law _____ smoking in public buildings.

9. concentration, concentrated, concentrate

   Most of a country's population tends to be _____ in urban areas.

10. promotion, promotional, promote

    The rock band is going on tour to _____ its new CD.

Nonacademic vocabulary *Match each **nonacademic word** in column 1 with its definition in column 2. Then, indicate each item's part of speech (n., v., or adj.).*

_____ 1. advancement _____

_____ 2. combustion _____

_____ 3. depletion _____

_____ 4. harness _____

_____ 5. install _____

_____ 6. absorb _____

_____ 7. pioneer _____

_____ 8. relentless _____

_____ 9. renewable _____

_____ 10. spur _____

a. soak up, take in
b. inexhaustible, replenishing
c. develop, break new ground
d. progress, improvement
e. stimulate, induce
f. exhaustion, reduction
g. persistent, never-ending
h. burning
i. place, put
j. utilize, make use of

Reading comprehension

Reading for main ideas *Answer the following questions in your own words.*

1. How important is the sun?

   _____

   _____

2. What are the consequences of increasing consumption of fossil fuels to produce energy?

   _____

   _____

3. What is passive solar energy, and what are its main uses?

   _____

   _____

4. What is photovoltaic solar technology, and what are its main uses?

   _____

   _____

5. What is concentrating solar power, and what are its main uses?

   _____

   _____

6. What are the principal issues in the debate over solar energy?

   _____

   _____

7. Where has solar energy made advances, and where has it not?

   _____

   _____

8. What is the future of solar energy?

   _____

   _____

Reading for details *For each of the following sentences, choose the correct answer to fill in the blank.*

1. Sunlight consists of _____ components.
   a. one
   b. two
   c. three

2. Eighty percent of commercial energy comes from _____.
   a. solar energy
   b. fossil fuels
   c. hydroelectricity

3. The world's first commercial solar building was built in _____.
   a. Germany
   b. Spain
   c. the United States

4. Waldpolenz Solar Park, near Leipzig, Germany, generates electricity using _____.
   a. passive solar energy
   b. photovoltaic cells
   c. concentrating solar power

5. Global sales of solar technology are predicted to reach _____ in the near future.
   a. $51 billion
   b. $51 trillion
   c. $51 million

6. Photovoltaic technology was first used in _____.
   a. water heaters
   b. power plants
   c. the space industry

Indicate which of the following statements are true (T) and which are false (F).

7. _____ Ultraviolet light is the largest constituent of sunlight.

8. _____ Solar energy can minimize CO_2 emissions.

9. _____ Photovoltaic solar technology is used to produce electricity on a large scale.

10. _____ PV cells are made from silicon derived from sand or quartz.

11. _____ The United States leads the world in the development and installation of solar technology.

12. _____ Solar technology is not practical in remote areas or developing countries.

Answer the following question.

13. Match each of the following applications with the most suitable type of solar technology: passive solar energy (PS), photovoltaic cells (PV), or concentrating solar power (CSP). More than one type of technology may be suitable to some applications.

   a. _____ Enhancing natural lighting

   b. _____ Powering calculators

   c. _____ Heating water and swimming pools

   d. _____ Large-scale electricity production

   e. _____ Powering satellites

   f. _____ Heating homes and buildings

   g. _____ Illuminating clocks and watches

Answer the following questions in complete sentences.

14. What are the main components of sunlight?

_____

15. What makes solar energy more environmentally sound than fossil fuel combustion?

_____

16. What event resulted in an increased interest in solar energy in the United States?

_____

17. What is responsible for the rising demand for solar energy in the United States?

_____

**EXERCISE
9·8**

Reading for interpretation and inference *Indicate which of the following statements from the reading text support (✓) or do not support (X) solar energy.*

1. _____ "Every day, 173,000 terawatts of energy—100,000 times more energy than humans use—strike the earth in the form of sunlight."

2. _____ "At 20 cents per kilowatt hour, energy produced by PV plants costs ten times more than energy generated by fossil fuel–burning plants."

3. _____ "A two-kilowatt off-grid private system can cost $20,800, and a ten-kilowatt system can cost up to $104,000."

4. _____ "Nevertheless, solar cell manufacturing has become more efficient and cheaper, and prices have been falling steadily since the 1970s."

5. _____ "Naysayers claim that solar energy is prohibitively expensive."

6. _____ "In the first quarter of 2012, solar panel installations increased 85 percent over the previous year's first quarter. . . ."

7. _____ ". . . by 1897, nearly a third of the homes in Pasadena, California, had installed a solar water heating system."

8. _____ "Buildings that take advantage of passive solar heating can cut their heating costs in half."

9. _____ ". . . commitment to solar energy has fluctuated with the price of oil, particularly in North America, where government energy policy is strongly influenced by oil companies."

10. _____ "Interest in [solar water heating] systems revived in the late 1970s, but in the mid-1980s, their popularity declined with energy prices and the expiration of a federal tax credit."

Reading strategies

Paraphrasing: Changing voice

Reading texts about technology often use the passive voice. One way to paraphrase sentences is to change the passive voice to the active. Here's an example:

PASSIVE VOICE   In the late 1950s, **solar cells were adopted by NASA** to power satellites.
ACTIVE VOICE   In the late 1950s, **NASA adopted solar cells** to power satellites.

The active voice is shorter and more direct than the passive voice. There can be a problem, however, if the agent (in the example above, NASA) is unknown or if the agent is very general or indefinite (for example, people, they, or someone), as in the following example:

PASSIVE VOICE   **The first water heater was patented** in the United States in 1891.

In this example, the name of the inventor is not known; therefore, an active sentence would not be an improvement.

Remember that it is not enough to simply change the order of the words in a sentence—you must also use *your own words*. The first example above might be written as follows:

NASA began using solar cells to run satellites at the end of the 1950s.

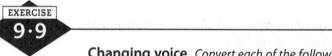

Changing voice *Convert each of the following passive sentences from the reading text to the active voice. The subject for each active-voice sentence is given in parentheses.*

1. "Throughout human history, the sun has been worshipped as a symbol of life and power." (people)

_____

_____

2. ". . . every day, 50 million barrels of oil are refined and converted to gasoline and other fuels." (companies)

_____

_____

3. "Passive solar energy is now being incorporated into environmentally friendly building designs. . . ." (architects)

_____

_____

4. "When sunlight strikes a PV cell's surface, electrons are knocked out of place, creating an electrical current." (sunlight)

_____

_____

5. "PV panels are most commonly seen on rooftops and walls. . . ." (we)

_____

6. "Solar panels are assembled into solar arrays. . . ." (manufacturers)

_____

7. ". . . over 20 to 30 years, these additional expenses are recovered in energy savings." (homeowners)

_____

_____

8. "By reducing overall energy consumption and incorporating further energy-saving features into homes and buildings, a return on investment can be realized much sooner." (lower energy usage and the integration of conservation measures in residences)

_____

_____

_____

9. "In 1956, the world's first commercial solar building was constructed in Albuquerque, New Mexico, by engineers Frank Bridgers and Don Paxton." (engineers Bridgers and Paxton)

_____

_____

10. ". . . government energy policy is strongly influenced by oil companies." (petroleum companies)

_____

_____

Now, scan other reading texts for passive sentences that you can convert to the active voice.

Organizing information

Read about the five principal issues in the debate on solar energy, then summarize their advantages and disadvantages by entering the most important details in the following chart.

Issue	Advantages	Disadvantages
Fuel supply		
Environmental impact		
Costs		
Energy payback		
Long-term energy savings		

Critical thinking

EXERCISE 9·10

Making evaluations *Indicate which of the following are suitable uses of solar energy (✓) and which are not (X). Give reasons for your answers.*

1. _____ Cars and buses

2. _____ Water heaters

3. _____ Supplying electricity to a city with a population exceeding one million

4. _____ Solar cookers for poor people

5. _____ Supplying electricity to a large hospital

6. _____ Powering robots on space missions

7. _____ Outerwear, such as parkas, jackets, and ski clothing, and outdoor equipment, such as tents

8. _____ Emergency radios and telephones

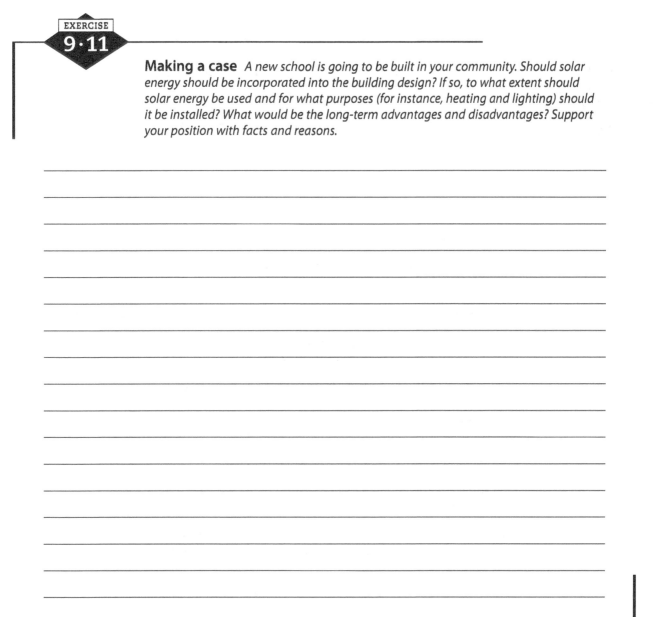

EXERCISE
9·11

Making a case *A new school is going to be built in your community. Should solar energy should be incorporated into the building design? If so, to what extent should solar energy be used and for what purposes (for instance, heating and lighting) should it be installed? What would be the long-term advantages and disadvantages? Support your position with facts and reasons.*

Bibliography

Jones, Susan, *Solar Power of the Future: New Ways of Turning Sunlight into Energy* (New York: Rosen Publishing Group, 2003).

Pierce, Erin R., "Top 6 Things You Didn't Know About Solar Energy" (U.S. Department of Energy, June 2012), http://energy.gov/articles/top-6-things-you-didnt-know-about-solar-energy.

Sherwood, Larry, *U.S. Solar Market Trends 2010* (Interstate Renewable Energy Council, June 2011), http://irecusa.org/wp-content/uploads/2011/06/IREC-Solar-Market-Trends-Report-June-2011-web.pdf.

Thomas, Isabel, *The Pros and Cons of Solar Power* (New York: Rosen Publishing Group, 2008).

Healing circles
A gentler justice

Pre-reading

Using the following questionnaire, interview your classmates, colleagues, family, and friends.

Questionnaire	A	B	C

Do you think the criminal justice system in your country does a good job of dealing with crime? Yes | No

How do you rate punishment for crimes in your country?
a. Too severe
b. Adequate
c. Not severe enough

Do you agree with capital punishment? Yes | No

Do you think the criminal justice system helps the victims of crimes? Yes | No

Do you think that the victim of a crime, his or her family, and the community should be included in decisions about the punishment of a criminal? Yes | No

What is the best way to deal with people who harm others?
a. Give them long prison sentences.
b. Make them apologize and pay something back to victims and their families.
c. Get them professional treatment for their behavior.
d. Have them do community service.
e. Try to understand the reasons for their actions and help them.
f. Other (specify: _____)

Predicting content

Considering the title of the chapter, predict which of the following topics will be mentioned in the reading text.

☐ Statistics on crime

☐ Involving victims in sentencing decisions

☐ Different types of punishment for criminal cases

☐ Examples of how crime is handled in different countries

☐ Alternatives to the traditional criminal justice system

Reading text

1 Life is a process of continuous change, and with change comes **conflict**. We have only to read a newspaper or watch the news on television to see the signs: vandalism, rioting, theft and robbery, hate crimes and bullying, drive-by shootings and gang warfare, drunk driving and road rage, mass killings, sexual assault, and many other offenses. In **response** to incidents of violence, we hear an outcry from the public and politicians for more police, tougher laws, and stiffer sentences.

2 FBI statistics show that from 2010 to 2011, violent crime in the United States fell by four percent. Nevertheless, the criminal justice system remains backed up, resulting in delayed, drawn-out, and even dismissed court cases. In the process, victims and the surviving families of victims feel abandoned by the courts. Racial and disadvantaged minorities, who are frequently the first to be arrested and who often receive inadequate legal representation and stiffer sentences, feel targeted, victimized, and criminalized. Although it is based on the principle of due and fair process, the criminal justice system pits right against wrong, prosecution against defense, plaintiff against accused—and the **outcome** is punishment rather than *restitution*. To bridge the gap between the legal system and the community, First Nations peoples and local justice officials in the Yukon Territory of Canada turned in the 1980s to the ancient *aboriginal* tradition of healing circles.

3 Originating with the indigenous peoples of North America, healing circles—also called talking, or peacemaking, circles—have been used for centuries to repair harm and rebuild peace in the community. In First Nations culture, the circle symbolizes life and the natural **cycles** that connect all living things. When people gathered, they traditionally sat in a circle around a fire to tell stories. As a vehicle for communication, the circle has evolved into an inclusive, nonconfrontational, and safe place for participants to share their experiences and their pain, as well as to **resolve** conflicts in a way that benefits everyone.

How healing circles work

4 According to the guiding **philosophy** of healing circles, helping individuals in need serves everyone involved in the process. By harnessing collective wisdom, the circle produces solutions of value to the broader community. In keeping with the belief that everyone and everything are connected, all participants are treated equally and respectfully and are given equal opportunity to speak in an open, honest dialogue. The **objectives** of healing circles are as follows:

◆ To support victims of a crime or harmful behavior
◆ To determine by **consensus** the **appropriate** sentence and to assist the offender in fulfilling the *obligations* of the sentence
◆ To **reinforce** the community's ability to prevent crime

5   Healing circles can be **adapted** to family situations, schools, the workplace, government agencies, churches, clubs, organizations, and prisons, and they embrace all ages, races, and walks of life. Whenever people need to make decisions, to resolve disagreements, to deal with harm done to others, to engage in teamwork, to learn from each other, or to celebrate, healing circles guide people toward achieving a greater understanding of each other and the issues.

6   The victim, offender, and community members sit in a circle without tables. The circle is opened by a **facilitator**, or keeper, in a ceremony that establishes the circle as a sacred place and makes the **transition** from daily life to the framework of the healing circle. One or more facilitators ensure that the participants follow the **guidelines** and maintain respect, and that each member feels safe to speak from the heart. Although the facilitators do not take an active part in the dialogue, they ask questions, make suggestions, and **refocus** the group in order to steer the process toward an outcome.

7   Healing circles follow a four-stage process:

1. The request for a healing circle is assessed, and if the situation is *deemed* suitable, all parties must be willing to take part.
2. The participants are informed, prepared, and trained in the process.
3. The circle is convened and consists of honest dialogue leading to some form of resolution. When the circle **convenes**, the group's first task is to establish relationships, which involves getting acquainted, building trust through sharing values and vision, and creating a sense of unity within the group. The second task is to set guidelines as to how participants will conduct themselves during the circle.
4. In the follow-up, progress is **monitored** to ensure that the decisions of the circle are carried out, that agreements are upheld, and that mistakes or failures are corrected.

8   A unique **feature** of talking circles is the use of a talking piece. The facilitator introduces an object of special meaning or symbolism, such as an eagle's feather, a stone, a crystal, or a figure, then passes it to the person on his or her left. Continuing in a clockwise direction, members of the circle take turns talking. Only the person holding the talking piece may speak, and he or she can choose to remain silent while holding the talking piece or pass it on without speaking. No one may attack or interrupt the person in possession of the talking piece, or use abusive, confrontational, or insulting language. Not only does the talking piece slow the conversation to a reflective, *deliberate* pace, but it *empowers* the speaker and gives the listeners time to reflect and respond thoughtfully rather than in anger or haste. In the process, the talking piece acts like a shuttle that weaves the group together in a fabric of truth.

9   In healing circles, participants are encouraged to tell their stories. A valued tradition in First Nations culture, storytelling communicates life experiences in a way that people can relate to emotionally and spiritually. Stories awaken compassion in people's hearts more readily than advice or judgment that is handed down or imposed by an outside authority.

10   At the conclusion of the healing circle, the group reaches a consensus decision that everyone can live with. Consensus decisions are arrived at through exploring the issues and possible solutions rather than through debate, argument, and persuasion. The decision can also include **assigning** responsibilities to participants to ensure that the decision is carried out. A closing ceremony recognizes the participants' efforts, reconfirms their interconnectedness, and expresses hope for the future.

Types and applications of healing circles

11   In *The Little Book of Circle Processes: A New/Old Approach to Peacemaking*, author Kay Pranis identifies nine types of healing circles:

1. **Talking circles** allow participants to exchange stories and explore issues without the necessity of arriving at a consensus.

2. **Circles of understanding** focus on getting at the underlying causes of a conflict or behavior, and generally do not concern themselves with decision making.
3. **Healing circles** provide support for people who have been victims of trauma or loss, and can include a plan of support.
4. **Sentencing circles** combine members of the community and the criminal justice system, as well as the offender, the victim, and the victim's family. The purpose is to examine the motive and circumstances that led to a crime, in addition to its harmful impact on the victim and the victim's family. Determined by consensus, the sentence can include responsibilities for its implementation and monitoring. Sentencing circles also determine ways to prevent the recurrence of a crime.
5. **Support circles** help people through times of personal loss or difficulty.
6. **Community-building circles** strengthen relationships and develop a common purpose.
7. **Conflict circles** aim to arrive at a consensus decision that will resolve a dispute.
8. **Reintegration circles** help repair relationships and *reconcile* estranged parties, or assist an individual to reenter the community after a period of incarceration.
9. **Celebration, or honoring, circles** recognize the accomplishments of community members and share their joy and success.

Challenges, rewards, and widespread adoption

12   Based on the simple concept of caring for others in need as we would have them care for us, the practice of healing circles comes with its challenges. Achieving justice is a time-consuming process in the traditional legal system, and healing circles are no exception. Participants must be trained and fully committed not only to a lengthy and painful process, but also to its aftermath. During the circle, they must put aside personal *prejudices* and learn to speak the truth and to listen with an open heart. When laymen and professionals have been raised and educated in a society that encourages competition, *confrontation,* and separation, making the shift to cooperation, sensitivity, and spiritual connection can be very difficult. Also, since consensus decisions require the agreement of all participants, some members may feel pressured to give in to the group.

13   No human process is perfect, but when healing circles and restorative justice, as they are known in their broader sense, succeed, the rewards *outweigh* the challenges. Since there are neither winners nor losers and participants have a vested interest in the outcome, everyone is more likely to work together to see a decision through. A 2007 metastudy of research conducted into restorative justice from 1986 to 2005 found that victims were able to resume a normal life and to sleep at night; that offenders were neither abusive toward their victims, nor were they likely to reoffend; and that the community felt more secure.

14   In 1991, Chief Judge Barry Stuart of the Territorial Court of Yukon introduced sentencing circles into the justice process in northern Canada. Since then, First Nations people have been training nonnative professionals in the use of healing circles, and they have met with success in the provinces of Saskatchewan and Manitoba. Since the 1980s, the Hollow Water First Nation Community Holistic Healing Circle in Hollow Water, Manitoba, has used healing circles to deal with cases involving alcoholism and sexual abuse. In 1996, the healing circle was applied for the first time in the United States in the Mille Lacs Circle Sentencing Project on the Mille Lacs Indian reservation in Minnesota. In various settings and situations involving both juvenile and adult offenders all over the world, healing circles and restorative justice are making their way from an ancient tradition to a modern worldwide movement, **ultimately** ensuring that justice serves all.

After reading

In the Pre-reading section, check to see if your predictions about the reading text were correct.

Vocabulary

EXERCISE

10·1

Thematic vocabulary *List 10 words related to criminal justice.*

_____   _____

_____   _____

_____   _____

_____   _____

_____   _____

EXERCISE

10·2

Academic vocabulary *Using a dictionary, complete the following chart with the correct part of speech and definition of each of the **academic words** in the reading text. If a word has multiple meanings, match the definition to the context in which the word is used in the text.*

Word	Part of speech	Definition
1. adapt	_____	_____
2. appropriate	_____	_____
3. assign	_____	_____
4. conflict	_____	_____
5. consensus	_____	_____
6. convene	_____	_____
7. cycle	_____	_____
8. facilitator	_____	_____
9. feature	_____	_____
10. guideline	_____	_____
11. monitor	_____	_____
12. objective	_____	_____
13. outcome	_____	_____
14. philosophy	_____	_____
15. refocus	_____	_____
16. reinforce	_____	_____
17. resolve	_____	_____

Word	Part of speech	Definition
18. response	_____	_____
19. transition	_____	_____
20. ultimate	_____	_____

EXERCISE
10·3

Using vocabulary *Complete each of the following sentences with the appropriate word(s) from the chart in Exercise 10-2. Be sure to use the correct form of each verb and to pluralize nouns, if necessary.*

1. At this stage, it is difficult to predict the _____ of the peace talks between the two countries.

2. The leader of the activity began by _____ different roles to all the participants.

3. If a _____ between two countries is not _____ quickly, the situation can lead to war.

4. The meeting is scheduled to _____ at 8 o'clock and to end at noon.

5. If you follow the dietary _____ in this booklet, you will eat well and stay healthy.

6. After a lengthy discussion, the group finally reached a _____ that everyone could accept.

7. The patient is hooked up to a machine that _____ her heart rate and blood pressure.

8. The students need to put their cell phones away and _____ on their work.

9. A circle symbolizes the natural _____ of life.

10. The main _____ of this book is to help you improve your reading skills.

11. It is not _____ to wear a baseball cap to a job interview.

12. When I asked him a question, his only _____ was to shrug his shoulders and grin.

13. Her _____ of life is to live and let live.

14. The man's aggressive behavior _____ my negative impression of him.

15. People who move to a foreign country have to _____ to another culture and lifestyle.

16. How long will it take to make the _____ to the new computer system?

17. Rather than giving orders and telling students what to do, a good teacher acts as a

_____ .

18. Most electronic gadgets have a lot of unnecessary _____ that no one ever uses.

19. Our _____ goal in life is to be healthy and happy.

EXERCISE
10·4

Nonacademic vocabulary *Match each **nonacademic word** in column 1 with its definition in column 2. Then, indicate each item's part of speech (n., v., or adj.).*

_____ 1. aboriginal _____

_____ 2. confrontation _____

_____ 3. deem _____

_____ 4. deliberate _____

_____ 5. empower _____

_____ 6. obligation _____

_____ 7. outweigh _____

_____ 8. prejudice _____

_____ 9. reconcile _____

_____ 10. restitution _____

a. a situation of angry disagreement or opposition
b. restore friendly relations between people
c. be more significant than
d. opinion not based on reason
e. inhabiting a land from the earliest times
f. done on purpose
g. regard or consider in a particular way
h. give authority or power to someone
i. restoration of something lost or stolen
j. something a person must do

Reading comprehension

EXERCISE
10·5

Reading for main ideas *Choose the boldface word or phrase that correctly completes each of the following statements. Some statements include more than one set of choices.*

1. Healing circles have a long tradition in **European** | **aboriginal** cultures and offer a **nonconfrontational** | **adversarial** alternative to the criminal justice process.

2. Healing circles serve **the community** | **only the individuals involved**, treat all participants **differently** | **equally**, and focus on **sentencing** | **peacemaking**.

3. Healing circles are conducted by a **facilitator** | **judge** who **takes** | **does not take** an active role in the process.

4. Healing circles are **formally** | **informally** structured in **three** | **four** stages, and they **encourage** | **discourage** storytelling.

5. The talking piece ensures **that the facilitator has control of the process** | **that everyone respects and listens to the speaker.**

6. Decisions are made by **the facilitator** | **consensus.**

7. Healing circles require **time** | **commitment** | **money** | **experts** | **prejudice** | **an open heart** | **lawyers.** (Choose three.)

8. Healing circles are **more likely** | **less likely** to be successful for **the victim** | **the offender** | **both victim and offender.**

9. Healing circles and restorative justice are used **only in Canada** | **internationally.**

Reading for details *For each of the following sentences, choose the correct answer to fill in the blank.*

1. Healing circles were first introduced into the criminal justice system in _____.
   a. the United States
   b. Australia
   c. Canada

2. In a healing circle, the talking piece is passed _____.
   a. clockwise
   b. counterclockwise
   c. crosswise

3. A healing circle focuses on _____.
   a. dialogue
   b. interrogation
   c. debate

4. Healing circles are *not* called _____.
   a. restorative justice
   b. peacemaking circles
   c. criminal justice

5. Healing circles were first used in the United States in _____.
   a. 1996
   b. 1991
   c. 1980

6. The Hollow Water First Nation Community Holistic Healing Circle in Manitoba has used healing circles to deal with _____.
   a. cases of sexual abuse
   b. cases of alcoholism
   c. cases of both sexual abuse and alcoholism

Indicate which of the following statements are true (T) and which are false (F).

7. _____ Healing circles work only in very specific and special circumstances.

8. _____ In aboriginal cultures, the circle symbolizes the natural cycles of life and the connections between all living beings.

9. _____ The traditional criminal justice system generally emphasizes restitution and understanding.

10. _____ Healing circles are concerned primarily with sentencing and punishing an offender.

11. _____ Healing circles set guidelines as to how participants will conduct themselves.

12. _____ People relate more compassionately to stories than to laws and regulations.

Answer the following questions in complete sentences.

13. What are the four stages of a healing circle?

    Stage 1 _____

    Stage 2 _____

    Stage 3 _____

    Stage 4 _____

14. List four duties of a facilitator in a healing circle.

    _____

    _____

    _____

    _____

15. What is a talking piece, and how does it work?

    _____

    _____

16. What did the 2007 metastudy conclude about the effectiveness of healing circles?

    _____

    _____

17. What is a consensus decision, and why is it the most desirable outcome?

    _____

    _____

EXERCISE
10·7

Reading for interpretation and inference *Choose the correct interpretation for each of the following statements from the reading text. Pay special attention to the boldface words and phrases.*

1. "In response to incidents of violence, we hear **an outcry** from the public and politicians for more police, tougher laws, and stiffer sentences."
   a. People want the law to be harder on criminals.
   b. People are sad when they hear about acts of violence.

2. "...the criminal justice system **pits** right **against** wrong, prosecution against defense, plaintiff against accused...."
   a. The criminal justice system is made up of two sides.
   b. The criminal justice system places one side in opposition to another.

3. "**To bridge the gap** between the legal system and the community, First Nations peoples and local justice officials in the Yukon Territory of Canada turned in the 1980s to the ancient aboriginal tradition of healing circles."
   a. Healing circles were introduced to bring people together.
   b. Healing circles were introduced to make up for a lack of understanding.

4. ". . . they embrace all ages, races, and **walks of life**. . . ."
   a. They include every kind of job or profession.
   b. They include every kind of experience.

5. ". . . each member feels safe to speak **from the heart**. . . ."
   a. Everyone speaks without thinking.
   b. Everyone says what he or she really feels or means.

6. "In the process, the talking piece acts **like a shuttle that weaves the group together in a fabric of truth**."
   a. The talking piece unites and unifies everyone.
   b. The talking piece is passed around the circle.

7. "Since there are neither winners nor losers and participants **have a vested interest** in the outcome, everyone is more likely to work together to see a decision through."
   a. Participants find the process interesting.
   b. Participants have something to gain personally from the process.

8. ". . . healing circles and restorative justice are making their way from an ancient tradition to a modern worldwide movement, ultimately ensuring that **justice serves all**."
   a. Everyone participates.
   b. Everyone benefits.

Reading strategies

Paraphrasing: Eliminating the passive

In the previous chapter, you practiced converting the passive voice to the active voice. Another way to paraphrase is to eliminate the passive altogether. You can do this by

- using the past participle as an adjective
- replacing the past participle with an adjective
- omitting the form of *to be* in the passive voice
- using a different subject, verb, or both in the active voice

In the following example, the past participle becomes an adjective and a different subject and verb are used.

PASSIVE	The screenplay **was adapted** from the best-selling novel and **turned into** a motion picture.
PARAPHRASE	The motion picture featured an **adapted** script.

The form of *to be* (for example, *had been*) can be eliminated, and the past participle used as an adjective. In the following example, synonyms are used for *bought, completely,* and *renovated.*

PASSIVE	We **bought** a house that **had been completely renovated**.
PARAPHRASE	We **purchased** a **totally upgraded** (or **remodeled**) house.

Eliminating the passive *Paraphrase each of the following statements from the reading text, using the techniques described above to eliminate the passive voice (shown underlined).*

1. "Originating with the indigenous peoples of North America, healing circles—also called talking, or peacemaking, circles—<u>have been used</u> for centuries to repair harm and rebuild peace in the community."

_____

_____

_____

2. ". . . all participants <u>are treated</u> equally and respectfully and are given equal opportunity to speak in an open, honest dialogue."

_____

_____

3. "Healing circles <u>can be adapted</u> to family situations, schools, the workplace, government agencies, churches, clubs, organizations, and prisons. . . ."

_____

_____

4. "The participants <u>are informed, prepared, and trained</u> in the process."

_____

5. "In healing circles, participants <u>are encouraged</u> to tell their stories."

_____

6. "Stories awaken compassion in people's hearts more readily than advice or judgment that <u>is handed down or imposed</u> by an outside authority."

_____

_____

7. "Consensus decisions <u>are arrived at</u> through exploring the issues and possible solutions rather than through debate, argument, and persuasion."

_____

_____

8. "In 1996, the healing circle <u>was applied</u> for the first time in the United States in the Mille Lacs Circle Sentencing Project on the Mille Lacs Indian reservation in Minnesota."

_____

_____

_____

Now, scan other reading texts for sentences in which you can eliminate the passive voice.

Organizing information

Organizing information *Scan the reading text, then enter the most important details about healing circles in the following chart.*

	Main idea	Important details
1. Origin		
2. Guiding philosophy		
3. The four stages		
4. Key features		
The facilitator		
The talking piece		
Storytelling		
Consensus decisions		
5. Types of circles and applications		
6. Benefits		
7. Challenges		
8. Examples of successes		

Critical thinking

Making evaluations *Referring to the section "Types and applications of healing circles" in the reading text, indicate which circle is best suited to resolving each of the following situations. Give reasons for your answers.*

1. A man has a serious drinking problem, which is seriously affecting his job and family life.

   _____

2. A family has lost a child, who died of a drug overdose.

   _____

3. Two teenage boys broke into the school and vandalized the computer lab.

   _____

4. A young boy is being bullied at school.

   _____

5. A group of people want to form an environmental action group to save a local stream where salmon spawn.

   _____

6. Two neighbors are constantly arguing, because one neighbor keeps unsightly junk in his yard.

   _____

7. A man has been released from prison after serving time for assault and other violent behavior under the influence of drugs and alcohol, and he wants to return to his family and community.

   _____

8. A woman who has been the victim of domestic abuse for years finally decides to leave her husband and move out with her children.

   _____

9. The residents of a community want to raise money to build a community library.

   _____

10. While under the influence of alcohol, a man with a history of drunk driving caused a car accident in which one person was killed.

    _____

11. An older member of the community has received an award for outstanding community service.

    _____

12. A low-income family has lost its home and possessions in a fire.

    _____

13. A young girl constantly runs away from home.

_____

14. A family has learned that their only son has been killed in a roadside bomb explosion while serving overseas in the army.

_____

15. The renters of a house have a complaint against their landlord, who has threatened to evict them because of their noisy parties.

_____

EXERCISE 10·11

Making a case _Consider the following statement by the Dalai Lama. Do you agree or disagree with this statement? How do healing circles reflect the statement? Support your opinion with information about healing circles and restorative justice from the reading text. Present situations or examples of how healing circles and restorative justice are used, or could be used, in your country._

"Learning to forgive is much more useful than merely picking up a stone and throwing it at the object of one's anger, the more so when the provocation is extreme. For it is under the greatest adversity that there exists the greatest potential for doing good, both for oneself and for others."

_____

_____

_____

_____

_____

_____

_____

_____

Bibliography

"About the Circle Process" (Living Justice Press), http://www.livingjusticepress.org/index.asp? Type=B_BASIC&SEC={51F9C610-C097-446A-8C60-05E8B4599FE7}.

Parker, Lynette, "Circles" (Restorative Justice Online, 2001), http://www.restorativejustice.org/ university-classroom/01introduction/tutorial-introduction-to-restorative-justice/processes/ circles/.

Pranis, Kay, _The Little Book of Circle Processes: A New/Old Approach to Peacemaking_ (Intercourse, PA: Good Books, 2005).

Umbreit, Mark, "Talking Circles" (Center for Restorative Justice & Peacemaking, University of Minnesota, 2003).

Medical technology
New frontiers in health care

Pre-reading

Using the following questionnaire, interview your classmates, colleagues, family, and friends.

Questionnaire	A	B	C

What do you do to stay healthy?
a. Eat a healthy diet
b. Exercise regularly and play sports
c. Take vitamin and mineral supplements
d. Go to the doctor for a regular check-up
e. Nothing in particular
f. Other (specify: _____)

How important is it to have a family doctor?
a. Very important
b. Important
c. Not important

How often do you see a doctor?
a. Only when I'm sick
b. Once a year
c. Two to four times a year
d. More than four times a year

How would you rate the quality of medical care where you live?
a. Excellent
b. Good
c. Average
d. Poor
e. Don't know

What is the most important medical service in a community?
a. A family doctor
b. Medical specialists
c. A hospital
d. Physiotherapists
e. Pharmacists
f. Other (specify: _____)

Which medical services does your community need more of?
a. Ambulance and emergency services
b. Home care services for the elderly
c. Medical testing and laboratory services
d. Other (specify: _____)

Predicting content

Considering the title of the chapter, predict which of the following topics will *not* be mentioned in the reading text.

☐ Common medical problems and their treatment

☐ When you should see a doctor

☐ How medicine will change in the future

☐ New kinds of medical treatment

☐ How medicine has changed in the past

☐ How computers are used in medicine

Reading text

1   It used to be that when a person went to see a doctor, the doctor listened to the patient's heartbeat with a stethoscope and measured blood pressure with a sphygmomanometer. Other simple instruments were used to test reflexes and check the ears and throat, but most importantly, the doctor relied on well-trained hands to feel for internal *abnormalities* during a physical examination. Although general **practitioners** still use these simple tools and time-tested **procedures** in their practices, technology is rapidly revolutionizing the way illness is diagnosed and treated.

2   Computer technology has **affected** the field of medicine as it has every aspect of our lives. Before computers became ubiquitous, medical records were handwritten and **filed** in drawers or cabinets. Doctors still keep handwritten records, but in large clinics and hospitals, where information is **accumulating** at a phenomenal rate, records are increasingly computerized for legal purposes and ease of access. Whereas physical records can get lost, compact digital records can be readily located, copied, distributed, and archived. In the not-so-distant future, electronic medical records will be stored on computer chips that patients will carry with them and update on an ongoing basis.

3   Computer technology has also vastly improved medical imaging. Three-dimensional X-rays and computer scans produce detailed reconstructions of anatomy. High-resolution scans using computer tomography (CT) and magnetic resonance imaging (MRI) can detect tumors and steer radiation, biopsy, and microsurgery with great precision. Stereotactic **interventions**, which can be compared to GPS navigation systems, are becoming so sophisticated that neurological diseases, such as Parkinson's, can be treated without the need for major brain surgery. Heads-up **displays** (HUDs), first developed for military, aviation, and auto racing purposes, can provide surgeons with an integrated picture of X-rays and monitors so that they do not need to look away from the patient on the operating table. As surface computing develops, doctors will be able to drag information onto a work table as they explore and analyze various medical data. **Visualization techniques** that integrate pictures, graphics, and data will enable doctors to react more quickly to *critical* developments in a patient's condition.

4   In hospitals, computer networks are making it easier for medical staff to monitor and supervise patient care, and they are shrinking the time and distances over which vital information has

to travel. In a telemedical intensive care unit (ICU), a patient's vital signs, laboratory findings, and medical notes are shown on displays, and cameras and microphones link medical staff to patients in their rooms. Besides having a complete overview of several patients simultaneously without having to be physically present at their bedsides, specialists can **confer** and communicate with each other more quickly in emergency situations. Radio-frequency identification (RFID) devices are used to track everything from misplaced instruments in an operating room to the whereabouts of doctors, pharmaceutical salespeople, and visitors in hospitals. Constantly vigilant smart alarms programmed with artificial intelligence can tell a doctor what is wrong with a patient and what needs to be done. Store-and-forward telemedical applications, useful in radiology, let physicians instantly transfer data, such as X-rays, to distant locations, thereby saving critical hours or even days.

5   In the future, computer networking infrastructure will allow housebound and bedridden patients to receive medical care without having to go out the door. A study of diabetes patients conducted by Columbia University revealed that, after a year, glucose management, blood pressure, and cholesterol levels in telemedical patients were better than in patients who received routine care. Digital health **equipment** of the future will be highly sophisticated, use artificial intelligence, and be integrated into the furniture, and telehealth units will include user-friendly health-oriented software with intelligent alarms, troubleshooting wizards, and patient access to educational medical websites. Of course, all of this will not happen overnight, due to the high costs of building infrastructure and the time involved, but the long-term savings to the health care industry and the convenience to patients make the **expansion** of computer use **inevitable**.

6   Beginning with intestinal laparoscopic surgery, also known as keyhole surgery, cutting-edge surgical techniques are **radically** changing how surgeons operate. Now used for plastic surgery, heart surgery, and brain surgery in addition to abdominal procedures, minimally *invasive* laparoscopic surgery results in less postoperative pain and scarring and reduces the risk of infection and *complications*. A further development is robotic surgery. Highly trained surgeons equipped with three-dimensional eyepieces and seated at a console can manipulate interchangeable mechanical robotic hands to perform difficult heart operations or delicate head and neck procedures on cancer patients. Multijointed insectlike robotic **appendages** are more flexible, *dexterous,* and sterile than human hands, and they can be programmed to eliminate tremor when sewing small vessels or nerves together. Robotic hands, however, cannot feel the tissue they are operating on, but scientists and engineers in the field of haptic engineering are working on solutions that will one day create tactile sensory *feedback* in robots. Although robotic technology is still very costly and surgeons face a steep learning curve, robotic surgery is the future. As telemedical robotic surgery progresses and **network** connections link the globe, surgeons will not have to be physically present to perform robotic surgeries on patients in remote and offshore locations.

7   Many of us have had personal experience with computer-based medical technology, or we do not find the idea of robots that clean floors and *sterilize* surgical instruments or function as nursing assistants all that far-fetched. Already, mobile medical robots exist to deliver drugs and allow doctors to make **virtual** patient rounds in ultra-modern hospitals. A leader in robotics and electronics, Japan has invested extensively in robotic technologies to provide care to a growing elderly population. On the other side of the technological coin, research in nanotechnology and stem cells is embarking on a journey that is as controversial as it is mind-boggling.

8   Defined as "the engineering of functional systems at the molecular scale," nanotechnology has already led to the manufacture of new metals, polymers, and composites. Still under development, nanoparticles, nanomaterials, and nanoceramics promise better, stronger, lighter, and more effective adhesives, bandages, epoxies, and bone substitutes. Nanomedicine aims to construct minuscule biomechanical machines—a nanometer measures one billionth of a meter—that are able to interact with cells at the molecular level and alter cellular processes that lead to cancer and

autoimmune diseases such as lupus. At this point, however, potential applications of nanotechnology are at the research stage. Current projects include the following:

- Nanoscale coatings for medical devices
- Nanotankers that supply tissues with oxygen
- Nanocontrast agents that illuminate specific cells in diseased tissue
- Nanoscaffolding that **aid** the three-dimensional growth of artificial organs
- Nanoscale cancer killing machines that travel through the body and selectively poison cancer cells
- Nanosensors that analyze the condition of tissue
- Nanosurgibots that perform surgery at the cellular level

Although major technical *obstacles* have yet to be overcome, the potential for nanotechnological applications appears limitless, and future nanomedicine is expected to be instrumental in diagnosing and treating cancer.

9   Another promising field, stem cell research, could eventually beat cancer and many debilitating genetic diseases. Thanks to embryonic stem cells, a single cell consisting of a sperm cell and an egg blossoms into a complex human embryo, with more than 200 different types of cells. In their DNA, these master cells contain the complete **instruction** manual for life, and they are responsible not only for an embryo's development, but for the renewal, regeneration, and repair of cells throughout an individual's lifetime. Since the late 1980s, bone marrow stem cells have successfully treated leukemia. More recently, they have been used for other blood-related disorders, metabolic and immune deficiency diseases, and cancers of the brain, kidneys, and breast, among others. International registries can match suitable donors with patients in need of bone marrow transplants. Because stem cells know exactly where to go when they are needed in the body and can live forever if frozen, the sky is the limit in how they could be used.

10   There are two types of stem cells: adult, or somatic, stem cells, which are found in existing tissue, and embryonic stem cells. Embryonic stem cells can be **extracted** only from unused in vitro embryos at fertility clinics or cloned embryos, which makes this practice the subject of heated debate. Stem cell research is generally considered vital in principle, and the United States government funds research with embryos created before 2001. However, individual states are responsible for regulation, and laws vary widely, from an outright *ban* to a policy of open encouragement. One proposal for getting around the ethical issue is to collect embryonic stem cells from the umbilical cord and to store and bank them for future use. In the meantime, it will take medical researchers years to learn how stem cells really work before they can produce viable medical cures.

11   When Dr. Christiaan Barnard performed the first heart transplant in 1967, it seemed like a miracle. Back then, few could imagine how commonplace organ transplants would become and how many lives they would save. When James Watson and Francis Crick discovered the double helix structure of DNA in 1953, who would have thought that 50 years later, the Human Genome Project would complete its mapping of 99% of the human genome? When the first artificial heart was *implanted* in Barney Clark in 1982, who would have believed that the cumbersome machinery used in that experimental operation would evolve into two pounds of plastic, polyurethane, and metal engineered to be resistant to clot formation? Whether it's artificial heart valves or pacemakers, laser eye surgery, artificial bionic limbs, biocomposite skin for burn victims, or any number of medical wonders, technology is changing the face of medicine.

12   As technology proceeds to break through new barriers, it will change lives and life itself. Who can guess where it will take us next?

After reading

In the Pre-reading section, check to see if your predictions about the reading text were correct.

Vocabulary

Thematic vocabulary *List 10 words or phrases related to medical care and disease.*

_____	_____
_____	_____
_____	_____
_____	_____
_____	_____

Academic vocabulary *Using a dictionary, complete the following chart with the correct forms and definitions of the **academic words** from the reading text. If a word has multiple meanings, match the definition to the context in which the word is used in the text.*

Noun	Adjective	Verb	Definition
1. expansion	_____	_____	_____
2. instruction	_____	_____	_____
3. intervention	_____	_____	_____
4. procedure	_____	_____	_____
5. visualization	_____	_____	_____
6. _____	virtual	_____	_____
7. _____	_____	accumulate	_____
8. _____	_____	affect, _____	_____
9. _____	X	extract	_____
10. appendage	X	_____	_____
11. network	X	_____	_____
12. display	X	_____	_____
13. equipment	X	_____	_____
14. _____	X	aid	_____
15. _____	X	confer	_____
16. _____	X	file	_____

Noun	Adjective	Verb	Definition
17. technique	X	X	_____
18. _____	inevitable	X	_____
19. _____	radical(ly)	X	_____
20. practitioner	X	_____	_____

EXERCISE
11·3

Using vocabulary *Complete each of the following sentences with the appropriate word(s) from the chart in Exercise 11-2. Be sure to use the correct form of each verb and to pluralize nouns, if necessary.*

1. To complete the test, you first need to read the _____ in order to know what to do.

2. People who never move out of their homes end up _____ a lot of useless stuff in their garages, basements, and attics.

3. Siemens, a German company, makes state-of-the-art diagnostic medical _____.

4. The patient's loss of blood pressure called for immediate _____.

5. Nowadays, laser eye surgery is a very common _____ that corrects shortsightedness.

6. _____ is an effective _____ that can help people remember things they associate with pictures.

7. My brother likes to play _____ reality video games in which he has to free people who are trapped or taken hostage by villains.

8. You can see the number of the last caller on your telephone's _____.

9. Drinking too much coffee can negatively _____ your ability to fall asleep.

10. The office _____ all patient records under their last names.

11. Robots have finger-like _____.

12. Sarah is an enthusiastic and dedicated _____ of Iyengar yoga.

13. Facebook is a popular social _____.

14. Some people believe that drinking schnapps or brandy after a heavy meal will _____ digestion.

15. The president _____ with his advisors before he spoke to the press.

16. In the wintertime, coming down with a cold or the flu is _____, especially if you travel on a public transportation system.

17. Thanks to technology, some surgeries on cancer patients are less _____ and disfiguring than they were in the past.

18. Vanilla is _____ from the vanilla bean.

19. The market for solar installations is undergoing a rapid _____ of over 80 percent.

Nonacademic vocabulary *Match each **nonacademic word** in column 1 with its definition in column 2. Then, indicate each item's part of speech (n., v., or adj.).*

_____ 1. abnormality _____
_____ 2. ban _____
_____ 3. complication _____
_____ 4. critical _____
_____ 5. dexterous _____
_____ 6. feedback _____
_____ 7. implant _____
_____ 8. invasive _____
_____ 9. obstacle _____
_____ 10. sterilize _____

a. showing skill
b. make something free of bacteria
c. insert into the body for medical purposes
d. feature or event that is not normal
e. introducing instruments into the body
f. something in the way
g. a condition that makes an existing one worse
h. extremely ill or at risk of dying
i. officially forbid or prevent
j. comments about performance

Reading comprehension

EXERCISE 11·5

Reading for main ideas *Choose the headline that corresponds with each of the following paragraphs. The answer for paragraph 1 has been provided.*

a. Robotic technology revolutionizes surgery
b. Stem cells could provide cures for cancer and debilitating genetic diseases
c. Computer technology improves medical imaging
d. Medical miracles will change our lives
e. Technology revolutionizes traditional medicine
f. Stem cell research gives rise to legal and ethical debate
g. Nanotechnology promises a range of medical applications
h. Computer networking brings medical care into the home
i. Medical robots provide services in hospitals
j. Computer networks facilitate patient supervision and speed up data transfer
k. Medical records become increasingly computerized

EXERCISE
11·6

Reading for details *For each of the following sentences, choose the correct answer to fill in the blank.*

1. Displays that give surgeons an integrated picture of patient data are called
   _____.
   a. HUDs
   b. MRIs
   c. RFIs

2. Store-and-forward technology is used to transfer _____ to distant locations.
   a. drugs
   b. X-rays
   c. surgical instruments

3. A doctor's most useful tool is _____.
   a. a stethoscope
   b. his or her hands
   c. a computer

4. _____ are also known as master cells.
   a. Blood cells
   b. Sperm and egg cells
   c. Stem cells

5. The first heart transplant was performed in _____.
   a. 1953
   b. 1967
   c. 1982

6. The field of engineering that is working on improving sensory feedback in robotic appendages is called _____.
   a. haptic engineering
   b. nanoengineering
   c. genetic engineering

Indicate which of the following statements are true (T) and which are false (F).

7. _____ Medical records are still written out by hand.

8. _____ In the future, people will carry their complete medical history on a computer chip.

9. _____ Medical staff must be physically present in the rooms of ICU patients in order to supervise their condition.

10. _____ A study showed that telemedical diabetes patients receive inferior care to diabetes patients treated in a doctor's practice.

11. _____ Robotic appendages perform delicate operations with less precision than a surgeon's hands.

12. _____ Stem cell research and its potential uses are a very controversial issue.

Answer the following questions in complete sentences.

13. Give four reasons why medical records are computerized.

_____

_____

_____

_____

14. How have robotics improved surgery?

_____

_____

15. What is the main disadvantage of using robotics in surgery?

_____

_____

16. What are the advantages of telemedical care in the home?

_____

_____

_____

17. Why is stem cell research a subject of debate?

_____

_____

_____

Reading for interpretation and inference *For each of the following statements from the reading text, choose the answer that is closer in meaning to the boldface word, phrase, or clause.*

1. "**Before computers became ubiquitous**, medical records were handwritten and filed in drawers or cabinets."
   a. Before computers became popular
   b. Before computers became common

2. "In the future, computer networking infrastructure will allow housebound and bedridden patients to receive medical care **without having to go out the door**."
   a. without leaving home
   b. without walking

3. "Although robotic technology is still very costly and surgeons **face a steep learning curve**, robotic surgery is the future."
   a. have to overcome danger
   b. need a long time to master it

4. "Of course, all of **this** [telehealth units in homes] **will not happen overnight**, due to the high costs of building infrastructure and the time involved, but the long-term savings to the health care industry and the convenience to patients make the expansion of computer use inevitable."
   a. this will take a long time
   b. this will take a few days

5. ". . . we do not find the idea of robots that clean floors and sterilize surgical instruments or function as nursing assistants **all that far-fetched**."
   a. unbelievable
   b. far into the future

6. "On the other side of the technological coin, research in nanotechnology and stem cells is embarking on a journey that is as controversial as it is **mind-boggling**."
   a. crazy
   b. overwhelming

7. "Because stem cells know exactly where to go when they are needed in the body and can live forever if frozen, **the sky is the limit** in how they could be used."
   a. everything is impossible
   b. anything is possible

8. "Back then, only few could imagine how **commonplace** organ transplants would become and how many lives they would save."
   a. usual
   b. unusual

Reading strategies
Paraphrasing: Transitional devices

Transitional devices are particularly useful paraphrasing tools. When using such a device, it is important to pay attention to how the particular word functions in a sentence.

- A **coordinating conjunction** joins two independent clauses.

    Computer networks are expensive, **but** their widespread use is inevitable.

- A **subordinating conjunction** begins a dependent clause (which is not a complete sentence in itself).

    Although computer networks are costly, their widespread use is inevitable.

- A **preposition** takes a noun as an object and cannot stand alone.

    Despite the high cost of computer networks, their widespread use is inevitable.

- A **transitional adverb** is used at the beginning of an independent clause and creates a logical connection between ideas.

    Computer networks are expensive; **however**, their widespread use is inevitable.

There are three main uses of transitional devices:

- Cause and effect

COORDINATING CONJUNCTION	*so*
SUBORDINATING CONJUNCTION	*because, since*
PREPOSITION	*because of, due to, as a result of*
TRANSITIONAL ADVERB	*therefore, hence, consequently*

- Contrast

COORDINATING CONJUNCTION	*but*
SUBORDINATING CONJUNCTION	*although, even though, while, whereas*
PREPOSITION	*despite, in spite of*
TRANSITIONAL ADVERB	*however, nevertheless, nonetheless*

- Adding information

COORDINATING CONJUNCTION	*and*
PREPOSITION	*in addition to, as well as, besides*
TRANSITIONAL ADVERB	*also, furthermore, moreover, additionally*

Transitional devices *Paraphrase each of the following statements from the reading text, using the transitional device in parentheses to replace the underlined word(s). Replace as many words as possible with synonyms.*

1. "Other simple instruments were used to test reflexes and check the ears and throat, <u>and</u> most importantly, the doctor relied on well-trained hands to feel for internal abnormalities during a physical examination." (in addition to)

_____

_____

_____

2. "<u>Although</u> general practitioners still use these simple tools and time-tested procedures in their practices, technology is rapidly revolutionizing the way illness is diagnosed and treated." (however)

_____

_____

_____

3. "Robotic hands, <u>however,</u> cannot feel the tissue they are operating on, but scientists and engineers in the field of haptic engineering are working on solutions that will one day create tactile sensory feedback in robots." (although)

_____

_____

_____

4. "<u>Although</u> major technical obstacles have yet be to overcome, the potential for nanotechnological applications appears limitless, and future nanomedicine is expected to be instrumental in diagnosing and treating cancer." (despite)

_____

_____

_____

5. "Of course, all of this will not happen overnight, <u>due to</u> the high costs of building infrastructure and the time involved. . . ." (because of)

_____

_____

6. "<u>Because</u> stem cells know exactly where to go when they are needed in the body and can live forever if frozen, the sky is the limit in how they could be used." (due to)

_____

_____

7. "Besides having a complete overview of several patients simultaneously without having to be physically present at their bedsides, specialists can confer and communicate with each other more quickly in emergency situations." (as well as)

_____

_____

_____

8. "In hospitals, computer networks are making it easier for medical staff to monitor and supervise patient care, and they are shrinking the time and distances over which vital information has to travel." (in addition to)

_____

_____

_____

9. ". . . minimally invasive laparoscopic surgery results in less postoperative pain and scarring and reduces the risk of infection and complications." (also)

_____

_____

10. "Stem cell research is generally considered vital in principle, and the United States government funds research with embryos created before 2001." (in addition to)

_____

_____

Organizing information

Scan the reading text for uses and advantages of medical technologies, then enter the information in the following chart.

Medical technology	Uses and advantages
Computer technology	
a. Record keeping	
b. Medical imaging	
c. Telemedical networks in hospitals	

Medical technology	Uses and advantages
d. Telemedical networks in homes	_____
	_____
	_____
Robotic technology	
a. Robotic surgery	_____
	_____
	_____
b. Medical robots	_____
	_____
	_____
Nanotechnology	_____
	_____
	_____
Stem cell research	_____
	_____
	_____

Critical thinking

EXERCISE
11·9

Making evaluations *Indicate which of the following technologies you think will be available (✓) or not available (X) in hospitals and health care centers in your city in the next decade. Give reasons to support your answers.*

1. _____ Complete personal medical records on computer chips

2. _____ Robots that deliver pharmaceuticals inside a hospital

3. _____ Home telehealth units

4. _____ Remote telemedical robotic surgery conducted by a surgeon located in another country or on another continent

5. _____ Nanoscale cancer-killing machines that travel through the body

6. _____ Artificial heart transplants

7. _____ Robotic brain surgery

8. _____ Smart alarms in hospitals that instruct doctors what to do in an emergency

Making a case *Do you think the government should permit or ban the cloning of embryonic stem cells for research purposes? Support your opinion with reasons, facts, and examples.*

_____

_____

_____

_____

_____

_____

_____

_____

_____

_____

_____

_____

_____

_____

_____

_____

_____

_____

_____

_____

_____

Bibliography

Hanson, C. William, *The Edge of Medicine: The Technology That Will Change Our Lives* (New York: Palgrave Macmillan, 2008).

The Enneagram
Understanding our personalities

Pre-reading

Using the following questionnaire, interview your classmates, colleagues, family, and friends.

Questionnaire	A	B	C
What is your best personality trait or traits?			
What is your worst personality trait or traits?			
Are you more introverted or extroverted?			
Are you more of an optimist or a pessimist?			
Are you more of a leader, a follower, or an individualist?			
Do you think that personality is determined by our genes or by our environment (upbringing, culture, education, and experiences)?			
Is your personality more like your mother's, your father's, or neither?			
What personality characteristic(s) do you value most in other people?			

Predicting content

Predict three things that you will learn about personality from the reading text.

_____

_____

_____

Reading text

1   No two people are the same. Even identical twins with the same genetic makeup are **distinct** in their thoughts, feelings, and behavior. The differences that make us unique are referred to as personality, which the *Oxford Dictionary* defines as "the characteristics or qualities that form a person's character." There are thousands of interesting personality *traits*, but more fascinating is what actually makes us think, feel, and behave the way we do.

2   The oldest **theory** of personality can be **credited** to the Roman surgeon Galen of Pergamon (129–c. 200 C.E.), who related the four body fluids, or humors—first identified by Hippocrates 500 years earlier—to four temperaments: melancholy, sanguine, choleric, and phlegmatic. Humorism, which was considered more an explanation of what causes disease, dominated Western thinking until the twentieth century, when **psychology** emerged and personality became the subject of scientific study. Since then, theories ranging from biological, behavioral, psychodynamic, humanist, and trait-based have been put forward. The controversial nature-nurture theory explains personality in terms of the influence of genetics (what we inherit from our parents) and our environment (our upbringing, culture, education, experiences, and so on). People have also been classified as Type A (active, outgoing, extroverted) and Type B (passive, withdrawn, introverted), or according to a five-**factor** model of extraversion, agreeableness, conscientiousness, neuroticism, and openness.

3   An ancient system rooted in Sufi mysticism, the Enneagram (Greek *ennea* for "nine" and *grammos* for "point") identifies nine major **aspects** of being. Unlike other personality theories, the Enneagram offers a model that symbolizes the unfolding of human consciousness. As individuals, we are born with one temperament or type, but we can see ourselves to some extent in all nine. While each type has certain attributes, it is organized around a chief feature of character or passion, which can become either a neurotic habit or an ally in **attaining** self-awareness.

4   Each type does not operate in **isolation** from the others. Based on the Law of Three, the nine types are **comprised** of three kinds of intelligence, or ways of receiving intuitive information, and characterized by three emotional *predispositions*:

- Types 1-8-9 are belly-based, or physical, with a predisposition toward anger.
- Types 2-3-4 are feeling-based, or emotional, with a predisposition toward not knowing one's true feelings.
- Types 5-6-7 are head-based, or mental, with a predisposition toward fear.

As the following diagram **illustrates**, each type is joined to the others by lines that indicate which types actively influence the predominating, or **inherent**, type under stressful or secure **circumstances**. When under stress, a Nine type, for example, will behave like a Three, and in a secure situation, like a Six. Each type has two **adjacent** wings, one of which will act as a complement, or second side, to the personality. A Nine has either a stronger Eight or a stronger One wing; a Four, a more dominant Three or Five wing; and so on. In some cases, both wings exert an equal influence, and in others they may exert minimal influence, or none at all. In addition to wings, each type consists of three subtypes that relate to issues in relationships: intimate and one-to-one, social, and self-preservation.

The Enneagram

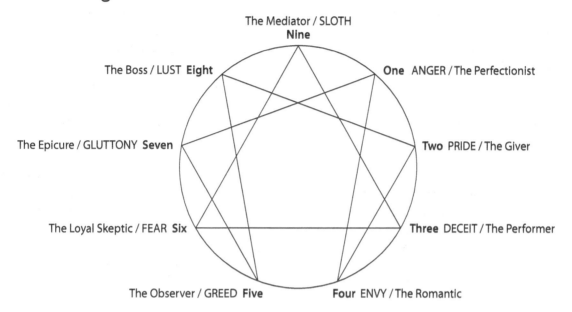

The Mediator / SLOTH **Nine**

One ANGER / The Perfectionist

The Boss / LUST **Eight**

Two PRIDE / The Giver

The Epicure / GLUTTONY **Seven**

Three DECEIT / The Performer

The Loyal Skeptic / FEAR **Six**

The Observer / GREED **Five**

Four ENVY / The Romantic

Type[1]	Intuition	Chief feature	Passion	Virtue	Stress	Security	Wings
One Perfectionist/ Reformer	Physical	Resentment	Anger	Serenity	Four	Seven	Nine/Two
Two Giver/Helper	Emotional	Flattery	Pride	Humility	Eight	Four	One/Three
Three Performer/ Achiever	Emotional	Vanity	Deceit	Honesty	Nine	Six	Two/Four
Four Romantic/ Individualist	Emotional	Melancholy	Envy	Equanimity (balance)	Two	One	Three/Five
Five Observer/ Investigator	Mental	Stinginess	Avarice	Detachment	Seven	Eight	Four/Six
Six Loyal Skeptic/ Loyalist	Mental	Cowardice	Fear	Courage	Three	Nine	Five/Seven
Seven Epicure/ Enthusiast	Mental	Planning	Gluttony	Sobriety	One	Five	Six/Eight
Eight Boss/ Challenger	Physical	Excess	Lust	Innocence	Five	Two	Seven/Nine
Nine Mediator/ Peacemaker	Physical	Indolence	Sloth	Action	Six	Three	Eight/One

---

[1] Names of types are those used by Helen Palmer and by Don Richard Riso and Russ Hudson.

Type One: The Perfectionist/Reformer

5   Ones are preoccupied with doing the right thing. Because they dread making mistakes, they tend to *procrastinate* when it comes to making decisions. Believing that there is one right way, Ones can be rigid, judgmental, and highly critical. They live in a "divided house" and have a habit of constantly monitoring themselves or making mental comparisons against a high ethical standard. Ones resent those who break the rules or take them lightly. By accepting their anger instead of bottling it up, Ones can find serenity and harness their considerable energy for humanitarian causes. At their best, Ones are organized, thorough, principled, purposeful, patient, and heroic.

Type Two: The Giver/Helper

6   Twos want to be loved and needed. To secure the affection of others, Twos will *suppress* their own feelings. They want to please others so badly that they develop several selves, and in the process they lose sight of their true selves. Twos want to feel important to others, and they pride themselves on being helpful and indispensable—the power behind the throne. When Twos give without expecting something in return, they can humbly give for the sake of giving. At their worst manipulative, seductive, and possessive, Twos give to get, but at their best they can be warm-hearted, generous, empathetic, thoughtful, and genuinely caring.

Type Three: The Performer/Achiever

7   Threes are go-getters, overachievers, and **status** seekers. They identify with their jobs, and although they have a reputation as workaholics, they are not always as productive as they appear. Vain and preoccupied with their image as winners, Threes derive their self-esteem from how others view them. Because Threes are continuously on the go, they tend to neglect their deeper feelings. Threes can benefit from learning to be honest so that they can recognize the difference between their true selves and the deceptive image they present for approval. Developed Threes possess self-assurance, charm, energy, optimism, adaptability, and the capacity to inspire others.

Type Four: The Romantic/Individualist

8   Fours fit the bill of the moody, sensitive, dramatic, and creative artist. Prone to swings of melancholy and hyperactivity, Fours live at opposite poles of the emotional *spectrum*. Their attraction to the unattainable and rejection of what is easily available are sources of intense suffering. Because they feel a sense of deprivation and loss, Fours are envious of those who enjoy love and satisfaction. When they can achieve a balance between the push-and-pull pattern of their relationships and focus completely on the here and now, Fours blossom with creativity. Their sensitivity and emotional depth make Fours able to help others through difficult periods of grief and pain.

Type Five: The Observer/Investigator

9   Fives prefer to retreat into the safety of their heads, where they can occupy themselves with ideas and avoid emotional risks. Intensely private in nature, Fives do not seek attention from other people for fear that emotional demands will be made on them. Minimalists by nature, Fives do not require wealth or material possessions, but they are as attached to their intellectual **pursuits** as a miser who counts his gold in secret. When Fives can detach themselves from their fear of getting involved or losing out, they can let go and experience peace at its fullest. Independent, innovative, inventive, self-reliant, and perceptive, Fives make excellent scholars, researchers, and decision makers.

Type Six: The Loyal Skeptic/Loyalist

10   Habitual doubters, Sixes fear power and authority. As a result, they either rebel and gravitate toward underdog causes, or toe the line. Afraid to act on their own, Sixes are given to procrastination and mental anguish. They shy away from success to avoid attention from hostile authorities, and they often change jobs or fail to complete projects. Suspicious to the point of *paranoia*, Sixes believe that they can see others' bad intentions. Once Sixes get out of their heads and free themselves from the turmoil of worst-case scenarios, they can find the courage to act. At their best reliable, resourceful, and responsible, Sixes will do all in their power for those they care about.

Type Seven: The Epicure/Enthusiast

11   Light-hearted, eternally optimistic, and enthusiastic, Sevens like adventure, and their appetite for excitement drives them to seek new experiences. Sevens have abundant energy and many talents, but they can become scattered and easily distracted, with their imagination swinging like a monkey from branch to branch. Sevens escape fear by planning and keeping their **options** open. When facing a potential conflict, their first line of defense is to turn on the charm. Undeveloped Sevens tend to be impulsive and narcissistic, and they will try to avoid pain by seeking pleasure. When Sevens settle down and get serious, they can channel their creative energy and accomplish great things.

Type Eight: The Boss/Challenger

12   Eights view themselves as protectors of the weak. Aggressive and assertive, they *thrive* on conflict and will start a fight or push others' buttons to test their weaknesses. Because they prefer **predictability**, Eights are preoccupied with being in control, and they become bored when not faced with a challenge. Given to excess, Eights will follow their *impulses* and indulge in extreme behavior in an all-or-nothing style, which causes suffering to themselves as well as to others. Eights who **approach** new situations unarmed can be generous, committed, self-confident, and strong leaders capable of choosing the right course of action.

Type Nine: The Mediator/Peacemaker

13   Born peacemakers, Nines can support and sympathize with all points of view. Nines find it hard to say no, and they will sometimes go along with what others want for the sake of harmony. When it comes to conflict, Nines sit on the fence or space out. Rather than taking a stand, Nines resort to stubborn inaction as a defense, and they avoid critical matters by busying themselves with trivialities or by hoping trouble will go away. Undeveloped Nines lazily let priorities slide and indulge in the comfort of food, sleep, or television. Developed Nines who do not let themselves be distracted or dulled, are attentive listeners, compassionate healers, skilled **mediators**, and trustworthy facilitators.

14   Our personalities are a complex and fascinating subject indeed, but why we are who we are need not elude us. Whereas many personality theories tend to offer simplistic formulas, the Enneagram approaches personality holistically, **comprehensively**, and dynamically. By recognizing our *preoccupations* and passions, we can learn to overcome our flaws—and return ultimately to our *essence*, our true selves. Through self-understanding, we can also gain insight into our family members, partners, associates, and humanity as a whole, and forge healthy, meaningful, and lasting relationships.

After reading

In the Pre-reading section, check to see if your predictions about the reading text were correct.

Vocabulary

Thematic vocabulary *List five positive and five negative personality traits.*

Positive   **Negative**

_____   _____

_____   _____

_____   _____

_____   _____

_____   _____

Academic vocabulary *Using a dictionary, complete the following chart with the correct part of speech and definition of each of the **academic words** in the reading text. If a word has multiple meanings, match the definition to the context in which the word is used in the text.*

Word	Part of speech	Definition
1. adjacent	_____	_____
2. approach	_____	_____
3. aspect	_____	_____
4. attain	_____	_____
5. circumstance	_____	_____
6. comprehensive	_____	_____
7. comprise	_____	_____
8. credit	_____	_____
9. distinct	_____	_____
10. factor	_____	_____
11. illustrate	_____	_____
12. inherent	_____	_____
13. isolation	_____	_____
14. mediator	_____	_____
15. option	_____	_____

Word	Part of speech	Definition
16. predictability	_____	_____
17. psychology	_____	_____
18. pursuit	_____	_____
19. status	_____	_____
20. theory	_____	_____

Using vocabulary, part 1 *Complete each of the following sentences with the appropriate word(s) from the chart in Exercise 12-2. Be sure to use the correct form of each verb and to pluralize nouns, if necessary.*

1. Successful businesspeople and doctors usually have a higher _____ in the community.

2. In order to master English grammar, you need a _____ book that covers all

   the different _____ from parts of speech to sentence structure.

3. Our class is _____ of international students who want to go on to study in a degree program.

4. Teachers need to know a lot about _____ to be able to understand and motivate their students.

5. The weather is an important _____ to consider when you are planning where to go on your vacation.

6. When we made our hotel reservation, we booked _____ rooms so that everyone in the wedding party could be together on one floor.

7. If you need to ask someone for a favor or money, you should choose a friendly and grateful

   _____.

8. Some people believe that because violence is _____ in human beings, there will never be an end to war.

9. You can receive financial assistance from the government, depending on your personal

   _____.

Using vocabulary, part 2 *For each of the following sentences, choose the correct form of the **academic word** to fill in the blank.*

1. attainment, attainable, attain

   Setting a world record is not a goal that every Olympic athlete can _____.

2. illustrations, illustrated, illustrate

   The _____ on these pages show us how the human heart works.

3. isolation, isolated, isolate

   Because the new student was so much younger than the others in her class, she felt very

   _____ at first.

4. Theory, Theoretically, Theorize

   _____, we could live on another planet, but there are all kinds of practical obstacles.

5. distinction, distinct, distinguish

   If you want to reduce your spending, you need to make a clear _____ between what you want and what you really need.

6. option, optional, opt

   In your first year of college, English is not _____.

7. predictability, predictable, predict

   The best way to _____ the weather is to look out the window.

8. pursuits, pursuant, pursue

   Motocross racing is one of my brother's latest _____.

9. creditor, credible, credited

   Sigmund Freud is _____ with the founding of psychoanalysis and dream interpretation.

10. mediator, mediated, mediate

    A _____ was called in to settle the labor dispute between the union and the company management.

Nonacademic vocabulary *Match each **nonacademic word** in column 1 with its definition in column 2. Then, indicate each item's part of speech (n., v., or adj.).*

_____ 1. essence _____
_____ 2. impulse _____
_____ 3. paranoia _____
_____ 4. predisposition _____
_____ 5. preoccupation _____
_____ 6. procrastinate _____
_____ 7. spectrum _____
_____ 8. suppress _____
_____ 9. thrive _____
_____ 10. trait _____

a. subdue, put down
b. delusion, persecution complex
c. range, scope
d. characteristic, attribute
e. urge, compulsion
f. flourish, prosper
g. obsession, concern
h. spirit, core
i. delay, postpone action
j. preference, inclination

Reading comprehension

EXERCISE
12·6

Reading for main ideas *Indicate which of the two statements in the following pairs contains a main idea (M) and which contains a supporting detail (SD).*

1. a. _____ Everyone has a unique personality.

   b. _____ Personality became a field of study in the twentieth century.

2. a. _____ Personalities can be classified as Type A or B, or according to extraversion, agreeableness, conscientiousness, neuroticism, and openness.

   b. _____ There are many theories that try to explain the origins and types of personalities.

3. a. _____ The Enneagram consists of nine types organized around a chief feature or passion and serves as a model for the development of human consciousness.

   b. _____ The term *Enneagram* comes from Greek.

4. a. _____ Each personality type can be broken down into three kinds of intelligence, three emotional predispositions, and three subtypes.

   b. _____ The Enneagram is based on the Law of Three.

5. a. _____ The nine types are the Perfectionist, the Giver, the Performer, the Romantic, the Observer, the Loyal Skeptic, the Epicure, the Boss, and the Mediator.

   b. _____ Although everyone has an inherent type, all personalities are linked to some extent.

Reading for details *For each of the following sentences, choose the correct answer to fill in the blank.*

1. The theory that explains personality in terms of genetics and the environment is called _____.
   a. A and B types
   b. the Enneagram
   c. the nature-nurture theory

2. The *ennea-* in *enneagram* comes from the Greek word for _____.
   a. nine
   b. points
   c. passion

3. The personality types of the Enneagram are organized around a chief feature or _____.
   a. ability
   b. passion
   c. neurosis

4. Types 1-8-9 have a predisposition toward _____.
   a. fear
   b. not knowing their true feelings
   c. anger

5. The adjacent personality types are called _____.
   a. wings
   b. chief features
   c. predispositions

6. The Enneagram has its roots in _____.
   a. Christianity
   b. astrology
   c. Sufi mysticism

Indicate which of the following statements are true (T) and which are false (F).

7. _____ The Enneagram is based on the Law of Three.

8. _____ Each personality type in the Enneagram is completely unrelated to the others.

9. _____ The Enneagram is an ancient system.

10. _____ Types 5-6-7 are fear types.

11. _____ The Mediator's passion is Gluttony.

12. _____ The wings of a personality type can have a wide range of influence.

Answer the following questions in complete sentences.

13. Name the three ways in which the personality types can receive intuitive information.

_____

_____

_____

14. Which personality type will a Four (the Romantic) behave like under stress?

_____

15. Which personality type will a Seven (the Epicure) behave like in a situation where he or she feels secure?

_____

16. What is the purpose of the Enneagram system?

_____

_____

Answer the following question.

17. Match each personality type in column 1 with its passion in column 2.

_____ (1) Boss/Challenger
_____ (2) Observer/Investigator
_____ (3) Epicure/Enthusiast
_____ (4) Perfectionist/Reformer
_____ (5) Mediator/Peacemaker
_____ (6) Performer/Achiever
_____ (7) Loyal Skeptic/Loyalist
_____ (8) Romantic/Individualist
_____ (9) Giver/Helper

a. Sloth
b. Envy
c. Anger
d. Lust
e. Fear
f. Avarice
g. Pride
h. Gluttony
i. Deceit

EXERCISE
12·8

Reading for interpretation and inference *Match each of the following statements with the appropriate personality type below.*

a. I prefer to keep my distance and not get involved.
b. I need a lot of excitement in my life.
c. I have deep feelings that make me different from others.
d. I try to do the right thing and avoid mistakes.
e. I want to please others and be loved.
f. I go along with other people's wishes.
g. I like to take charge and be in control.
h. I try to excel at what I do and look good to others.
i. I expect the worst to happen and mistrust authority.

_____ 1. Perfectionist/Reformer

_____ 2. Giver/Helper

_____ 3. Performer/Achiever

_____ 4. Romantic/Individualist

_____ 5. Observer/Investigator

_____ 6. Loyal Skeptic/Loyalist

_____ 7. Epicure/Enthusiast

_____ 8. Boss/Challenger

_____ 9. Mediator/Peacemaker

Reading strategies
Summarizing: Eliminating relative clauses and appositives

Writing a summary of a reading text is one of the most useful skills you can develop. Having practiced paraphrasing passages from the reading texts and organizing key information, you should be able to restate the most important information in your own words.

A good summary

• restates the main ideas of the reading text *in your own words*
• includes only *the most essential details* and omits superfluous examples, facts, and statistics
• condenses the original text to approximately one third of its length
• reflects the author's purpose and point of view

Your summary does not need to follow the order in which the main ideas are presented in the reading text, but it is easier and logical to do so. Remember that copying the author's words is plagiarism.

When writing a summary, you need to condense the original text by eliminating repetition and nonessential details. Relative clauses, also called adjective clauses, are used to avoid repetition of nouns or pronouns. Because relative clauses beginning with *who, which, that, whose,* and *whom* contain additional information, they can be either eliminated or condensed in summaries.

The differences **that make us unique** are referred to as personality.
Our unique differences are referred to as personality.

An appositive is a word that restates information about an adjacent noun; the appositive is separated from the noun by a comma. Like relative clauses, appositives provide additional information that may not be essential to a summary, and they can be omitted.

~~Habitual doubters,~~ Sixes fear power and authority.

EXERCISE
12·9

Eliminating relative clauses and appositives, part 1 *Summarize each of the following statements from the reading text, eliminating the underlined relative clause.*

1. "Unlike other personality theories, the Enneagram offers a model <u>that symbolizes the unfolding of human consciousness.</u>"

_____

_____

2. "While each type has certain attributes, it is organized around a chief feature of character or passion, <u>which can become either a neurotic habit or an ally in attaining self-awareness.</u>"

_____

_____

3. "Each type has two adjacent wings, <u>one of which will act as a complement, or second side, to the personality.</u>"

_____

_____

4. "Ones resent those <u>who break the rules or take them lightly.</u>"

_____

_____

5. "Eights <u>who approach new situations unarmed</u> can be generous, committed, self-confident, and strong leaders capable of choosing the right course of action."

_____

_____

6. "Developed Nines <u>who do not let themselves be distracted or dulled</u>, are attentive listeners, compassionate healers, skilled mediators, and trustworthy facilitators."

_____

_____

Eliminating relative clauses and appositives, part 2 *Summarize each of the following statements from the reading text by striking through the least important noun phrase and any other unnecessary words.*

1. "The oldest theory of personality can be credited to the Roman surgeon Galen of Pergamon. . . ."

2. "An ancient system rooted in Sufi mysticism, the Enneagram (Greek *ennea* for "nine" and *grammos* for "point") identifies nine major aspects of being."

3. "Minimalists by nature, Fives do not require wealth or material possessions, but they are as attached to their intellectual pursuits as a miser who counts his gold in secret."

4. "Born peacemakers, Nines can support and sympathize with all points of view."

Organizing information

Organizing information *Scan the reading text for descriptions of the nine personality types, then enter the details in the following chart.*

Type One: The Perfectionist/Reformer

Chief feature _____

Passion _____

Virtue _____

Positive traits _____

Negative traits _____

Type Two: The Giver/Helper

Chief feature _____

Passion _____

Virtue _____

Positive traits _____

Negative traits _____

Type Three: The Performer/Achiever

Chief feature _____

Passion _____

Virtue _____

Positive traits _____

Negative traits _____

Type Four: The Romantic/Individualist

Chief feature _____

Passion _____

Virtue _____

Positive traits _____

Negative traits _____

Type Five: The Observer/Investigator

Chief feature _____

Passion _____

Virtue _____

Positive traits _____

Negative traits _____

Type Six: The Loyal Skeptic/Loyalist

Chief feature _____

Passion _____

Virtue _____

Positive traits _____

Negative traits _____

Type Seven: The Epicure/Enthusiast

Chief feature _____

Passion _____

Virtue _____

Positive traits _____

Negative traits _____

Type Eight: The Boss/Challenger

    Chief feature _____

    Passion _____

    Virtue _____

    Positive traits _____

    Negative traits _____

Type Nine: The Mediator/Peacemaker

    Chief feature _____

    Passion _____

    Virtue _____

    Positive traits _____

    Negative traits _____

Critical thinking

EXERCISE
12·12

Making evaluations *Indicate which personality type(s) would be most suited to the following jobs. Give reasons to support your answers.*

1. A police officer _____

2. A stand-up comedian _____

3. The CEO of a company _____

4. A good teacher _____

5. The leader of a country _____

6. A medical doctor _____

7. A scientific researcher _____

8. An actor or actress _____

9. A psychologist _____

10. A secretarial assistant _____

11. The coach of a basketball team _____

12. A defense lawyer _____

13. A television talk-show host _____

14. A travel agent _____

15. A negotiator _____

Making a case *Which personality type are you? Give reasons to support your opinion.*

Bibliography

Palmer, Helen, *The Enneagram: Understanding Yourself and the Others in Your Life* (San Francisco: Harper & Row, 1988).

Artificial Intelligence
Can machines think?

Pre-reading

Using the following questionnaire, interview your classmates, colleagues, family, and friends.

Questionnaire	A	B	C

What is the most important machine to you?
a. A computer
b. A cell phone
c. A car
d. Other (specify: _____)

What machine could you live without?
a. A washing machine
b. A television
c. A microwave
d. Other (specify: _____)

How many hours a day do you use a computer?
a. Under 2
b. 2 to 4
c. 4 to 6
d. More than 6

What electronic devices besides a computer
and cell phone do you use on a regular basis?

Have you ever seen or used a robot? Yes | No

If "yes," what did the robot do?

What kind of robot would you like to have?
a. A house cleaner
b. A chess player
c. An animal
d. Other (specify: _____)

Predicting content

Considering the title of the chapter, predict which of the following topics will be mentioned in the reading text.

☐ What Artificial Intelligence means

☐ Who developed the first robots

☐ How robots are built

☐ How much robots cost to make

☐ What robots are used for

Reading text

1   Nowadays, we use so many machines that life is unimaginable without them. Because of machines, we can travel farther and faster. We can **access** and process greater quantities of information at ever-increasing speeds. We can *perform* dangerous and complicated tasks more safely, efficiently, and precisely. In our homes, schools, hospitals, factories, stores, and offices, there are machines from the simplest gadgets to the most sophisticated electronic systems. In fact, we would have to travel very far indeed to find a place on this earth where we wouldn't encounter a machine of some kind.

2   The invention of machines and their widespread *adoption* have **transformed** human society. Simple tools fashioned from wood or stone allowed early humans to conquer their environment and improve their chances of survival. Ten thousand years ago, the first crude hand plow led to the agricultural revolution, followed **approximately** 15 centuries later by the wheel, which evolved over time into animal-drawn carts and farm implements. Beginning with the steam engine in 1705, the Industrial Revolution brought about massive economic and social changes that continued into the twentieth century. With the train and automobile came increasing urbanization and mobility, and the telegraph—and later the telephone, radio, and television—**enabled** people to communicate over long distances.

3   Technological progress that had been thousands of years in the making accelerated rapidly with the advent of the electronic computer in 1941. Eight years later, the stored-program computer vastly improved programming procedures. As computer science took off in universities, far-fetched ideas that had once belonged to the realm of science fiction became realities. One such idea was to build mechanical creatures that could think and act independently. After World War II, English mathematician Alan Turing worked on programming intelligent machines, but it was American visionary and computer scientist John McCarthy who coined the term *artificial intelligence* (AI) in 1956 at an international conference that paved the way for future research.

4   The idea of **mechanical** men has fascinated thinkers and inventors for centuries. In the early 1600s, Renaissance genius and painter Leonardo da Vinci designed a mechanical humanoid robot, which was never built due to the technical limitations of the time. Elaborate mechanical toys and sophisticated creatures, such as a mechanical body that could write and draw, were **constructed** in France in the eighteenth and nineteenth centuries, but such inventions, as amazing as they were, ended up in various museums as objects of curiosity. The idea of mechanical men, or robots,[1] surfaced in a play written in 1921 by a Czech playwright about a mad scientist who creates artificial men to do manual **labor**. After they are bought by nations at war, the robots end up wiping out humanity and taking over the world. The theme of crazed, uncontrollable killing machines bent on their creators' destruction continued in the science-fiction novels and movies of the 1950s.

---

[1] *Robot* comes from the Czech word *robota*, meaning hard work or drudgery.

5   In the meantime, with cheaper, faster computer technology at their disposal, scientists could take up the quest for *autonomous* machines that philosophers and mathematicians could only imagine a century earlier. In the 1940s, American-born British neurophysiologist W. Grey Walter constructed some of the first autonomous electronic robots at the Burden Neurological Institute. The size of a shoebox, these tortoiselike robots could move about on three wheels and respond to a light source. Later models contained reflex circuits, which Walter used to condition them to flee or display simple behavior at the sound of whistles.

6   In the late 1960s, microprocessors radically reduced the size of computers, making it possible to build mobile robots with an onboard "brain" linked to a mainframe computer. At Stanford Research Institute in California, a team of researchers programmed a small adult-sized robot named Shakey to sense colored blocks and wedges with an onboard camera and to push them around a carefully constructed set of rooms. As part of NASA's Apollo program to land a man on the moon, scientists at Stanford University built a four-wheeled vehicle to test the moon's surface. The Stanford Cart never made it to the moon, but at the Stanford Artificial Intelligence Laboratory (SAIL), where the first video game, electric robot arms, and computer-generated music were also produced, graduate students under John McCarthy's supervision tried to make the Cart into an automatically driven automobile. Although the Cart could sense what was in front of it, follow a white line and eventually **compute** the best path to its goal, it functioned poorly in an uncontrolled environment.

7   Real progress with robots was made in the field of manufacturing. The first industrial robot, the Unimate, was a hydraulically powered arm that transported and welded die castings on automobiles. Soon to become standard equipment on car manufacturing assembly lines, the robotic arm eliminated human error, reduced costs, and **automated** production. Research labs such as SAIL also became **involved** in working on electrically powered arms with more humanlike joints. As companies, particularly those in Japan, developed the technology, these arms evolved into programmable universal manipulation arm (PUMA) robots, the most *pervasive* electric arms used in mass production. Ideally suited to replace human workers in dangerous and dirty industrial environments, advanced robotic systems and custom-built robots perform repetitive jobs around the clock that require a high degree of precision and flawlessness.

8   Remote-controlled robots are also *indispensable* in space and underwater exploration, military reconnaissance, and search-and-rescue operations. Robotic probes such as the Pioneer and, later, the Voyager series have been used since the early days of space exploration to gather information and radio data back to Earth. Mobile robots with insectlike appendages can investigate the craters of active volcanoes and **survey** ocean floors. Autonomous underwater vehicles can patrol extreme ocean depths, relay video and sonar pictures to the surface, and carry out delicate jobs such as **adjusting** valves on underwater oil pipelines. Police and military forces employ joystick-controlled demolition robots to defuse bombs and clear mine fields. In nuclear power plants, where accidents can produce life-threatening levels of radiation, robots can enter unsafe areas and help scientists **assess** the damage. When mines or buildings **collapse**, as happened during the 9/11 terrorist attacks in the United States, robots are sent in to locate trapped people.

9   From manufacturing and exploration, robots have begun making their way into our personal lives. Finely tuned medical robots can perform delicate operations, such as heart and eye surgery, with greater precision and control than a surgeon's hand. As these devices become smaller and more sophisticated, their use will make many medical procedures less invasive and risky to patients. **Components** originally designed for robotic joints and limbs can be incorporated into bionic prosthetics that will **eventually** restore normal function to disabled people. Already, there are floor-cleaning robots on the market, but so far their limited ability to navigate around the house and do a thorough job has made them more of an amusing luxury. At the rate technology is developing, robots could quite **conceivably** relieve us of many chores in eldercare facilities and hospitals, as well as in our homes.

10   Despite the amazing accomplishments in robotics, the ultimate goal still remains the creation of an independently thinking humanoid robot—in other words, a machine made in man's image. In the 1970s in Japan, Professor Hirokazu Kato built Wabot-1, a robot that walked on two legs, *grasped* simple objects with both hands, and was capable of basic speech interaction. A later and more lifelike version, Wabot-2, was equipped with a TV camera for a head and could sight-read and play music while it sat on a piano bench. In 1997, Honda introduced the remote-controlled P2, followed by the P3 in 1998, which *resembled* a human being in a space suit, carried a battery backpack, and walked and climbed stairs. In 2001, Honda introduced Asimo, a child-sized humanoid that could walk, reach, grasp, talk to people, and understand simple commands. Built for amusement parks, Asimo remained a remote-controlled puppet rather than a truly autonomous creature.

11   Although research into humanoid robots has exploded around the world, the final product is far from reach. Walking comes naturally to human beings, but coordinated, elegant movement is not nearly as simple for a robot, whose vision system and brain cannot collect and process information in the same complex way that humans can. Balance is another problem, one that humans master because of their delicately constructed inner ear. Vision systems equipped with a video camera can distinguish colors, but cannot tell the difference between a baseball and an orange. To demonstrate real intelligence, a robot's computer brain would have to contain gargantuan databases and operate like the human nervous system. An advanced ability called parallel processing enables robotic systems to break down complex problems according to patterns of **logic**, and it is already being used in AI systems that update flight information at airports or pre-approve mortgage applications online. Scientists are working on neural network programs for robots, and should they succeed, robots of the future may be able to learn from experience and generate creative thought.

12   While it is possible to construct a robot with a human form and one that can even communicate and *mimic* human behavior, the creation of a truly sentient, intelligent, and autonomous machine is another story. Despite numerous advancements, it has not been possible to create from silicon, metal, and tissue a machine that can reproduce itself, feel emotions and empathy, survive on its own instincts, understand the consequences of its actions, or operate with the same level of purpose or understanding that humans **exhibit**. A machine is still a machine, and in the final analysis, a machine lacks the spark of life.

13   On the other hand, there is a movement of extropians, those who believe that human life can be extended by downloading consciousness into computers or robots. Although this may be possible in principle, the value of living forever inside a machine seems questionable, if not ridiculous. Conceivably, however, humans and machines could *merge* in the future like the cyborgs of science fiction, as robotic components are integrated into our bodies for medical purposes or as a means of enhancing our abilities to see, hear, and move. In any case, machines and robots will likely **assume** a greater, rather than a lesser, role in our lives. The question is, Will we humans still control machines, or will machines eventually control us?

After reading

In the Pre-reading section, check to see if your predictions about the reading text were correct.

Vocabulary

EXERCISE
13·1

Thematic vocabulary *List 10 words or phrases related to machines.*

_____ _____

_____ _____

_____ _____

_____ _____

EXERCISE
13·2

Academic vocabulary *Using a dictionary, complete the following chart with the correct forms and definitions of the **academic words** from the reading text. If a word has multiple meanings, match the definition to the context in which the word is used in the text.*

	Noun	Adjective	Verb	Definition
1.	_____	_____	access	_____
2.	_____	_____	adjust	_____
3.	_____	_____	automate	_____
4.	_____	_____	collapse	_____
5.	_____	_____	compute	_____
6.	_____	_____	construct	_____
7.	_____	X	involve	_____
8.	_____	_____	transform	_____
9.	labor	_____	_____	_____
10.	_____	approximate(ly)	_____	_____
11.	_____	conceivable (conceivably)	_____	_____
12.	_____	mechanical	_____	_____
13.	_____	X	assess	_____
14.	_____	X	assume	_____
15.	_____	X	enable	_____
16.	_____	X	exhibit	_____
17.	component	_____	X	_____

Noun	Adjective	Verb	Definition
18. logic	_____	X	_____
19. _____	eventual(ly)	X	_____
20. _____	X	survey	_____

EXERCISE 13·3

Using vocabulary *Complete each of the following sentences with the appropriate word from the chart in Exercise 13-2. Be sure to use the correct form of each verb and to pluralize nouns, if necessary.*

1. Computers _____ us to process and store a large amount of information.

2. The new subway line operates without drivers and is completely _____.

3. A monitor is just one _____ of a computer system.

4. Learning a second language _____ a lot of time and effort.

5. Is it _____ that one day ordinary people will be able to travel into outer space and visit Mars?

6. It is illegal to steal people's personal data and _____ their identity.

7. If you try hard enough, you will _____ find a job.

8. Under the influence of alcohol or drugs, people _____ abnormal and sometimes aggressive behavior.

9. Men are usually better at _____ skills than women.

10. The damage from the storm was _____ at $1.6 billion.

11. Before divers went down to explore the sunken ship, a robotic device was used to _____ the wreck and the terrain.

12. Would you like to have a robot that did most of the household _____?

13. To solve this mathematical problem, you have to use _____ and reason.

14. If buildings are not seismically upgraded, there is a danger that they will _____ during an earthquake.

15. After the long dry period, the rain _____ the gardens into an abundance of flowers.

16. Your plane will be ready for boarding in _____ 30 minutes.

17. Due to an error in the program, the figures we entered did not _____.

18. You cannot _____ your Facebook account without a valid password.

19. You may have to _____ your seatbelt so that it fits tightly.

20. Do you know how long ago the Parliament buildings were _____?

Nonacademic vocabulary *Match each **nonacademic word** in column 1 with its definition in column 2. Then, indicate each item's part of speech (n., v., or adj.).*

_____ 1. adoption _____
_____ 2. artificial _____
_____ 3. autonomous _____
_____ 4. grasp _____
_____ 5. indispensable _____
_____ 6. merge _____
_____ 7. mimic _____
_____ 8. perform _____
_____ 9. pervasive _____
_____ 10. resemble _____

a. hold something firmly
b. combine into a whole
c. spreading widely
d. made as a copy of something natural
e. be similar to someone or something
f. absolutely necessary
g. function or do something
h. use or putting into effect
i. take on the appearance of someone or something
j. self-governing or independent

Reading comprehension

Reading for main ideas *Write the topic sentence of each of the paragraphs of the reading text. The topic sentence of paragraph 1 has been provided.*

Paragraph 1 *Nowadays, we use so many machines that life is unimaginable without them.* _____

Paragraph 2 _____

Paragraph 3 _____

Paragraph 4 _____

Paragraph 5 _____

Paragraph 6 _____

Paragraph 7 _____

Paragraph 8 _____

_____

Paragraph 9 _____

_____

Paragraph 10 _____

_____

Paragraph 11 _____

_____

Paragraph 12 _____

_____

Paragraph 13 _____

_____

EXERCISE
13·6

Reading for details *For each of the following sentences, choose the correct answer to fill in the blank.*

1. The _____ led to the Industrial Revolution.
   a. wheel
   b. steam engine
   c. plow

2. Mathematicians and computer scientists began working on artificial intelligence _____.
   a. after World War I
   b. after World War II
   c. during the Industrial Revolution

3. The term *artificial intelligence* was first used by _____.
   a. Leonardo da Vinci
   b. Alan Turing
   c. John McCarthy

4. The first adult-sized robot was developed at _____.
   a. the Stanford Research Institute
   b. the Burden Neurological Institute
   c. NASA

5. The Unimate was used in _____.
   a. space exploration
   b. medical surgery
   c. manufacturing

6. In 2001, Honda introduced a humanoid robot called _____.
   a. Asimo
   b. Shakey
   c. Wabot

Indicate which of the following statements are true (T) and which are false (F).

7. _____ The Industrial Revolution mechanized manufacturing.

8. _____ The first robots were built and used as soldiers in Czechoslovakia.

9. _____ Robots cannot understand the consequences of their actions.

10. _____ Robots are able to walk, run, and climb stairs like humans.

11. _____ Floor-cleaning robots have been commercially successful and popular.

12. _____ Robotic systems can analyze problems logically.

Answer the following questions in complete sentences.

13. What is the origin of the word *robot,* and where was it first used?

   _____

   _____

14. How did the invention of microprocessors lead to the development of robots?

   _____

   _____

15. Give five reasons why robots have become such an integral component of car manufacturing.

   _____

   _____

   _____

   _____

   _____

16. In what dangerous situations are robots indispensable?

   _____

   _____

17. What important functions are robots not able to perform in the way that humans can?

   _____

   _____

Reading for interpretation and inference *Indicate which of the following statements about robots are positive (+) and which are negative (−).*

1. _____ "The theme of crazed, uncontrollable killing machines bent on their creators' destruction continued in the science-fiction novels and movies of the 1950s."

2. _____ ". . . such inventions, as amazing as they were, ended up in various museums as objects of curiosity."

3. _____ "Although the Cart could sense what was in front of it, follow a white line and eventually compute the best path to its goal, it functioned poorly in an uncontrolled environment."

4. _____ ". . . advanced robotic systems and custom-built robots perform repetitive jobs around the clock that require a high degree of precision and flawlessness."

5. _____ "Built for amusement parks, Asimo remained a remote-controlled puppet rather than a truly autonomous creature."

6. _____ "Vision systems equipped with a video camera can distinguish colors, but cannot tell the difference between a baseball and an orange."

7. _____ "A machine is still a machine, and in the final analysis, a machine lacks the spark of life."

8. _____ ". . . humans and machines could merge in the future like the cyborgs of science fiction, as robotic components are integrated into our bodies for medical purposes or as a means of enhancing our abilities to see, hear, and move."

Reading strategies
Summarizing

Summarizing *Condense and summarize each of the following passages from the reading text, using techniques covered in Chapters 6 through 12.*

1. "Beginning with the steam engine in 1705, the Industrial Revolution brought about massive economic and social changes that continued into the twentieth century. With the train and automobile came increasing urbanization and mobility, and the telegraph—and later the telephone, radio, and television—enabled people to communicate over long distances."

_____

_____

_____

2. "Elaborate mechanical toys and sophisticated creatures, such as a mechanical body that could write and draw, were constructed in France in the eighteenth and nineteenth centuries, but such inventions, as amazing as they were, ended up in various museums as objects of curiosity."

_____

_____

_____

3. "After World War II, English mathematician Alan Turing worked on programming intelligent machines, but it was American visionary and computer scientist John McCarthy who coined the term *artificial intelligence* (AI) in 1956 at an international conference that paved the way for future research."

_____

_____

_____

4. "In the 1940s, British neurophysiologist W. Grey Walter constructed some of the first autonomous electronic robots at the Burden Neurological Institute. The size of a shoebox, these tortoiselike robots could move about on three wheels and respond to a light source. Later models contained reflex circuits, which Walter used to condition them to flee or display simple behavior at the sound of whistles."

_____

_____

_____

5. "As part of NASA's Apollo program to land a man on the moon, scientists at Stanford University built a four-wheeled vehicle to test the moon's surface. The Stanford Cart never made it to the moon, but at the Stanford Artificial Intelligence Laboratory (SAIL), where the first video game, electric robot arms, and computer-generated music were also produced, graduate students under John McCarthy's supervision tried to make the Cart into an automatically driven automobile. Although the Cart could sense what was in front of it, follow a white line and eventually compute the best path to its goal, it functioned poorly in an uncontrolled environment."

_____

_____

_____

6. "As companies, particularly those in Japan, developed the technology, these arms evolved into programmable universal manipulation arm (PUMA) robots, the most pervasive electric arms used in mass production. Ideally suited to replace human workers in dangerous and dirty industrial environments, advanced robotic systems and custom-built robots perform repetitive jobs around the clock that require a high degree of precision and flawlessness."

_____

_____

_____

7. "In the 1970s in Japan, Professor Hirokazu Kato built Wabot-1, a robot that walked on two legs, grasped simple objects with both hands, and was capable of basic speech interaction. A later and more lifelike version, Wabot-2, was equipped with a TV camera for a head and could sight-read and play music while it sat on a piano bench. In 1997, Honda introduced the remote-controlled P2, followed by the P3 in 1998, which resembled a human being in a space suit, carried a battery backpack, and walked and climbed stairs. In 2001, Honda introduced Asimo, a child-sized humanoid that could walk, reach, grasp, talk to people, and understand simple commands. Built for amusement parks, Asimo remained a remote-controlled puppet rather than a truly autonomous creature."

_____

_____

_____

8. "Walking comes naturally to human beings, but coordinated, elegant movement is not nearly as simple for a robot, whose vision system and brain cannot collect and process information in the same complex way that humans can. Balance is another problem, one that humans master because of their delicately constructed inner ear. Vision systems equipped with a video camera can distinguish colors, but cannot tell the difference between a baseball and an orange. To demonstrate real intelligence, a robot's computer brain would have to contain gargantuan databases and operate like the human nervous system."

_____

_____

_____

Organizing information

Scan the reading text for details that support the main ideas in the following chart, then enter the information in the chart. Don't copy directly from the text; use your own words as much as possible.

Main ideas	Important details
The development of robots and Artificial Intelligence	_____ _____ _____ _____
The use of robots in manufacturing	_____ _____ _____ _____
The use of robots in dangerous situations	_____ _____ _____ _____

Main ideas	Important details
Medical and personal uses of robots	_____
	_____
	_____
	_____
The development of humanoid robots	_____
	_____
	_____
	_____
Problems and obstacles	_____
	_____
	_____
	_____
The future of robots	_____
	_____
	_____
	_____

Critical thinking

EXERCISE
13·9

Making evaluations *Indicate which of the following would be useful and feasible (✓) in the future and which would not (X). Give reasons to support your answers.*

1. _____ Robotic babysitters

2. _____ Robotic gardeners

3. _____ Robotic surgeons

4. _____ Robotic dog walkers

5. _____ Robotic housekeepers

6. _____ Robotic short-order cooks

7. _____ Robotic agents at airport information counters

8. _____ Robotic tour guides in museums

EXERCISE
13·10

Making a case *Do you think that it will be possible in the future to create superhuman people who are part human and part robot? What would be the advantages and disadvantages of such superhuman people? Are there dangers or ethical considerations? Give reasons to support your opinions.*

Bibliography

Brooks, Rodney A., *Flesh and Machines: How Robots Will Change Us* (New York: Pantheon Books, 2002).

Fritz, Sandy, *Robotics and Artificial Intelligence* (North Mankato, MN: Byron Preiss Publications, 2003).

"An Introduction to the Science of Artificial Intelligence" (Oracle ThinkQuest Education Foundation), http://library.thinkquest.org/2705/.

McCarthy, John, "What Is Artificial Intelligence?" (Stanford University, 2007), http://www-formal.stanford.edu/jmc/whatisai/whatisai.html.

Voluntary simplicity
Making more out of less

Pre-reading

Using the following questionnaire, interview your classmates, colleagues, family, and friends.

Questionnaire	A	B	C

How much stress do you have in your life?
a. Too much
b. Not very much
c. None

How much time do you have to do the things you really enjoy doing?
a. Lots of time
b. Always enough time
c. Never enough time
d. No time at all

What makes you happy?
a. Money
b. Success
c. Family relationships
d. Friends
e. New experiences
f. Other (specify: _____)

How important are "things" to you?
a. Very important
b. Somewhat important
c. Not very important

Why do you buy things?
a. Because I need them
b. Because I want them
c. Because everyone else has them
d. Because I can't say no
e. Because I saw an advertisement or commercial
f. Other (specify: _____)

How much "stuff" do you have?
a. Too much
b. Enough
c. Not very much
d. Only what I really need

Predicting content

Read only the first paragraph of the reading text, then make three predictions about the content of the entire text.

_____

_____

_____

Reading text

1   In 1988, American vocalist Bobby McFerrin **released** "Don't Worry, Be Happy." **Accompanied** by an entertaining video featuring comic actors Robin Williams and Bill Irwin, McFerrin's _a cappella_ song had a catchy tune, but it was the simple, upbeat message that lifted it to No. 1 on the Billboard Hot 100. As stated in the American Declaration of Independence of 1776, life, liberty, and the pursuit of happiness are inalienable rights. Happiness motivates us; without it, our lives would be empty and meaningless.

2   Of course, what makes a person happy differs greatly from **individual** to individual. For some it's money, fame, or power; for others, it's family, relationships, work, adventure, creativity, or peace of mind. In its short refrain, "Don't Worry, Be Happy" offers a **straightforward formula** for happiness—one that most people would agree with—but not worrying and being happy aren't always so easy. Or is it possible that by simplifying our lives, by reducing the _clutter_ that worries and burdens us, we can find true happiness?

3   The **majority** of people have always lived simply, and most of humanity still struggles on a daily basis to eke out a meager existence under dire circumstances. Only in _affluent_ industrialized countries do people have the luxury of more goods and services than they need to survive. On the basis of material wealth, North Americans and Europeans should be the happiest people on earth, but according to the 2012 Happy Planet **Index** (HPI), they are not.

4   Introduced in 2006 by the New Economics Foundation as a challenge to the Gross Domestic Product (GDP) and the Human Development Index (HDI) as measures of a country's well-being, the Happy Planet Index assesses happiness in terms of life expectancy, experienced well-being, and the country's ecological footprint. The results are astounding. The top five _ranking_ countries are Costa Rica, Vietnam, Colombia, Belize, and El Salvador, in that order; these poor countries also have a minimal ecological footprint between 1.4 and 2.4. The least happy of the 161 countries listed are Mali, the Central African Republic, Qatar, Chad, and Botswana. Except for oil-rich Qatar with an ecological footprint of 11.7, these countries are poor and have an ecological footprint between 1.4 and 2.8. Wealthy countries show the following results:

Country	Rank	Ecological footprint
Switzerland	34	5.0
United Kingdom	41	4.7
Japan	45	4.2
Germany	46	4.6
Canada	64	6.4
Australia	76	6.7
United States	105	17.2

5   Not only are Americans, Canadians, Britons, Germans, Australians, the Swiss, and the Japanese less happy than their counterparts in Central and Latin American countries, but—ironically—in the last few decades, some people, particularly in North America, have been turning away from consumerism and embracing a simpler, more natural lifestyle. During the counter-

culture era of the 1960s, there was a trend for mostly young people to reject the "American Dream" and the White Anglo-Saxon Protestant (WASP) work ethic. Even professionals and intellectuals were "dropping out" of society and moving "back to the land" to commune with nature. In the 1980s, surveys conducted in the United States revealed that 25 percent of the adult population had simplified how they lived and worked. The results of a 1991 *Time*-CNN survey **published** in *Time* magazine showed that 69 percent of participants wanted to slow down and enjoy a more relaxed lifestyle, and that 60 percent found that work made it difficult to enjoy life.

6   What had begun as an experimental lifestyle evolved into a quiet revolution that spread the word through books such as Duane Elgin's best-selling *Voluntary Simplicity: Toward a Way of Life That is Outwardly Simple, Inwardly Rich* (1981), as well as numerous magazines, alternative communities of the like-minded, and, later, Internet websites. Combined with a growing awareness of the environmental consequences of consumerism, the voluntary simplicity movement sought to reduce the consumption of goods and energy and to minimize one's personal impact on the environment. "Voluntary" **denotes** a free and conscious choice to make appropriate changes that will enrich life in a deeper, spiritual sense. "Simplicity" refers to the lack of clutter, that is, eliminating all those things, patterns, habits, and ideas that take control of our lives and distract us from our inner selves.

7   Voluntary simplicity is not to be confused with poverty, which is involuntary, degrading, and debilitating. Neither does it mean that people must live on a farm or **reject** progress or technology, or do without what is necessary for their comfort and **welfare**. For example, we need food and shelter, but we don't necessarily need to eat steak and lobster or to live in a palace. In today's world, most of us need a computer and an Internet connection for work and school, but at home we don't need a computer in every room—and we don't need to spend our time endlessly surfing the Internet.

8   To practice voluntary simplicity, one must differentiate between what one *wants* (psychological desires) and what one *needs* (basic requirements of life), and **seek** a healthy *balance* that is **compatible** with both. In a consumer society where advertising bombards us with the message that without this, that, and the other product, we are unsuccessful, undesirable, and unimportant, being clear on what you really need and resisting what you don't can be an ongoing struggle.

9   The beauty of voluntary simplicity is that it is a philosophy, and not a dogma. How one goes about it depends on individual character, cultural background, and climate. Although there is no single right way to practice voluntary simplicity, there are some general guidelines that one can apply to one's individual circumstances:

1. **Take stock** Before you make any changes, you must examine your life. Do you spend your time and energy on activities that fulfill you, or do you let other people or pressures control you? Do you use your time effectively, or do you waste it on activities that bring neither satisfaction nor results? How much stuff do you own? Do you use what you have on a regular basis, or do most of your possessions just take up space?

2. **Set priorities** Once you have taken stock, you can identify what you value most and what you can definitely dispense with. Making a list and assigning a numerical value to each item can help you sort things out. Next, you can decide how much time and energy you will dedicate to your **priorities**. If family is important, how will you make sure that you give your loved ones your full attention? If learning a new skill means a lot to you, how can you free up your schedule to accommodate taking a course?

3. **Reduce, recycle, and reuse** The three Rs represent the best way to get a handle on rampant consumerism. In economies driven by the quest for ever more, living with less is **erroneously equated** with poverty and social inferiority. By conserving energy, for instance, you are actually ensuring that more resources are available for future use. By making a *frugal budget* and sticking to it, you can eliminate unnecessary expenses. Recycling paper, metal, plastic, and

glass and reusing building materials and old clothing keep materials in the loop and out of landfills.

4. **Share, give away, and use public resources** Pooling skills and resources through barter networks not only saves money, but sharing with others establishes **bonds** and *fosters* a sense of community. You can donate what you no longer use to charitable organizations or give it away to someone in need, rather than throwing usable items into the trash. You can also **utilize** public libraries, public transportation, and other public facilities.

5. **Choose quality over quantity** With the glut of cheap goods that are usually designed for obsolescence, quality products that last are becoming progressively harder to find. In the long run, a more expensive but *durable* and repairable item or even an older used item that is still in good condition is a better investment than a brand new piece of junk that will only break down and end up in the trash.

6. **Resist pressure** We are raised to believe that more and bigger are synonymous with better, and that without lots of money, a big house, a new car, and the latest fashions, we are nobody. What we are never told is that all these things come with an enormous price tag, and that we have to sacrifice much of our lives chasing after the dollars we need to pay for them. Choosing a simpler life means going against the grain of mainstream society, and you must be committed in order to withstand the pressures that society, the media, and even sometimes family and friends exert on you to **conform**.

7. **Take time** They say that time is money, but time is actually more precious than money. You do not have to change your life or your habits overnight. Not only is it impossible, but like crash diets, rash behavior is sure to backfire. Only by taking small, reasonable steps and giving yourself sufficient time to adjust and evaluate your progress will you be able to commit yourself to your choices and see them through.

8. **Be grateful** People chase after more because they either have accumulated the wrong things or do not appreciate what they have. If you can be genuinely *grateful* for what you have, you will always have enough.

10   At the heart of voluntary simplicity is the conscious realization that less is really more. Less consumption means more resources for future generations. Less activity that brings little satisfaction or reward is more time for yourself and your loved ones. Less stuff is more space to move around in. Less **stress** means more relaxation and better health. Less worry provides more enjoyment and more *fulfillment* in life. How we live our lives is essentially our choice, but one choice we can make is simple enough: in the words of Bobby McFerrin, "Don't worry, be happy."

After reading

In the Pre-reading section, check to see if your predictions about the reading text were correct.

Vocabulary

EXERCISE 14·1

Thematic vocabulary *List 10 words or phrases related to social and cultural values.*

_____   _____

_____   _____

_____   _____

_____   _____

_____   _____

EXERCISE 14·2

Academic vocabulary *Using a dictionary, complete the following chart with the correct forms and definitions of the **academic words** from the reading text. If a word has multiple meanings, match the definition to the context in which the word is used in the text.*

Noun	Adjective	Verb	Definition
1. _____	_____	equate	_____
2. _____	X	publish	_____
3. _____	X	release	_____
4. _____	X	utilize	_____
5. index	X	_____	_____
6. stress	_____	_____	_____
7. _____	erroneous(ly)	_____	_____
8. individual, _____	_____	_____	_____
9. _____	X	accompany	_____
10. _____	X	conform	_____
11. _____	X	denote	_____
12. _____	X	reject	_____
13. X	X	seek	_____
14. bond, bonding	X	_____	_____
15. priority	X	_____	_____

Noun	Adjective	Verb	Definition
16. formula	_____	X	_____
17. majority	_____	X	_____
18. _____	compatible	X	_____
19. welfare	X	X	_____
20. X	straightforward	X	_____

EXERCISE

14·3

Using vocabulary *Complete each of the following sentences with the appropriate word from the chart in Exercise 14-2. Be sure to use the correct form of each verb and to pluralize nouns, if necessary.*

1. Meditation can help you reduce your _____ level and find a sense of balance.

2. The Consumer Price _____ reflects spending patterns and indicates inflationary trends.

3. If you have a library card, you can _____ all of its resources.

4. The _____ between mother and child is one of the strongest human relationships.

5. Individualists find it difficult to _____ to the rules of society, especially if the rules do not make sense.

6. The president won the election by a large _____.

7. The bride will be _____ to the altar by her father and three bridesmaids.

8. It is _____ to believe that everyone can become rich.

9. J. K. Rowling has just _____ her first adult novel.

10. It is better to be _____ than beat around the bush.

11. The symbols ♀ and ♂ _____ female and male, respectively.

12. The government is responsible for the safety and _____ of its citizens.

13. People often _____ money with happiness.

14. If you do not want to keep on wasting your time and energy, you need to sit down and set your _____.

15. The Bill of Rights protects the democratic rights of every _____.

16. There is no simple _____ for success or happiness.

17. At the end of the semester, a lot of college students will be _____ a summer job.

18. When Sally flatly refused to go on a date with Harry, he felt deeply hurt and

     _____.

19. When is the band going to _____ its latest CD and video?

20. My roommate and I get along, because our interests are so _____.

Nonacademic vocabulary *Fill in the part of speech for each of the **nonacademic words** below, then indicate which of the words best conveys the meaning of the underlined word or phrase in each sentence that follows. Be sure to use the correct form of each verb and to change an adjective to an adverb, if necessary.*

affluent _____   balance _____   budget _____   clutter _____   durable _____

foster _____   frugal _____   fulfillment _____   grateful _____   rank _____

1. I would be very <u>appreciative</u> if you could help me with this project.

     _____

2. A person who has a stressful and demanding job finds it difficult to <u>put in an equal position</u> family and work.

     _____

3. Mrs. Johnson gets a lot of <u>satisfaction</u> out of volunteering in the community.

     _____

4. Massachusetts Institute of Technology <u>holds a top position</u> among the world's top universities.

     _____

5. If you have trouble making ends meet, you need to sit down and make a <u>plan of income and expenditures</u>.

     _____

6. Josephine's family lives in a very <u>wealthy</u> neighborhood.

     _____

7. I don't know how you can stand the <u>untidy jumble</u> of papers and stuff on your desk.

     _____

8. Student exchange programs <u>promote the development of</u> cultural understanding and a spirit of cooperation.

     _____

9. People who have to raise a family on a low income have to live <u>using as little money as possible</u>.

     _____

10. If you want to go hiking in the mountains, you need to get a good <u>hardwearing</u> pair of hiking boots.

_____

Reading comprehension

EXERCISE
14·5

Reading for main ideas *Choose the boldface word or phrase that correctly completes each of the following statements. Some statements include two sets of choices.*

1. **Wealth | Happiness** is what gives our lives true meaning, but there **is | isn't** a simple, straightforward formula for achieving it.

2. According to the Happy Planet Index, people living in affluent countries **are | are not** the happiest people on earth.

3. According to the Happy Planet Index, the happiest people live in countries with the **lowest | highest** ecological footprint.

4. Voluntary simplicity originated in **North America | Central and South America** as a counterculture that evolved into an alternative lifestyle movement.

5. Voluntary simplicity seeks to **reduce | increase** consumption patterns and personal impact on the environment.

6. Voluntary simplicity **equates | differentiates between** "wants" and "needs."

7. Voluntary simplicity is a **philosophy | dogma** that depends on **individual circumstances | societal pressures**.

EXERCISE
14·6

Reading for details *For each of the following sentences, choose the correct answer to fill in the blank.*

1. A *Time-Life* survey found that _____ percent of participants wanted a more relaxed lifestyle.
   a. 25
   b. 60
   c. 69

2. According to the 2012 Happy Planet Index, the happiest countries are in _____.
   a. North America
   b. Central and South America
   c. Europe

3. According to the 2012 Happy Planet Index, the least happy countries are in
   _____.
   a. North America
   b. Africa
   c. Asia

4. Of the least happy countries, all have a low ecological footprint except _____.
   a. Qatar
   b. Mali
   c. Chad

5. Voluntary simplicity began as a movement in the _____.
   a. 1960s
   b. 1970s
   c. 1980s

6. Surveys conducted in the 1980s in the United States showed that _____ percent of adults had simplified their lifestyle and work.
   a. 69
   b. 60
   c. 25

Indicate which of the following statements are true (T) and which are false (F).

7. _____ People in wealthy countries are the happiest people on earth.

8. _____ The happiest countries have a low ecological footprint.

9. _____ It is not possible to apply voluntary simplicity both to your life and to your work.

10. _____ Bobby McFerrin wrote a book about voluntary simplicity.

11. _____ People don't have to live on a farm or in the country to practice voluntary simplicity.

12. _____ People who practice voluntary simplicity reduce, recycle, and reuse.

Answer the following questions in complete sentences.

13. What is the definition of *voluntary simplicity*?

   _____

   _____

14. What is the difference between "wants" and "needs"?

   _____

   _____

15. What three factors does the Happy Planet Index measure?

   _____

   _____

   _____

16. What are the two main goals of the voluntary simplicity movement?

_____

_____

17. What influences make it difficult for people to reduce their consumption patterns?

_____

_____

EXERCISE
14·7

Reading for interpretation and inference *Match each of the following guidelines with the appropriate explanation below.*

a. Take stock.
b. Set priorities.
c. Reduce, recycle, and reuse.
d. Share, give away, and use public resources.
e. Choose quality over quantity.
f. Resist pressure.
g. Take time.
h. Be grateful.

_____ 1. Buy things that last instead of cheap junk.

_____ 2. Don't consume needlessly, waste resources, or throw useful things away.

_____ 3. Look at all you have and give thanks.

_____ 4. Do things because you believe in them, not because others expect it of you.

_____ 5. Look closely at your life and ask yourself how much you really get out of what you have and do.

_____ 6. Make changes thoughtfully and without being in a big hurry.

_____ 7. Contribute to the community instead of accumulating things for selfish purposes.

_____ 8. Decide what is really important to you and use your time, energy, and resources accordingly.

Reading strategies

Summarizing *Summarize the reading text, using the following questions as a guide. First, answer the questions in bullet points, then write sentences and organize them into paragraphs.*

1. How important is happiness to most people, and what is the relationship between material wealth and happiness?

2. What does the term *voluntary simplicity* mean?

3. How did the movement get its start, and what are its goals?

4. What is the difference between "wants" and "needs"?

5. What can people do to simplify their lives?

6. What are the challenges and rewards of voluntary simplicity?

Critical thinking

Making evaluations *Indicate which of the following choices conform (✓) to the philosophy of voluntary simplicity and which do not (X).*

1. _____ a. Living in a mansion

   _____ b. Living in a small apartment

2. _____ a. Buying a brand new car

   _____ b. Buying a good used car

3. _____ a. Driving to work or school

   _____ b. Organizing a car pool with colleagues who live in the same neighborhood

4. _____ a. Buying clothes that match

   _____ b. Buying clothes that are fashionable but don't go with anything that you have in your wardrobe

5. _____ a. Making a schedule to manage your time

   _____ b. Doing things on the fly

6. _____ a. Buying a new product because it is advertised on television

   _____ b. Buying a new product because it is effective and useful

7. _____ a. Shopping locally and buying food that is in season

   _____ b. Buying expensive and exotic products that are imported from far away

8. _____ a. Sharing tools or machines with friends

   _____ b. Buying a brand new item even if you are going to use it only once or very rarely

9. _____ a. Borrowing books from the library

   _____ b. Buying every book you are interested in reading

10. _____ a. Going for a long walk on the beach

    _____ b. Working overtime to earn money to pay off your credit card debt

Making a case *Give the meaning of each of the following quotations, and explain how it relates to the concept of voluntary simplicity. Do you agree or disagree with the quotations? Give reasons to support your opinion.*

1. *Only give up a thing when you want some other condition so much that the thing no longer has any attraction for you.*—Mahatma Gandhi

_____

_____

_____

2. *A man is rich in proportion to the number of things he can afford to let alone.*
—Henry David Thoreau

_____

_____

_____

3. *The simplest things are often the truest.*—Richard Bach

_____

_____

_____

4. *With a few flowers in my garden, half a dozen pictures and some books, I live without envy.*
—Lope de Vega

_____

_____

_____

5. *Use it up, wear it out, make do or do without.*—New England Puritans

_____

_____

_____

6. *Nothing can bring you peace but yourself. Nothing can bring you peace but the triumph of principles.*—Ralph Waldo Emerson

_____

_____

_____

Bibliography

Elgin, Duane, *Voluntary Simplicity: Toward a Way of Life That is Outwardly Simple, Inwardly Rich* (New York: William Morrow and Company, Inc., 1981).

Future directions
Ecology or technology?

Pre-reading

Using the following questionnaire, interview your classmates, colleagues, family, and friends.

Questionnaire	A	B	C

Which do you think is more important to the future of the planet—ecology or technology?

How do you view the future of the planet?
a. Positively
b. Negatively
c. Don't know

Rate the following problems in terms of their seriousness.
_____ Pollution
_____ Population
_____ Energy supply
_____ Global warming
_____ Poverty
_____ Hunger
_____ Disease
_____ Other (specify: _____)

Who do you think should be responsible for solving the world's problems?
a. Governments
b. International organizations, such as the United Nations
c. Corporations
d. Individual citizens
e. Other (specify: _____)

What are you prepared to do personally to ensure the future of the planet?
a. Conserve energy and consume fewer resources
b. Live a more moderate lifestyle
c. Help the poor
d. Join an organization that works for people and/or the environment
e. Other (specify: _____)

Predicting content

Considering the title of the chapter, predict which of the following topics will be mentioned in the reading text.

☐ The major problems facing the world

☐ An important book that discusses the problems facing the world

☐ The reasons for the problems

☐ What governments are doing to solve the problems

☐ The importance of technology in solving the problems

Reading text

1   In 1954, Canadian artist Alex Colville finished what is probably his most famous painting, *Horse and Train*. Set against a stark, surrealistic background, the painting depicts a horse galloping down the middle of the railroad tracks toward an oncoming train. Colville's painting is subject to many interpretations, but whether the horse and the train symbolize instinct versus **rationality**, nature versus man, or ecology versus technology, the artist warns that unless something **intervenes** to alter the course, tragedy is *imminent*.

2   In 1972, the appearance of the book *The Limits to Growth* unleashed a controversy concerning the future of the planet. **Commissioned** by the Club of Rome[1] and conducted by researchers/ authors Donella Meadows, Jørgen Randers, Dennis Meadows, and William W. Behrens III, the project applied systems dynamics and computer modeling to **simulate** 12 scenarios based on the interactions of population, food production, industrial production, pollution, and consumption of nonrenewable natural resources. Using the World3 computer **model** developed at Massachusetts Institute of Technology, the authors projected the implications of the data **input** and concluded that if human society continued on the path of *exponential* growth and **unrestrained** consumption and resource exploitation, the planet's physical carrying capacity would be exceeded by the middle of the twenty-first century. The only way humanity could avoid inevitable collapse was to reduce its ecological footprint[2] through far-reaching technological, cultural, and institutional changes. Although their predictions appeared *dire*, they believed that disaster was avoidable. They warned, however, that unless people and policy makers tackled the **underlying** causes of the problem—and the sooner the better—the less likely they would be to turn things around.

3   *The Limits to Growth*'s **explicit** message *provoked* strong reactions. Economists, politicians, and industrialists were outraged at the suggestion that people should have to impose **constraints** on their pursuit of growth, growth, and more growth. Since the Industrial Revolution, growth has been driving the global socioeconomic system, and to this day, growth is still equated with progress, profit, improvement, prosperity, and success. To question growth, let alone challenge the corporate world's quest for unlimited profit, was next to heresy. Those who didn't deny *The Limits to Growth*'s findings tried to debunk the team's methodology or *disseminate* scare stories based on misinterpretations and misrepresentations of the book's conclusions. One example is the false claim that the authors predicted global collapse by the end of the twentieth century.

4   On the other side of the political-economic fence, those who had neither power nor profits to lose regarded *The Limits to Growth* as groundbreaking and courageous. Environmentalists,

---

[1] Founded in 1968, the Club of Rome is an informal think tank comprised of 100 international business people, statesmen, thinkers, and scientists who share a commitment to the future of humanity and the planet.

[2] In this context, *ecological footprint* is the total area of productive land that humanity requires to provide resources and absorb wastes divided by the geographical area available. The ideal ecological footprint is 1.

scientists, and thinkers applauded Donella Meadows and her colleagues for caring deeply enough about the planet to initiate an *urgent* discussion on its future. Inspired by the book, President Jimmy Carter supported energy conservation, resource management, and social values over material gain, but his policies **posed** a threat to corporate America and he lost his bid for a second term in office to Ronald Reagan, who went on to implement a program of widespread tax cuts, decreased social spending, increased military spending, and deregulation of domestic markets.

5   Translated into 26 languages, *The Limits to Growth* became the all-time best-selling book on environment issues. In addition to bringing the **notion** of sustainability to the *forefront* of environmental consciousness, *The Limits to Growth* earned Donella Meadows, a Pulitzer Prize–nominated author and respected scientist, the No. 3 spot on the (En)Rich List of top sustainability thinkers. *The Limits to Growth* was updated in 1992, the year of the Rio global summit on environment and development; after two decades, the team's only revision was their observation that "humanity had already overshot the limits of Earth's support capacity." In 2004, three years after Donella Meadows's sudden death, a 30-year update was published with the purpose of restating the original argument for a new generation, showing what had actually occurred since 1972, and inspiring widespread action. Their conclusions, again, were unaltered.

6   At the **core** of *The Limits to Growth* are the concepts of overshoot and sustainability. Overshoot happens when a course of action goes too far and exceeds its physical limits. Imagine what would happen if you drank too much alcohol, or if a timber company practiced clear-cut logging. Common sense tells us that we cannot drink excessively without passing out, getting sick, and ending up with a horrendous hangover, and that we cannot cut down a forest without decimating the ecosystem. On a larger scale, overshoot is the result of rapid, uncontrolled growth, and when no one pays attention to or responds to the problem, **coupled** with the lack of accurate data and the **persistent** belief that there is no tomorrow, the consequences of overshoot are collapse. Overshoot can be compared to the bubble that occurs on the stock market when irrational exuberance for a particular stock, such as dot.com companies at the turn of this century, *inflates* prices until the bubble bursts and the market crashes.

7   *The Limits to Growth* identifies the growth of the global population and the material economy as exerting the highest demand on Earth's finite resources. Of particular concern is exponential growth, which occurs when something doubles and redoubles. Yeast, for example, multiplies exponentially. In 1650, it took 240 years for the global population of 0.5 billion to double; in 1965, it took only 36 years for the global population to increase from 3.3 billion to 6.13 billion. In 1950, the population of Nigeria was 36 million; in 2000, a mere 50 years later, it had more than tripled to 125 million. Although global birth rates (the ratio of births compared to population) have been decreasing slightly and women are bearing fewer children, when the global population numbers 7.1 billion (as of this writing), fewer women giving birth still *incrementally* produces a lot of people.

8   More people require more food, but only so much agricultural land is available to grow it. To produce more goods for more people, more resources are consumed, but resources come in limited supply. Since the late 1980s, more nonrenewable resources have been consumed on a yearly basis than can be generated within the same year, and renewable resources have not been produced fast enough to replace them. More people and the consumption of more resources generate more pollution and waste, but the planet's sinks can absorb waste only so fast without overflowing. At the turn of the millennium, humanity had already overshot the planet's limits by 20 percent.

9   The alternative to overshoot is sustainability, first defined by the 1987 Brundtland Commission as development that "meets the needs of the present without compromising the ability of future generations to meet their own needs." According to economist Herman Daly, sustainability can be achieved by meeting three widely **acknowledged** conditions:

1. Renewable resources cannot be consumed faster than they can be regenerated.
2. Nonrenewable resources cannot be used up faster than they can be replaced by a renewable resource.
3. Pollution cannot exceed the environment's capacity to absorb waste or to render it harmless.

In practical terms, sustainability means limiting human reproduction to two children per couple, reducing consumption rates in affluent countries so that poorer countries can have a fair share, and bringing human activity into balance with the environment.

10   Sustainability does not mean, as many naysayers and critics would argue, zero growth, economic paralysis or stagnation, rigid political control, cultural **uniformity**, or the end of democracy. It does mean responsible management of resources, long-term planning, and a more equitable redistribution of food, services, and capital so that everyone has enough to live comfortably and with dignity.

11   Whereas technology can be of great service in protecting land and soil, reducing pollution, and making more efficient use of resources, real change can come about only with a change in people's hearts and minds. A new **ideology** is in order: one that values human well-being above wealth, favors long-term development over short-term growth, satisfies social and spiritual needs before material wants, and ensures that people do not take more from the earth than it can give.

12   Since its first publication, *The Limits to Growth* has held its ground. In 2008, the Australian Commonwealth Scientific and Industrial Research Organization revisited *The Limits to Growth*'s scenarios and compared 30 years of historical data to its World3 scenarios. Their findings **confirmed** that "the global system is on an unsustainable *trajectory* unless there is substantial and rapid reduction in consumptive behavior, in combination with technological progress." It is **crucial**, therefore, that we ask ourselves: do we stand on the sidelines, gazing helplessly at a horse and a train on a collision course, or do we take our lives and the future of our children into our hands and set a new direction?

After reading

In the Pre-reading section, check to see if your predictions about the reading text were correct.

Vocabulary

EXERCISE
15·1

Thematic vocabulary *List 10 words or phrases related to the negative consequences of unlimited growth.*

_____   _____

_____   _____

_____   _____

_____   _____

_____   _____

Academic vocabulary *Using a dictionary, complete the following chart with the correct part of speech and definition of each of the **academic words** in the reading text. If a word has multiple meanings, match the definition to the context in which the word is used in the text.*

Word	Part of speech	Definition
1. acknowledge	_____	_____
2. commission	_____	_____
3. confirm	_____	_____
4. constraint	_____	_____
5. core	_____	_____
6. couple	_____	_____
7. crucial	_____	_____
8. explicit	_____	_____
9. ideology	_____	_____
10. input	_____	_____
11. intervene	_____	_____
12. model	_____	_____
13. notion	_____	_____
14. persistent	_____	_____
15. pose	_____	_____
16. rationality	_____	_____
17. simulate	_____	_____
18. underlying	_____	_____
19. uniformity	_____	_____
20. unrestrained	_____	_____

Using vocabulary *Complete each of the following sentences with the appropriate word from the chart in Exercise 15-2. Be sure to use the correct form of each verb and to pluralize nouns, if necessary.*

1. Reliable and accurate data is _____ to any scientific analysis.

2. The test results _____ the doctor's diagnosis.

3. In order to complete the task, the group requires _____ from each of its members.

4. _____ with stress, an unhealthy diet and lack of exercise can lead to a heart attack.

5. When the reporter raised his hand to ask a question, the speaker _____ him with a nod.

6. A well-constructed argument is based on _____ rather than personal opinions and bias.

7. Any organized group encourages _____ from its members.

8. The Green Party's _____ embraces environmental protection and the development of renewable energy.

9. The architect's team built a _____ of the proposed building.

10. Before we can tackle the problem, we need to determine the _____ causes.

11. In order to succeed, you have to be _____ and not give up on your dreams.

12. Not everyone has the same _____ of what constitutes happiness.

13. The police _____ to break up the fight between the two gang members.

14. At the _____ of a problem is people's general reluctance to face the truth.

15. The teacher gave the class _____ directions on how to carry out the experiment, but they failed because they didn't listen.

16. Due to the growing national debt, the government will have to impose _____ on social spending.

17. The purpose of role play is to _____ a real-life situation in which participants learn communication skills.

18. Air pollution _____ a serious threat to our health.

19. _____ consumption of drugs and alcohol can lead to serious social and physical consequences.

20. The government _____ a portrait of the queen in honor of her diamond jubilee.

Nonacademic vocabulary *Fill in the part of speech for each of the **nonacademic words** below, then indicate which of the words best conveys the meaning of the underlined word or phrase in each sentence that follows. Be sure to use the correct form of each verb and noun and to change an adjective to an adverb, if necessary.*

dire _____   disseminate _____   exponential _____   forefront _____

imminent _____   increment _____   inflate _____   provoke _____

trajectory _____   urgent _____

1. The crime scene investigators traced the bullet's <u>path</u> to find the location from which it had been fired.

   _____

2. If you invest your money in a certificate that pays compound interest, it will increase <u>more and more rapidly.</u>

   _____

3. I'm sorry to interrupt the meeting, but I've just received a(n) <u>requiring immediate action</u> message from the hospital.

   _____

4. During tornado season, meteorologists try to warn people of <u>fast-approaching</u> natural disasters.

   _____

5. Urban slum dwellers live under <u>seriously grim</u> conditions, without clean water or proper sanitation.

   _____

6. Bullies always try to <u>set in motion</u> fights.

   _____

7. You can use a pump to <u>fill with air</u> the air mattress.

   _____

8. MIT has a reputation of being at the <u>foremost position</u> of technological research.

   _____

9. Over the next five years, the workers will receive a pay raise in <u>regular increases</u> of 1.5 percent.

   _____

10. Nowadays, viral marketers use the Internet and social networking to <u>spread very quickly</u> information about a specific product.

    _____

Reading comprehension

Reading for main ideas *Answer the following questions in complete sentences.*

1. What is the message behind *Train and Horse* and *The Limits to Growth*?

   _____

   _____

   _____

2. How did the authors of *The Limits to Growth* arrive at their conclusions about the future of the planet?

   _____

   _____

   _____

3. What was the reaction to the book?

   _____

   _____

   _____

4. What is the book's publishing history?

   _____

   _____

   _____

5. What is overshoot, and what factors could cause it?

   _____

   _____

   _____

6. How can sustainability prevent overshoot?

   _____

   _____

   _____

7. What do people need to do to achieve an effective turnaround?

   _____

   _____

   _____

Reading for details *For each of the following sentences, choose the correct answer to fill in the blank.*

1. *The Limits to Growth* was written by _____.
   a. Alex Colville
   b. Herman Daly
   c. Donella Meadows, Jørgen Randers, Dennis Meadows, and William W. Behrens III

2. The conclusions set down in *The Limits to Growth* were confirmed by _____.
   a. the Club of Rome
   b. the Australian Commonwealth Scientific and Industrial Research Organization
   c. the Brundtland Commission

3. In 2000, humanity had already overshot the planet's carrying capacity by
   _____.
   a. 2 percent
   b. 12 percent
   c. 20 percent

4. World3 is a _____.
   a. computer model
   b. book
   c. painting

5. *The Limits to Growth* presented _____ different scenarios for the future of the planet.
   a. 12
   b. 10
   c. 3

6. Overshoot is caused by _____.
   a. pollution
   b. exponential growth
   c. political indecision

Indicate which of the following statements are true (T) and which are false (F).

7. _____ *The Limits to Growth* predicted global collapse by the end of the twentieth century.

8. _____ *The Limits to Growth* was published out of humanitarian concerns.

9. _____ Sustainable growth means zero growth and economic stagnation.

10. _____ Politicians and industrialists embraced the findings of *The Limits to Growth*.

11. _____ *The Limits to Growth* suggested that it was possible for humanity to avoid collapse.

12. _____ *The Limits to Growth* has been updated twice.

Answer the following questions in complete sentences.

13. What is exponential growth?

_____

14. What is overshoot?

_____

15. What is sustainability?

_____

16. What three conditions must be met in order to achieve sustainability?

_____

_____

_____

17. To produce the World3 scenario, what five factors were analyzed?

_____

_____

_____

_____

_____

EXERCISE
15·7

Reading for interpretation and inference *For each of the following statements from the reading text, choose the boldface word or phrase in the sentence below that more accurately reflects the meaning of the underlined phrase in the statement.*

1. "They warned, however, that unless people and policy makers tackled the underlying causes of the problem—and <u>the sooner the better</u>—the less likely they would be to turn things around."

   People **can | cannot** wait to make changes.

2. "To question growth, let alone challenge the corporate world's quest for unlimited profit, was <u>next to heresy</u>."

   The book's message **went against popular beliefs | told lies.**

3. "Environmentalists, scientists, and thinkers applauded Donella Meadows and her colleagues for <u>caring deeply enough about the planet</u> to initiate an urgent discussion on its future."

   Donella Meadows and her colleagues wrote the book **to become famous | for humanitarian reasons.**

4. "President Jimmy Carter supported energy conservation, resource management, and social values over material gain, but his policies posed a threat to corporate America and he <u>lost his bid for a second term in office</u> to Ronald Reagan. . . ."

President Carter's policies were **popular** | **unpopular** with voters.

5. "On a larger scale, overshoot is the result of rapid, uncontrolled growth, and when no one pays attention to or responds to the problem, coupled with the lack of accurate data and the persistent belief that <u>there is no tomorrow</u>, the consequences of overshoot are collapse."

People thought that **they could go on doing the same things forever** | **the world was going to end soon**.

6. "Although global birth rates (the ratio of births compared to population) have been decreasing slightly and women are bearing fewer children, when the global population numbers 7.1 billion (as of this writing), <u>fewer women giving birth still incrementally produces a lot of people</u>."

The population continues to increase because **more women are having children** | **it takes fewer women giving birth to keep the population growing**.

7. ". . . real change can come about only with a change in <u>people's hearts and minds</u>."

People have to do something about their **beliefs** | **health**.

8. A new ideology is in order: one that values human well-being above wealth, favors long-term development over short-term growth, satisfies social and spiritual needs before material wants, and ensures that <u>people do not take more from the earth than it can give</u>.

People have to use the earth's resources **wisely** | **freely**.

Reading strategies

Summarizing *Using your answers to Exercise 15-5, write a summary of the reading text. Include only the most important details, and use the paraphrasing techniques you learned in Chapters 6 to 12. Your summary should not exceed 500 words.*

_____

_____

_____

_____

_____

_____

_____

_____

_____

_____

_____

_____

_____

_____

_____

_____

_____

_____

_____

_____

_____

Critical thinking

EXERCISE
15·9

Making evaluations *Indicate which of the following actions represent (✓) or do not represent (X) a move toward sustainability. Give reasons to support your answers.*

1. _____ Oil and gas exploration in environmentally sensitive areas, such as the Arctic or wilderness preserves

2. _____ Clearing woodlands and hillsides to build luxury single-family homes

3. _____ Limiting the number of children to two per couple and promoting family planning and birth control

4. _____ Rezoning agricultural land for commercial uses, such as shopping malls and big-box stores

5. _____ Buying locally grown food in season and providing spaces in urban areas for apartment dwellers to grow gardens

6. _____ Changing building codes to require the incorporation of solar energy and energy-conservation features in new construction

7. _____ Manufacturing cheap goods that cannot be repaired, serviced, or recycled, and that have a limited life span

8. _____ Creating carfree and pedestrian-friendly inner cities, and linking walkways and bike paths with public transportation

9. _____ Collecting organic waste in cities and using it for compost in public parks and gardens

10. _____ Building more nuclear power plants

EXERCISE 15·10

Making a case *Give the meaning of each of the following quotations, and explain how it relates to the ideas presented in the reading text. Which of the two quotations do you agree with? Give reasons to support your opinion.*

1. *There are no limits to growth and human progress when men and women are free to follow their dreams.*—Ronald Reagan

2. *An age of expansion is giving way to an age of equilibrium.*—Lewis Mumford

_____

_____

_____

_____

_____

_____

_____

_____

_____

_____

_____

_____

_____

_____

_____

_____

_____

_____

_____

_____

Bibliography

Dietz, Rob, "The Influence of Donella Meadows and the Limits to Growth" (Center for the Advancement of the Steady State Economy, *The Daly News*), http://steadystate.org/influence-of-donella-meadows/.

Meadows, Donella, Jørgen Randers, and Dennis Meadows, *Limits to Growth: The 30-Year Update* (White River Junction, VT: Chelsea Green Publishing Company, 2004).

Turner, Graham, "A Comparison of the Limits to Growth with Thirty Years of Reality" (Socio-Economics and the Environment in Discussion, CSIRO Working Paper Series, 2008-2009), http://www.csiro.au/files/files/plje.pdf.

Answer key

1 Ecotourism: Another way to see the world

1·1   *Suggested answers:* destination, travel agency, ship, airplane, online booking service, adventures, sightseers, globetrotters, tourist, commercial tour operators, hotels, palm-lined beaches, travel, souvenirs, tour guides, resort, parks, traveler

1·2   *Consult a dictionary for definitions.*
1. accommodation, accommodating
2. conversion, convertible
3. disposal, disposable
4. enforcement, enforceable
5. integration, integral
6. initiation, initial
7. minimum, minimal
8. beneficial, benefit
9. diverse, diversify
10. exploitative/exploitable, exploit
11. commitment, commit
12. sustainability, sustain
13. implementation
14. projection
15. convention
16. impact
17. environmental
18. resourceful
19. —
20. —

1·3
1. integrate
2. committed
3. convert
4. implement
5. conventional
6. enforce
7. accommodate
8. minimize
9. impact
10. projects
11. initiate
12. benefit
13. diversification, revenue
14. commodity
15. sustainable
16. resource
17. environment
18. dispose of
19. exploitation

1·4
1. c (v.)
2. h (n.)
3. g (v.)
4. j (v.)
5. f (v.)
6. a (n.)
7. d (adj.)
8. i (v.)
9. e (v.)
10. b (adj.)

1·5   *Suggested answers:*

Paragraph 2: Tourism will continue to grow at a rapid rate.
Paragraph 3: Tourism has become a major economic factor.
Paragraph 4: Tourism is a serious threat to the environment.
Paragraphs 5 and 6: Ecotourism has developed as a popular alternative over the last two decades.
Paragraph 7: Ecotourism aims to protect the environment, conserve resources, use alternative energy, support local economies, and preserve cultural traditions.
Paragraphs 8 and 9: Many successful examples of ecotourism exist in Madagascar, the Philippines, Nepal, and Costa Rica.
Paragraph 10: The increased demand for ecotourism can lead to further destruction of the environment and a greenwashing of tourist operations.
Paragraph 11: The success of ecotourism depends on the commitment of governments, the tourism industry, and the individual traveler to the environment.

1·6
1. a
2. c
3. c
4. b
5. c
6. a
7. T
8. T
9. F
10. T
11. F
12. F
13. Villages are turned into sprawling tourist playgrounds, hotels line beaches, fields are converted into golf courses, beaches become dirty, traffic is noisy, road construction increases, forest lands are cleared, ecosystems are destroyed, wildlife is endangered, and people are displaced.
14. Some countries depend heavily on the revenue, foreign investment, employment, and development.
15. Sí Como No runs on solar power, recycles, conserves water, and practices environmental gray water management. Its staff is trained in environmental awareness, and time and money are invested in programs that benefit the environment and the community.
16. Ecotourism is meant to protect the environment and support local communities and culture, while sustainable tourism is meant to provide for future generations and does not specifically focus on the environment.
17. Hotels under the IHEI have joined with the United Nations Environment Program and the International Hotel & Restaurant Association to develop a program to conserve energy and water, reduce waste and emissions, and promote environmental management.

1·7
1. 4,000 percent
2. heavily
3. major
4. many

1·8
1. c
2. a
3. b
4. a

1·9
1. ✓   6. ✓
2. X   7. ✓
3. ✓   8. X
4. ✓   9. ✓
5. X   10. ✓

1·10   *Answers will vary.*

2 The Human Genome Project: Writing the book of life

Questionnaire

1. b
2. b
3. a
4. b
5. b
6. c

2·1   *Suggested answers:* DNA, chromosome, gene, trait, splice, split, genome, parent, offspring, double helix, recombinant RNA

2·2   *Consult a dictionary for definitions.*
1. allocation
2. denial
3. discrimination, discriminatory
4. emergence, emergent
5. interpretation, interpretive
6. revelation, revealing
7. revolution, revolutionary
8. specification, specific
9. transmission, transmissible
10. undertaking
11. elimination
12. enhancement
13. estimation
14. empiricism
15. ethics
16. fundament
17. potential
18. evident
19. —
20. —

2·3
1. widespread
2. ethical
3. empirical
4. potential
5. eliminate
6. evidence
7. undertook
8. definitive
9. transmitted
10. fundamental

2·4
1. c
2. b
3. a
4. b
5. c
6. a
7. c
8. a
9. a
10. b

2·5
1. c (n.)
2. f (v.)
3. j (n.)
4. i (v.)
5. g (v.)
6. b (n.)
7. e (adj.)
8. a (adj.)
9. h (n.)
10. d (n.)

2·6
Paragraph 2: e
Paragraph 3: n
Paragraph 4: c
Paragraph 5: g
Paragraph 6: j
Paragraph 7: b
Paragraph 8: i
Paragraph 9: l
Paragraph 10: f
Paragraph 11: a
Paragraph 12: m
Paragraph 13: d
Paragraph 14: k

2·7 1. c
2. a
3. a
4. c
5. b
6. b
7. T
8. T
9. F
10. F
11. T
12. F
13. The main goals of the Human Genome Project were to lead to the understanding of genetic diseases, to create effective pharmaceuticals and medical treatments, and to prevent human suffering due to genetically transmitted diseases.
14. Mendel's experiments established that traits were passed from parents to offspring in an organized and predictable way; Charles Darwin developed the theory of evolution.
15. The Human Genome Project was made possible by recombinant DNA, the PCR machine, computer technology, and the Internet.
16. The Genetic Information Nondiscrimination Act made discrimination on the basis of genetic information illegal for employers, insurers, courts, schools, and other entities.

2·8 1. a   6. b
2. b   7. c
3. a   8. a
4. c   9. a
5. a   10. c

2·9 *Suggested answers:*
Paragraph 5
Main idea: Rapid technological advances allow researchers to process and store greater amounts of genetic information.
Supporting details:
1. Recombinant DNA and PCR machines allowed researchers to slice and copy DNA
2. The silicon semiconductor chip made analyzing and storing data faster and cheaper
Paragraph 9
Main idea: HGP promises to revolutionize how doctors test and treat patients and diagnose disease.
Supporting details:
1. More sophisticated diagnostic tests for genetic profiles and patient counseling
2. Computerized and portable patient files
Paragraph 10
Main idea: HGP promises revolutionary new drugs and reduced health care costs.
Supporting details:
1. Development of thousands of customized drugs with fewer side effects and successful results
2. Potential for cloned transplant organs and lifesaving advances

2·10 *Suggested answers:*
1. +   5. –
2. –   6. –
3. +   7. +
4. –   8. +

2·11 *Answers will vary.*

3 Near-death experiences: Fact or fantasy?

3·1 *Suggested answers:* die, heaven, hell, nirvana, paradise, resurrections, ghosts, dead, pronounce dead, suicide, the other side, the afterlife, kill, clinically dead, cardiac arrest, consciousness, close brush with death

3·2
1. cessation, ceaseless
2. conclusion, conclusive
3. document/documentation, documentary
4. establishment, established
5. evolution, evolutionary
6. survival/survivor, survivable
7. transportation/transport, transportable
8. concept, conceptual, conceive
9. validation, valid, validate
10. (ir)reversibility, reverse
11. alteration
12. compilation
13. encounter
14. trigger
15. aware
16. elemental
17. incidental
18. insightful
19. phenomenal
20. researcher, research

3·3
1. awareness
2. conclude
3. triggered
4. altered
5. insight
6. documented
7. encountered
8. compiled
9. research
10. phenomenon

3·4
1. b
2. a
3. b
4. c
5. a
6. a
7. c
8. c
9. a
10. a

3·5 *Consult a dictionary for definitions.*
1. n.
2. v.
3. adj.
4. v.
5. n.
6. adj.
7. v.
8. v.
9. n.
10. v.

3·6
1. are not
2. have been
3. nearly die
4. a very similar pattern, regardless of
5. scientific research
6. pleasant
7. does not have to
8. have not successfully proven
9. positive
10. can

3·7
1. b
2. c
3. c
4. a
5. b
6. F
7. T
8. T
9. F
10. T
11. F
12. *Near-death experience* means what people who are seriously ill or injured consciously experience when they seem to die but come back to life.
13. They are afraid that their doctor will not believe them.
14. The International Association for Near-Death Studies and the Near Death Experience Research Foundation were established to carry out NDE research.
15. The person feels himself leaving his body.
16. A person is pronounced "clinically dead" when the heart has stopped long enough for brain activity to cease and the person has lost consciousness.
17. A "life review" occurs when a person sees her life pass before her eyes, as if she is watching a movie.

3·8
1. a		4. a	
2. b		5. a	
3. b		6. b	

3·9
1. X		6. X	
2. ✓		7. X	
3. ✓		8. ✓	
4. X		9. ✓	
5. ✓		10. X	

3·10 *Answers will vary.*

4 Genetically modified organisms: Breadbasket or Pandora's box?

4·1 *Suggested answers:* farmers, seed, livestock, crop, yield, garden peas, breeding, cross-fertilization, wheat hybrids, grain, agronomist, varieties, cereal grains, irrigation, farm machinery, fertilizers, pesticides, fields, corn, soybeans, canola, cotton, potatoes, squash, tomatoes, dairy cows, weeds, plants, pest, farming methods, planting season, organic farming, soil

4·2 *Consult a dictionary for definitions.*
1. adj.	11. v.
2. n.	12. n.
3. v.	13. v.
4. adj.	14. n.
5. v.	15. v.
6. n.	16. n.
7. adj.	17. v.
8. adj.	18. adj.
9. v.	19. adj.
10. v.	20. v.

4·3
1. controversial	6. adequate
2. ensure	7. significant
3. complexity	8. so-called
4. insert	9. conducting
5. precision	10. finite

4·4	1. a	6. b
	2. c	7. a
	3. b	8. c
	4. c	9. c
	5. a	10. b

4·5	1. c (v.)	6. a (n.)
	2. j (n.)	7. i (v.)
	3. f (n.)	8. e (adj.)
	4. h (adj.)	9. g (adj.)
	5. b (adj.)	10. d (adj.)

4·6	Paragraph 2: f	Paragraph 8: a
	Paragraph 3: l	Paragraph 9: b
	Paragraph 4: k	Paragraph 10: j
	Paragraph 5: c	Paragraph 11: i
	Paragraph 6: g	Paragraph 12: d
	Paragraph 7: e	Paragraph 13: h

4·7
1. b
2. a
3. c
4. b
5. b
6. a
7. T
8. F
9. T
10. T
11. F
12. F
13. Terminator crops are sterile and cannot produce seed.
14. GE crops and foods have not been proven safe and are harmful to the environment.
15. GE crops mature earlier, contain more nutrients, resist pesticides and herbicides, and produce higher yields.
16. Most of the studies are conducted by the companies that produce GE seeds and products.
17. Organic farming increases yields, improves soil quality, reduces pests and disease, restores traditional breeds, and produces better-tasting, more nutritious food.

4·8	1. ✓	4. ✓
	2. ✓	5. X
	3. X	6. X

4·9	1. b	4. a
	2. b	5. b
	3. a	

4·10
1. a. ✓   b. X
2. a. ✓   b. X
3. a. X   b. ✓
4. a. X   b. ✓
5. a. ✓   b. X
6. a. X   b. ✓

4·11 *Answers will vary.*

4·12 *Answers will vary.*

5   Men and women: Long live the difference

Questionnaire

1. Men	6. Men
2. Women	7. Women
3. Men	8. Women
4. Men	9. Women
5. Women	10. Men

5·1   *Suggested answers:* lovers, sexes, female, male, feminine, masculine, hormones, sexual development, ovaries, testes, estrogen, progesterone, testosterone, oxytocin, mother, father, caregiver, feminism, battle of the sexes, Mr., Mrs.

5·2   *Consult a dictionary for definitions.*

1. n.	11. n.
2. v.	12. n.
3. v.	13. v.
4. v.	14. adj.
5. v.	15. v.
6. v.	16. adj.
7. n.	17. v.
8. v.	18. n.
9. adj.	19. v.
10. v.	20. n.

5·3

1. process	6. matured
2. metaphors	7. gender
3. function	8. theme
4. primary	9. role
5. Intrinsic	10. passive

5·4

1. a	6. c
2. b	7. b
3. c	8. a
4. c	9. b
5. c	10. c

5·5

1. d (v.)	6. e (n.)
2. a (v.)	7. h (n.)
3. i (n.)	8. j (v.)
4. f (v.)	9. c (n.)
5. b (n.)	10. g (n.)

5·6

1. ✓	7. ✓
2. X	8. ✓
3. ✓	9. X
4. X	10. ✓
5. ✓	11. X
6. ✓	12. ✓

5·7
1. b
2. a
3. b
4. a
5. c
6. b
7. F
8. T
9. F
10. T
11. T
12. F
13. Men and women come from different planets, and therefore they speak different languages and have different needs.
14. Feminism and the women's liberation movement, plus the availability of birth control and legalized abortion, changed women's roles.
15. a. W   b. M   c. W   d. M   e. W   f. W   g. M   h. W   i. M   j. W   k. M   l. M

5·8   *Suggested answers:*
1. In order for love to grow and flourish, it needs to be nurtured and cared for.
2. Sometimes, men like to be close and intimate, but they also need to pull away and feel independent.
3. Women's emotional state moves up and down between feeling good about themselves and feeling depressed and vulnerable.
4. Men like to be alone in their own space to think things out for themselves without being bothered by anyone else.
5. Men offer solutions to problems.
6. Women like to give advice even when they are not asked for advice.
7. Men are more aggressive and active, like the Roman god of war.
8. Women are more caring and nurturing, like the Roman goddess of love.

5·9   *Answers will vary.*

5·10
1. W	6. M
2. M	7. W
3. M	8. W
4. W	9. M
5. W	10. W

5·11   *Answers will vary.*

6 Electric cars: Greener, cleaner driving

6·1 *Suggested answers:* vehicle, miles, automobile, engine, gas/gasoline, acceleration, traffic, highway, roads, parking lots, shoulder belts, headrests, catalytic converters, air bag, economy cars, exhaust, driving range, drivers, carmakers, trucks, internal combustion engine, taxis, delivery vehicles, buses, rental cars, service station, hybrids, sedan, coupe, SUV, pickup

6·2 *Consult a dictionary for definitions.*
1. stable, stabilize
2. legislative, legislate
3. globe, globalize
4. abandonment
5. consideration, considerable
6. consumption, consumable
7. excess, excessive
8. generation, generative
9. maintenance/maintainability, maintainable
10. registration
11. termination/terminal, terminal
12. contribution, contributory, contribute
13. decline
14. fluctuation
15. range
16. vehicular
17. —
18. —
19. —
20. converse

6·3
1. consider	11. consume
2. annual	12. versions
3. Conversely	13. vehicles
4. terminate	14. generate
5. declining	15. fluctuate
6. contributors	16. abandon
7. maintain	17. legislation
8. range	18. devices
9. global	19. exceed
10. stability	20. register

6·4
1. c (n.)	6. h (adj.)
2. g (v.)	7. d (n.)
3. j (n.)	8. i (n.)
4. f (n.)	9. e (n.)
5. b (v.)	10. a (v.)

6·5
1. increasing, faster
2. major
3. has not been
4. The price of oil, government regulation
5. were not, pressure from the automotive and oil industries
6. are
7. has proven
8. making cars more energy-efficient and environmentally friendly
9. unlikely

6·6

1. b
2. c
3. a
4. b
5. b
6. c
7. T
8. T
9. F
10. F
11. T
12. F
13. The price of gasoline quadrupled, and people started buying more economical Japanese and European cars, which forced American carmakers to produce economy cars.
14. In 1990, CARB stipulated that two percent of all cars sold in California be zero-emission in 1998, and ten percent in 2003. The automobile industry tried to fight CARB, and only GM developed an electric car to meet the mandate's requirements.
15. A series hybrid uses a small gasoline or diesel engine to generate the power that drives an electric motor and recharges the battery pack; a parallel hybrid switches between a gasoline engine and an electric motor.
16. Electric cars have zero emissions, are cheaper to operate, have 90 percent efficiency, and reduce dependency on oil.
17. Hybrid cars are light, compact, quiet, and fuel- and energy-efficient, and shut off automatically at traffic lights.

6·7

1. b
2. b
3. a
4. b
5. a
6. a
7. b
8. b
9. a
10. b

6·8 *Suggested answers:*

1. In 60 years, the number of registered vehicles and miles driven per household increased twice as fast as the number of households.
2. In 50 years, the number of American households owning three or more cars increased nearly tenfold.
3. Japan produced one third of the world's cars in 2008. Car sales in China are projected to grow tenfold / to skyrocket.
4. In 20 years, CO_2 emissions from the U.S. transportation sector increased measurably.
5. The price of gasoline quadrupled.
6. Five times as many zero-emission cars had to be sold in California by 2003.
7. EV1s had a limited driving range.
8. It would take significantly more EVs to produce the same amount of CO_2 emitted by one conventional automobile.

6·9 *Answers will vary.*

6·10 *Answers will vary.*

7 DNA fingerprinting: Condemning evidence

7·1 *Suggested answers:* crime scene, crime-solving, police detective, forensic technician, evidence, hearing, offender, innocent, guilty, execute, prison, commit a crime, murderer, fingerprint, convicted, criminal, rape, murder, suspect, confess, killer, perpetrator, arrest, accused, defendant, defend, lawyer, investigator, detective, FBI, RCMP, law enforcement, judges, court, cold case, prison sentence, sexual assault, sentence, charged, victim

7·2 *Consult a dictionary for definitions.*
1. detectable, detect
2. evaluative, evaluate
3. investigation, investigative, investigate
4. sequential, sequence
5. legality, legalize
6. violence, violate
7. analysis, analytical
8. assemblage
9. challenge, challenging/challenged
10. exclusion, exclusive
11. identification, identifiable
12. location
13. implication, implicating
14. removal, removable
15. accurate
16. expert, expert
17. regional
18. availability, avail
19. consequence
20. obtainable

7·3
1. expertise	6. challenged
2. assembled	7. evaluation
3. sequence	8. obtained
4. analyze	9. accuracy
5. implicated	10. remove

7·4
1. b	6. a
2. a	7. b
3. a	8. a
4. c	9. c
5. a	10. a

7·5
1. d (n.)	6. g (n.)
2. a (adj.)	7. j (v.)
3. i (adj.)	8. e (n.)
4. h (adj.)	9. b (n.)
5. c (v.)	10. f (n.)

7·6   Paragraph 2: Before DNA arrived on the scene, digital fingerprints were the key to determining an individual's identity.

Paragraph 3: DNA testing would not be where it is today without the discoveries of British geneticist Alec Jeffreys and American biochemist Kary Mullis.

Paragraph 4: In 1987, RFLP was used for the first time in the investigation into the rape and murder of two young girls.

Paragraph 5: While Alec Jeffreys was carrying out his lengthy research, Kary Mullis worked out, one night in 1983, an ingenious method to increase the amount of DNA available for testing.

Paragraph 6: Before DNA testing became a standard feature of the criminal justice system, legal hurdles had to be cleared.

Paragraph 7: Without standardization or scientific evaluation of their methods, these companies were engaged more in competing for dominance in a very profitable field than in ensuring the quality of their services.

Paragraph 8: In the late 1980s, DNA testing achieved legitimacy with the involvement of governmental agencies.

Paragraph 9: In 1992, a two-year federally funded National Research Council study recommended that DNA evidence continue to be used in courts, and in 1994, the scientific and law enforcement communities agreed that DNA evidence should be considered legitimate and admissible in court.

Paragraph 10: The widespread acceptance of DNA fingerprinting led to the establishment of DNA databases, beginning in Great Britain, where DNA evidence had been more widely embraced from the start.

Paragraph 11: In the United States, a law passed in 1994 laid the groundwork for the formation of a nationwide database.

Paragraph 12: DNA fingerprinting was not only bringing criminals to justice, but was also freeing wrongly convicted persons from long prison sentences.

Paragraph 13: Despite DNA fingerprinting's usefulness, significant issues temper its success.

Paragraph 14: While lawmakers debate the legal uses of DNA fingerprinting, the science will continue to prove itself outside the crime lab and court of law.

7·7
1. b
2. c
3. a
4. b
5. a
6. b
7. F
8. T
9. T
10. F
11. F
12. T
13. DNA is present in all human cells and cannot be easily removed from the scene by the criminal.
14. Innocent people are wrongly convicted of crimes because of mistaken identity, police misconduct, sloppy forensics, an incompetent defense, and a false confession made under pressure.
15. Mullis discovered the process of polymerase chain reaction, which made it possible to create billions of copies of DNA in a very short time.
16. Civil liberties organizations consider mandatory DNA testing an invasion of privacy and warn of the dangers of such information being made available to employers or insurance companies.
17. DNA testing can be used to establish paternity and family relationships, to identify the remains of soldiers missing in action, to match organ donors with potential recipients, to protect endangered plants and animals, and to reconstruct human history through genetics.

7·8
1. a   4. b
2. a   5. a
3. b   6. b

7·9
1. b   4. a
2. a   5. b
3. a

7·10 *Suggested answers:*
  Paragraph 2: Before DNA technology appeared, mainly digital fingerprints identified criminals.
  Paragraph 3: DNA technology wouldn't exist without the work of a British geneticist and an American biochemist.
  Paragraph 4: Police employed RFLP in the late 1980s in order to solve two sexual assault and homicide cases.
  Paragraph 5: Mullis discovered how to duplicate DNA in greater quantities for processing at the same time that Jeffries was carrying out his investigations.
  Paragraph 6: Legal issues had to be settled before DNA was accepted as a common procedure.
  Paragraph 7: In the absence of regulations, commercial laboratories put more effort into competition for profits than providing accurate test results.
  Paragraph 8: In the late 1980s, government action led to the recognition of DNA technology.
  Paragraph 9: In 1992, a federally sponsored study supported the use of DNA evidence in court, and two years later, scientists and police officials agreed to acknowledge its legitimacy as evidence.
  Paragraph 10: The recognition of DNA fingerprinting resulted in the creation of DNA databases in Great Britain, where it had been accepted from the outset.
  Paragraph 11: In the United States, 1994 legislation enabled the establishment of a national database.
  Paragraph 12: In addition to convicting criminals, DNA evidence was getting innocent prisoners out of prison.

7·11 *Answers will vary.*

7·12 *Answers will vary.*

8 Eco-cities: Building sustainable urban communities

8·1 *Suggested answers:* communities, population, urban, home, dwellers, megacities, residents, suburban centers, public transportation, traffic, garbage, metropolitan, citizens, slums, living conditions, city management, municipal government, municipalities, settlements, buildings, urban sprawl, public services, green areas, parks, architects, planners, residential apartments

8·2 *Consult a dictionary for definitions.*
  1. administrative, administer
  2. aggregate, aggregate
  3. communal, commune
  4. immigration, immigrant, immigrate
  5. invest
  6. residence, residential, reside
  7. secure, secure
  8. trendy, trend
  9. visible/visionary, envision
  10. demonstration, demonstrative
  11. incorporation
  12. achievement, achievable
  13. link
  14. concentrate
  15. fund/funds, fund
  16. phase in
  17. shift
  18. principal
  19. —
  20. —

8·3 1. phases
  2. consists of
  3. funding
  4. concentration
  5. community
  6. infrastructure, investment
  7. links
  8. shift
  9. principles

8·4
1. a. administration   b. administrative
2. a. demonstrate   b. demonstrations
3. a. immigrated   b. immigrants
4. a. investment   b. invest
5. a. achieve   b. achievement
6. a. resident   b. reside
7. a. incorporate   b. incorporation
8. a. vision   b. envisions
9. a. security   b. secure
10. a. trendy   b. trend

8·5   *Consult a dictionary for definitions.*
1. n.   6. v.
2. adj.   7. v.
3. v.   8. n.
4. v.   9. n.
5. n.   10. v.

8·6
1. a. M   b. SD
2. a. SD   b. M
3. a. SD   b. M
4. a. M   b. SD
5. a. M   b. SD
6. a. SD   b. M
7. a. M   b. SD
8. a. SD   b. M

8·7
1. c
2. a
3. c
4. a
5. b
6. b
7. F
8. T
9. T
10. F
11. T
12. F
13. *Urbanization* is the demographic shift of a population from rural areas to urban centers.
14. People are attracted to cities because of their developed infrastructure, public transportation system, employment opportunities, better health care and education, and wide range of services.
15. The area required to meet the city's resource requirements and to absorb waste is divided by the city's geographical area.
16. The major problems facing modern cities are pollution, traffic congestion, waste production, and environmental destruction.
17. In Curitiba, a population explosion was brought on by immigration.
18. In Hammarby Sjöstad, residents began moving back to the city from the country.

8·8
1. f   6. j
2. a   7. d
3. e   8. h
4. c   9. g
5. i   10. b

8·9   *Suggested answers:*
Principle 2: Build communities that harmonize with the environment.
Principle 3: Develop the area in accordance with natural conditions.
Principle 4: Build cities that take up less space and use public transportation.
Principle 5: Save energy and integrate conservation technology into building.
Principle 6: Support the local economy.
Principle 7: Create a safe, healthy community.
Principle 8: Get local people involved in decisions.
Principle 9: Encourage citizen participation and democracy.
Principle 10: Support cultural diversity.

8·10

1. X	6. X
2. X	7. ✓
3. ✓	8. ✓
4. ✓	9. X
5. X	10. ✓

8·11   *Answers will vary.*

9   Solar energy: Power for the future

9·1   *Suggested answers:* power, terawatt, watt, sunlight, infrared radiation, heat, oil, coal, natural gas, heating, lighting, fossil fuels, combustion, generate, gasoline, electricity, electrical current, power grid, steam, turbine, electrical generator, water heater, power plant, thermal

9·2   *Consult a dictionary for definitions.*

1. conj.	11. n.
2. adj.	12. n.
3. n.	13. adj.
4. n.	14. adj.
5. v.	15. v.
6. v.	16. v.
7. n.	17. v.
8. n.	18. n.
9. adj.	19. n.
10. v.	20. adj.

9·3

1. subsidies	6. output
2. offset	7. albeit
3. capacity	8. source
4. incentive	9. policy
5. alternative	10. principal

9·4

1. constitutes	6. vary
2. distribution	7. equivalent
3. intense	8. prohibits
4. recovery	9. concentrated
5. Refined	10. promote

9·5

1. d (n.)	6. a (v.)
2. h (n.)	7. c (v.)
3. f (n.)	8. g (adj.)
4. j (v.)	9. b (adj.)
5. i (v.)	10. e (v.)

9·6 *Suggested answers:*

1. The sun is the most plentiful source of energy, and all life on Earth depends on sunlight.
2. Increasing consumption of fossil fuels results in their depletion and in pollution and global warming.
3. Passive solar energy occurs when sunlight passes through windows or is absorbed by walls; it can be used for lighting and heating.
4. PV solar technology uses solar cells, containing silicon, to convert sunlight into energy; it produces electricity on a small or large scale.
5. CSP concentrates the sun's radiation, using mirrors or collectors, to heat water or gas and drive a turbine or generator; it is used to produce large amounts of electricity for power grids. Smaller collectors heat water.
6. The principal issues are the supply of fuel, the impact on the environment, costs, energy payback, and long-term energy savings.
7. Solar energy has been more popular in Europe, Japan, and remote areas; it has not been popular in the United States, where the oil industry has a large influence on energy policy.
8. Because of global warming and consumer consciousness, the demand for solar energy is expected to grow significantly in the future.

9·7
1. c
2. b
3. c
4. b
5. a
6. c
7. F
8. T
9. T
10. T
11. F
12. F
13. a. PS   b. PS   c. CSP   d. PV, CSP   e. PV   f. PS, PV, CSP   g. PV
14. The main components of sunlight are visible light, ultraviolet light, and infrared radiation.
15. Solar energy doesn't produce CO_2 or pollution.
16. The 1973–74 OPEC oil embargo increased interest in solar energy in the United States.
17. The rising demand for solar energy in the United States is due to an increasing awareness of global warming, consumer demand, and government tax incentives.

9·8
1. ✓		6. ✓
2. X		7. ✓
3. X		8. ✓
4. ✓		9. X
5. X		10. X

9·9 *Suggested answers:*

1. Historically, people have honored the sun as an emblem of vigor and vitality.
2. Companies process 50 million barrels of oil into gasoline and other fuels daily.
3. Architects are integrating passive solar energy into environmental construction plans.
4. Sunlight dislocates electrons as it contacts the surface of a PV cell and releases electrical energy.
5. We often see PV panels on the walls and roofs of buildings.
6. Manufacturers construct solar arrays from smaller sections.
7. Homeowners get their money back in the energy they conserve within two to three decades.
8. Lower energy usage and the integration of conservation measures in residences achieve an earlier payback on initial outlay.
9. Engineers Bridgers and Paxton constructed the world's first commercial solar building in Albuquerque, New Mexico, in 1956.
10. Petroleum companies have a major impact on government energy decisions.

9·10 *Answers will vary.*

9·11 *Answers will vary.*

10   Healing circles: A gentler justice

10·1   *Suggested answers:* conflict, vandalism, rioting, theft, robbery, hate crimes, drive-by shootings, gang warfare, drunk driving, road rage, mass killing, sexual assault, offenses, violence, police, laws, sentencing, court cases, arrested, sentence, prosecution, defense, plaintiff, accused, justice officials, judge, offender, victim

10·2   *Consult a dictionary for definitions.*

1. v.	11. v.
2. adj.	12. n.
3. v.	13. n.
4. n.	14. n.
5. n.	15. v.
6. v.	16. v.
7. n.	17. v.
8. n.	18. n.
9. n.	19. n.
10. n.	20. adj.

10·3

1. outcome	11. appropriate
2. assigning	12. response
3. conflict, resolved	13. philosophy
4. convene	14. reinforced
5. guidelines	15. adapt
6. consensus	16. transition
7. monitors	17. facilitator
8. refocus	18. features
9. cycle	19. ultimate
10. objective	

10·4

1. e (adj.)	6. j (n.)
2. a (n.)	7. c (v.)
3. g (v.)	8. d (n.)
4. f (adj.)	9. b (v.)
5. h (v.)	10. i (n.)

10·5

1. aboriginal, nonconfrontational
2. the community, equally, peacemaking
3. facilitator, does not take
4. formally, four, encourage
5. that everyone respects and listens to the speaker
6. consensus
7. time, commitment, an open heart
8. more likely, both victim and offender
9. internationally

10·6
   1. c
   2. a
   3. a
   4. c
   5. b
   6. c
   7. F
   8. T
   9. F
  10. F
  11. T
  12. T
  13. In stage 1, the request for a healing circle is made. In stage 2, participants are informed, prepared, and trained. In stage 3, the circle is convened and there is dialogue and resolution. In stage 4, progress is monitored and mistakes are corrected.
  14. The facilitator opens the circle; establishes the circle as a sacred place; ensures that participants follow guidelines, maintain respect, and feel safe; and steers the process toward an outcome.
  15. The talking piece is an object of symbolic value. It is passed clockwise from person to person. The person holding it may speak or remain silent. The members of the healing circle must respect and listen to the person in possession of the talking piece.
  16. The metastudy's conclusion was that victims were able to carry on a normal life again, offenders didn't commit their crimes again or harass their victims, and the community felt safer.
  17. A consensus decision is one in which everyone arrives at the decision collectively and agrees to it. When everyone contributes to the decision and has a vested interest, it is more likely to succeed.

10·7
   1. a   5. b
   2. b   6. a
   3. b   7. b
   4. a   8. b

10·8 *Suggested answers:*
   1. In North America, aboriginal healing, talking, and peacemaking circles heal communities and restore harmony.
   2. Members have the same chance to express themselves directly in a respectful exchange.
   3. People can modify (or tailor) healing circles to personal, educational, occupational, and various institutional situations.
   4. Members receive background information, orientation, and instruction.
   5. Healing circles foster storytelling.
   6. Stories open people's hearts sooner and more effectively than forced recommendations or decisions from external sources.
   7. People come to mutual decisions by discussing problems and solutions instead of trying to convince each other through formal argument.
   8. The 1996 Mille Lacs Circle Sentencing Project introduced the first healing circle in Minnesota.

10·9 *Answers will vary.*

10·10
   1. Circle of understanding
   2. Support circle
   3. Sentencing circle
   4. Talking circle
   5. Community-building circle
   6. Conflict circle
   7. Reintegration circle
   8. Healing circle
   9. Community-building circle
  10. Sentencing circle
  11. Celebration circle
  12. Support circle
  13. Circle of understanding
  14. Healing circle
  15. Conflict circle

10·11 *Answers will vary.*

11 Medical technology: New frontiers in health care

11·1 *Suggested answers:* stethoscope, sphygmomanometer, blood pressure, physical examination, X-rays, blood and urine tests, general practitioners, diagnose, treat, clinics, hospitals, patient, computer tomography, magnetic resonance imaging, tumors, biopsy, surgery, intensive care unit, physician, radiology, diabetes, glucose management, cholesterol levels, health care, surgeon, cancer, surgical instruments, nurses, nursing assistants, bandages, autoimmune disease

11·2 *Consult a dictionary for definitions.*
1. expansive, expand
2. instructive/instructional, instruct
3. interventional, intervene
4. procedural, proceed
5. visual, visualize
6. virtuality, virtualize
7. accumulation, accumulative
8. effect, effective, effect
9. extraction
10. append
11. network
12. display
13. equip
14. aid
15. conference
16. file
17. —
18. inevitability
19. radical
20. practice

11·3
1. instructions
2. accumulating
3. equipment
4. intervention
5. procedure
6. Visualization, technique
7. virtual
8. display
9. affect
10. files
11. appendages
12. practitioner
13. network
14. aid
15. conferred
16. inevitable
17. radical
18. extracted
19. expansion

11·4
1. d (n.)
2. i (v.)
3. g (n.)
4. h (adj.)
5. a (adj.)
6. j (n.)
7. c (v.)
8. e (adj.)
9. f (n.)
10. b (v.)

11·5
Paragraph 2: k
Paragraph 3: c
Paragraph 4: j
Paragraph 5: h
Paragraph 6: a
Paragraph 7: i
Paragraph 8: g
Paragraph 9: b
Paragraph 10: f
Paragraph 11: d

11·6
1. a
2. b
3. b
4. c
5. b
6. a
7. T
8. T
9. F
10. F
11. F
12. T
13. Medical records are increasing in volume and complexity. When they are computerized, they are easier to store and access; cannot get easily lost; and can be easily copied, stored, and archived.
14. Surgeons can perform delicate surgical procedures with increased accuracy. Robotic appendages can eliminate tremor.
15. Robotic appendages cannot feel the tissue they are operating on.
16. People who are bedridden or housebound do not have to leave home to receive care, and they can monitor their own treatment by using software, troubleshooting wizards, and user-friendly medical websites.
17. Stem cells can be collected only from unused or cloned embryos. Some people believe that these embryos are living beings, while others question how stem cells will be used.

11·7
1. b	5. a
2. a	6. b
3. b	7. b
4. a	8. a

11·8 *Suggested answers:*
1. In addition to basic instruments to examine patients, the doctor uses her expert hands to discover internal irregularities in her patients.
2. Doctors continue to use traditional instruments and methods; however, technology is significantly changing how they determine the cause of sickness and appropriate therapies.
3. Although robotic appendages have no tactile sensation, technicians are in the process of enhancing their sensory capacities.
4. Despite significant technical challenges, nanotechnology seems to offer the hope of boundless possibilities in the field of cancer diagnosis and therapy.
5. Understandably, it will take considerable time because of expensive construction costs and a long time frame. . . .
6. There is no end to the potential uses of stem cells, due to their ability to locate diseased areas of the body and to keep indefinitely when frozen.
7. Specialists can oversee their patients and carry on a dialogue from remote locations, as well as keep in touch to discuss urgent cases.
8. In addition to facilitating the delivery of medical care in hospitals, computer networks shorten the travel time and distance for critical data exchange.
9. Laparoscopic surgery lessens a patient's suffering after a procedure; it also decreases the potential side effects of surgery.
10. In addition to financing research on embryos generated prior to 2001, the U.S. government believes in the essential value of stem cell research.

11·9 *Answers will vary.*

11·10 *Answers will vary.*

12 The Enneagram: Understanding our personalities

12·1 *Suggested answers:*
Positive traits: organized, thorough, principled, purposeful, patient, heroic, warm-hearted, generous, empathetic, thoughtful, caring, self-assurance, charm, energy, optimism, adaptability, inspiring, creative, sensitive, independent, innovative, inventive, self-reliant, perceptive, reliable, resourceful, optimistic, enthusiastic, productive, committed, strong, compassionate, attentive, trustworthy.
Negative traits: rigid, judgmental, highly critical, manipulative, seductive, possessive, moody, dramatic, miserly, detached, paranoid, cowardly, impulsive, narcissistic

12·2 *Consult a dictionary for definitions.*
1. adj.	11. v.
2. n.	12. adj.
3. n.	13. n.
4. v.	14. n.
5. n.	15. n.
6. adj.	16. n.
7. v.	17. n.
8. v.	18. n.
9. adj.	19. n.
10. n.	20. n.

12·3
1. status
2. comprehensive, aspects
3. comprised
4. psychology
5. factor
6. adjacent
7. approach
8. inherent
9. circumstances

12·4
1. attain	6. optional
2. illustrations	7. predict
3. isolated	8. pursuits
4. Theoretically	9. credited
5. distinction	10. mediator

12·5
1. h (n.)	6. i (v.)
2. e (n.)	7. c (n.)
3. b (n.)	8. a (v.)
4. j (n.)	9. f (v.)
5. g (n.)	10. d (n.)

12·6
1. a. M b. SD
2. a. SD b. M
3. a. M b. SD
4. a. SD b. M
5. a. SD b. M

12·7
1. c
2. a
3. b
4. c
5. a
6. c
7. T
8. F
9. T
10. T
11. F
12. T
13. Intuitive information can be belly-based, or physical; feeling-based, or emotional; or head-based, or mental.
14. A Four will behave like a Two under stress.
15. A Seven will behave like a Five in a situation where he or she feels secure.
16. The Enneagram system's purpose is to find our true selves through understanding our passions and preoccupations, and to develop meaningful relationships.
17. (1) d   (2) f   (3) h   (4) c   (5) a   (6) i   (7) e   (8) b   (9) g

12·8
1. d
2. e
3. h
4. c
5. a
6. i
7. b
8. g
9. f

12·9 *Suggested answers:*
1. The Enneagram uniquely symbolizes human consciousness.
2. The principal feature of each distinct type can become a neurotic habit or an ally in achieving self-knowledge.
3. Every type has two complementary, neighboring wings.
4. Ones object to rule-breakers.
5. Unguarded Eights can be giving, dedicated, and self-assured, and lead toward appropriate action.
6. Evolved, focused Nines listen carefully, soothe, and guide others.

12·10
1. The oldest theory of personality can be credited to ~~the Roman surgeon~~ Galen of Pergamon. . . .
2. ~~An ancient system rooted in Sufi mysticism,~~ the Enneagram (Greek *ennea* for "nine" and *grammos* for "point") identifies nine major aspects of being.
3. ~~Minimalists by nature,~~ Fives do not require wealth or ~~material~~ possessions, but they are ~~as~~ attached to their intellectual pursuits ~~as a miser who counts his gold in secret~~.
4. ~~Born peacemakers,~~ Nines can support ~~and sympathize with~~ all points of view.

12·11   Type One: The Perfectionist/Reformer
   Chief feature: Resentment
   Passion: Anger
   Virtue: Serenity
   Positive traits: Organized, thorough, principled, purposeful, patient, heroic
   Negative traits: Rigid, judgmental, highly critical
Type Two: The Giver/Helper
   Chief feature: Flattery
   Passion: Pride
   Virtue: Humility
   Positive traits: Warm-hearted, generous, empathetic, thoughtful, genuinely caring
   Negative traits: Manipulative, seductive, possessive
Type Three: The Performer/Achiever
   Chief feature: Vanity
   Passion: Deceit
   Virtue: Honesty
   Positive traits: Self-assured, charming, energetic, optimistic, adaptable, inspiring
   Negative traits: Vain, preoccupied with image, dishonest, deceptive
Type Four: The Romantic/Individualist
   Chief feature: Melancholy
   Passion: Envy
   Virtue: Equanimity (balance)
   Positive traits: Creative, sensitive, emotionally deep
   Negative traits: Moody, dramatic
Type Five: The Observer/Investigator
   Chief feature: Stinginess
   Passion: Avarice
   Virtue: Detachment
   Positive traits: Independent, innovative, inventive, self-reliant, perceptive
   Negative traits: Private, fearful
Type Six: The Loyal Skeptic/Loyalist
   Chief feature: Cowardice
   Passion: Fear
   Virtue: Courage
   Positive traits: Reliable, resourceful, responsible
   Negative traits: Suspicious, paranoid
Type Seven: The Epicure/Enthusiast
   Chief feature: Planning
   Passion: Gluttony
   Virtue: Sobriety
   Positive traits: Light-hearted, eternally optimistic, enthusiastic, adventurous, energetic
   Negative traits: Distracted, impulsive, narcissistic
Type Eight: The Boss/Challenger
   Chief feature: Excess
   Passion: Lust
   Virtue: Innocence
   Positive traits: Generous, committed, self-confident, strong leader
   Negative traits: Aggressive, assertive, controlling, impulsive, excessive
Type Nine: The Mediator/Peacemaker
   Chief feature: Indolence
   Passion: Sloth
   Virtue: Action
   Positive traits: Attentive, compassionate, trustworthy
   Negative traits: Distracted, avoiding, lazy

12·12   *Answers will vary.*

12·13   *Answers will vary.*

13 Artificial Intelligence: Can machines think?

13·1 *Suggested answers:* gadget, electronic system, hand plow, wheel, Industrial Revolution, carts, train, automobile, telephone, radio, television, computer, mechanical, inventors, robot, toys, technology, circuits, device, hydraulically powered arm, assembly lines, industrial environment, mass production, components, valves

13·2 *Consult a dictionary for definitions.*
1. access, accessible
2. adjustment, adjustable
3. automation, automatic
4. collapse, collapsible
5. computation/computer, computational
6. construction, constructive
7. involvement
8. transformation, transformative
9. laborious, labor
10. approximation, approximate
11. conception, conceive
12. mechanics/mechanization, mechanize
13. assessment
14. assumption
15. enablement
16. exhibit/exhibition
17. component
18. logical
19. eventuality
20. survey

13·3
1. enable
2. automated
3. component
4. involves
5. conceivable
6. assume
7. eventually
8. exhibit
9. mechanical
10. assessed
11. survey
12. labor
13. logic
14. collapse
15. transformed
16. approximately
17. compute
18. access
19. adjust
20. constructed

13·4
1. h (n.)
2. d (adj.)
3. j (adj.)
4. a (v.)
5. f (adj.)
6. b (v.)
7. i (v.)
8. g (v.)
9. c (adj.)
10. e (v.)

13·5   Paragraph 2: The invention of machines and their widespread adoption have transformed human society.
Paragraph 3: Technological progress that had been thousands of years in the making accelerated rapidly with the advent of the electronic computer in 1941.
Paragraph 4: The idea of mechanical men has fascinated thinkers and inventors for centuries.
Paragraph 5: In the meantime, with cheaper, faster computer technology at their disposal, scientists could take up the quest for autonomous machines that philosophers and mathematicians could only imagine a century earlier.
Paragraph 6: In the late 1960s, microprocessors radically reduced the size of computers, making it possible to build mobile robots with an onboard "brain" linked to a mainframe computer.
Paragraph 7: Real progress with robots was made in the field of manufacturing.
Paragraph 8: Remote-controlled robots are also indispensable in space and underwater exploration, military reconnaissance, and search-and-rescue operations.
Paragraph 9: From manufacturing and exploration, robots have begun making their way into our personal lives.
Paragraph 10: Despite the amazing accomplishments in robotics, the ultimate goal still remains the creation of an independently thinking humanoid robot—in other words, a machine made in man's image.
Paragraph 11: Although research into humanoid robots has exploded around the world, the final product is far from reach.
Paragraph 12: While it is possible to construct a robot with a human form and one that can even communicate and mimic our behavior, the creation of a truly sentient, intelligent, and autonomous machine is another story.
Paragraph 13: Although this may be possible in principle, the value of living forever inside a machine seems questionable, if not ridiculous.

13·6   1. b
2. b
3. c
4. a
5. c
6. a
7. T
8. F
9. T
10. F
11. F
12. T
13. *Robot* comes from the Czech word *robota*; it was used in a play about a mad scientist who created artificial men.
14. Microprocessors made it possible to build robots with an onboard brain.
15. Robots eliminate human error, reduce manufacturing costs, perform monotonous jobs with precision, work around the clock, and speed up production.
16. Robots are used in space and underwater exploration, military reconnaissance, and search-and-rescue missions. They are used to investigate volcanoes, to adjust valves on underwater pipelines, to defuse bombs and clear mine fields, to assess damage after a nuclear accident, and to find people trapped in collapsed buildings or mines.
17. Robots can't see or maintain balance, reproduce, feel emotions and empathize, survive by their instincts, understand the consequences of their actions, or operate with purpose or understanding.

13·7   1. –   5. –
2. –   6. –
3. –   7. –
4. +   8. +

13·8 *Suggested answers:*

1. The invention of the steam engine—and later, the train, automobile, telephone, radio, and television—revolutionized the economy, human society, and long-distance communication.
2. Early attempts at creating mechanical creatures became museum exhibits.
3. Alan Turing and John McCarthy were responsible for opening up research into Artificial Intelligence after World War II.
4. A British neurophysiologist built the first mobile robots that could react to light and sound stimuli, and later to whistles in a conditioned response.
5. SAIL researchers pioneered the development of a robotic vehicle for space exploration. Despite their attempts to achieve automatic performance, it could operate only under controlled conditions.
6. Developed mostly in Japan, PUMA robots became commonplace in mass production, where they carried out dangerous, high-precision, and routine tasks on an around-the-clock basis.
7. A Japanese professor developed the first walking, talking, and piano-playing robots. Later, Honda built a small humanoid robot to perform basic, but limited, humanlike functions in amusement parks.
8. Obstacles to creating an intelligent, autonomous robot include overcoming a lack of balance, coordination, and natural movement, as well as constructing an independently functioning brain with sufficient capacity to process and store information like humans.

13·9 *Answers will vary.*

13·10 *Answers will vary.*

14 Voluntary simplicity: Making more out of less

14·1 *Suggested answers:* happiness, life, liberty, money, fame, power, family, relationships, work, adventure, creative, peace of mind, simplicity, affluence, well-being, consumerism, lifestyle, counterculture, nature, priorities, community, fashion

14·2 *Consult a dictionary for definitions.*

1. equation, equal
2. publication/publishing
3. release
4. utility/utilization
5. index
6. stressful, stress
7. error, err
8. individuality, individual, individualize
9. accompaniment
10. conformity
11. denotation
12. rejection/reject
13. —
14. bond
15. prioritize
16. formulaic
17. major
18. compatibility
19. —
20. —

14·3

1. stress		11. denote
2. Index		12. welfare
3. utilize		13. equate
4. bond		14. priorities
5. conform		15. individual
6. majority		16. formula
7. accompanied		17. seeking
8. erroneous		18. rejected
9. published		19. release
10. straightforward		20. compatible

14·4

1. grateful (adj.)
2. balance (v.)
3. fulfillment (n.)
4. ranks (v.)
5. budget (n.)
6. affluent (adj.)
7. clutter (n.)
8. foster (v.)
9. frugally (adv.)
10. durable (adj.)

14·5

1. Happiness, isn't
2. are not
3. lowest
4. North America
5. reduce
6. differentiates between
7. philosophy, individual circumstances

14·6

1. c
2. b
3. b
4. a
5. a
6. c
7. F
8. T
9. F
10. F
11. T
12. T
13. *Voluntary simplicity* means choosing freely and consciously to change one's life in a spiritual sense by getting rid of anything that controls one's life and takes away from what is really important for happiness and well-being.
14. "Wants" are what we desire, and "needs" are absolute necessities for survival and well-being.
15. The Happy Planet Index measures longevity, experienced well-being, and a country's ecological footprint.
16. The goals of the voluntary simplicity movement are to reduce consumption patterns and to minimize our personal impact on the environment.
17. Pressures from advertising, society, the media, family, and friends make it difficult for people to cut back on accumulating stuff.

14·7

1. e
2. c
3. h
4. f
5. a
6. g
7. d
8. b

14·8 *Answers will vary.*

14·9 *Answers will vary.*

14·10 *Answers will vary.*

15 Future directions: Ecology or technology?

15·1   *Suggested answers:* tragedy, collapse, dire, disaster, scare stories, overshoot, decimate, bubble, burst, crash, overflowing, trajectory

15·2   *Consult a dictionary for definitions.*

1. v.	11. v.
2. v.	12. n.
3. v.	13. n.
4. n.	14. adj.
5. n.	15. v.
6. v.	16. n.
7. adj.	17. v.
8. adj.	18. adj.
9. n.	19. n.
10. n.	20. adj.

15·3

1. crucial	11. persistent
2. confirmed	12. notion
3. input	13. intervened
4. Coupled	14. core
5. acknowledged	15. explicit
6. rationality	16. constraints
7. uniformity	17. simulate
8. ideology	18. poses
9. model	19. Unrestrained
10. underlying	20. commissioned

15·4

1. trajectory (n.)
2. exponentially (adv.)
3. urgent (adj.)
4. imminent (adj.)
5. dire (adj.)
6. provoke (v.)
7. inflate (v.)
8. forefront (n.)
9. increments (n.)
10. disseminate (v.)

15·5

1. Both warn us that humanity is on a path that could lead to disaster.
2. They used a computer model and fed data on population, food production, industrial production, pollution, and consumption of natural nonrenewable resources into a computer model that analyzed how the data interacted and came up with 12 projected scenarios. On that basis, they predicted that if humanity did not make significant changes, it would exhaust the planet's limits and face ecological collapse.
3. The political and business community tried to discredit the findings, because they were contrary to their notions of growth and profit, while others, including President Jimmy Carter, welcomed and supported the book.
4. *The Limits to Growth* became an international best-seller, and although it has been updated twice, its conclusions remain unchanged.
5. The exponential growth of population and the material economy could exhaust the planet's limited resources, increase pollution beyond tolerable levels, and exceed the planet's carrying capacity, which would result in overshoot. If no one pays attention or begins to act in time, overshoot could cause collapse.
6. Sustainability can prevent overshoot if humanity manages the consumption of nonrenewable resources, replaces them with renewable resources, and reduces pollution so that everyone will have enough to live on and future generations will be able to meet their needs.
7. People can use technology to make changes, but most importantly they have to change their values and the way they think about growth and the environment.

15·6
1. c
2. b
3. c
4. a
5. a
6. b
7. F
8. T
9. F
10. F
11. T
12. T
13. Exponential growth occurs when an entity doubles in number, then rapidly redoubles.
14. Overshoot occurs when an activity exceeds its physical limits.
15. Sustainability occurs when the needs of the present generation are met without compromising the ability of future generations to meet their needs.
16. To achieve sustainability, renewable resources cannot be used at a greater rate than they can be produced, nonrenewable resources cannot be consumed at a greater rate than they can be replaced by renewable resources, and pollution cannot be produced at a greater rate than the Earth can absorb or detoxify it.
17. The five factors were population, food production, industrial production, pollution, and consumption of nonrenewable natural resources.

15·7
1. cannot
2. went against popular beliefs
3. for humanitarian reasons
4. unpopular
5. they could go on doing the same things forever
6. it takes fewer women giving birth to keep the population growing
7. beliefs
8. wisely

15·8   *Answers will vary.*

15·9
1. X   6. ✓
2. X   7. X
3. ✓   8. ✓
4. X   9. ✓
5. ✓   10. X

15·10   *Answers will vary.*